JAPANESE
Army Handbook
1939–1945

George Forty

Sutton Publishing

First published in 1999 by
Sutton Publishing Limited · Phoenix Mill
Thrupp · Stroud · Gloucestershire · GL5 2BU

British Library Cataloguing in Publication Data
A catalogue record for this book is available from the British Library.

ISBN 0-7509-1688-5

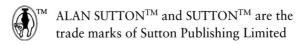
ᵀᴹ ALAN SUTTONᵀᴹ and SUTTONᵀᴹ are the
trade marks of Sutton Publishing Limited

Typeset in 10/13pt Sabon.
Typesetting and origination by
Sutton Publishing Limited.
Printed in Great Britain by
Butler & Tanner, Frome, Somerset.

CONTENTS

Acknowledgements iv

Introduction v

1. Historical Background 1
2. Mobilization and Conscription 13
3. Training 23
4. Higher Organizations 33
5. Field Organizations 43
6. The Combat Arms 66
7. The Services 79
8. The Soldier 93
9. Weapons 133
10. Vehicles 159
11. Miscellaneous Equipment 189
12. Tactics 204
13. Personalities 223
14. The Kempeitai 232

Annex A: Japanese Military Conventional Signs 241
Annex B: Army Abbreviations 259
Annex C: Japanese Ground Radio Equipment 264

Bibliography 268
Index 269

ACKNOWLEDGEMENTS

First and foremost I must thank the National Archives of America for allowing me to quote from their wartime training manuals, which has permitted me to put in considerably more detail than would otherwise have been possible. I must also thank the Photographic Department at the IWM and the Tank Museum for their invaluable assistance in allowing me to search their archives for suitable photographs. Individually I must thank Mr Richard Fuller for all his help and kindness, especially with the photographs of Japanese personalities; also Bill Norman of RHQ The Duke of Wellington's Regiment for providing the excellent photograph of a young Japanese tank commander. Finally, I must thank Dr Kazuo Tamayama for allowing me to quote from his book *Japanese Soldiers of the Burma Campaign*, Mr Lamont-Brown and those other authors from whose works I have quoted, and last but not least my son Jonathan, for his invaluable help with all the drawings and diagrams.

George Forty
Bryantspuddle
August 1998

INTRODUCTION

THE LEGEND OF INVINCIBILITY

'Lack of information is a most fertile source of exaggeration, distortion and legend which, if unrefuted, eventually assumes the stature of accepted fact.' Thus begins the opening chapter of a handy little pocket-sized US Army manual, *Soldier's Guide to the Japanese Army*. It goes on: 'For years the Japanese were taken lightly as military antagonists, and the confidence of the Western World in its disdainful appraisal of their military and naval capabilities seemed justified by the Japanese failure to achieve decisive victory in the Chinese war. Then, following the outbreak of war with the United States and Britain, a succession of speedy and apparently easy victories stimulated the rise of the legend of invincibility of the Japanese soldier. He allegedly was unconquerable in jungle terrain; his fanatical, death-courting charges and last-ditch defenses were broadcast until popular repute invested the Japanese soldier with almost superhuman attributes. Several years of combat experience against the Japanese have replaced such fanciful notions by more realistic evaluation. While the military capabilities of the Japanese soldier still are appreciated, it is now realized that he has pronounced weaknesses. As a soldier his good qualities are not innate but are the result of careful training and preparation for specific tactical

Banzai! *('May the Emperor live for 10,000 years!') Typical photograph of IJA infantry jubilantly raising their rifles in salute after clashes with Chinese forces in North China during July 1937. The signed unit flag has bold patriotic sayings on it for good luck. Among the raised rifles with their long bayonets fitted is one 50mm grenade discharger. (IWM: NYT 70962)*

'I surrender!' A very unusual photograph of a wounded IJA soldier being taken prisoner in Burma. Even in the last days of the war, Japanese soldiers would normally rather kill themselves than surrender. (IWM: IND 3145)

situations. Hence an accurate appraisal of the Japanese soldier must give adequate attention to the Japanese system of military training and show its effect on his physical, mental and temperamental characteristics.'

OBEDIENCE AND FEROCITY

To be fair both to the Japanese soldier and to the person who wrote that appraisal one must remember that the handbook was deliberately written as a morale booster to the GIs who undoubtedly held the Imperial Japanese Army (IJA) in some awe. However, this and other comments in the handbook certainly do not always do justice to the undoubted fighting prowess of the average Japanese soldier, of whom Gen Slim, the famous commander of the British XIVth Army, wrote in his book *Defeat into Victory*: 'He fought and marched till he died. If 500 Japanese were ordered to hold a position, we had to kill four hundred and ninety five before it was ours – and the last five killed themselves. It was this combination of obedience and ferocity that made the Japanese Army, whatever its condition, so formidable. It would make a European army invincible.'

AIR AND NAVAL FORCES

In order to keep this handbook within manageable proportions I have omitted all but brief reference to Japanese air and sea (naval land) forces. However, a brief explanation is necessary here:

Japanese Air Service. During the Second World War, Japan did not have an independent air force, the Japanese Army Air Service being an integral part

The last resting place for this Japanese officer was near Tamu, just across the Burmese frontier in the Kabaw Valley. Note his tropical helmet on the stone pile above the grave. (IWM: IND 3667)

of the IJA. In the same way, the Japanese Naval Air Service was an integral part of the Navy. There was a separate Inspector General of Aviation, who was on the same level as the Inspector General of Military Training.

Naval Land Forces. The Japanese used special naval landing forces in China from 1932 onwards, then during the Second World War they employed naval land forces to occupy Pacific island bases such as Wake Island. Special naval landing forces (instead of the Army) were also used in the defence of a number of outlying bases. These forces were organized and equipped with weapons similar to those of the Army, but their uniform was navy blues and canvas leggings, with 'Special Naval Landing Force' (in Japanese characters) on their naval caps. The Imperial Japanese Navy (IJN) took a continuing interest in the design and production of certain armoured fighting vehicles (AFVs), in particular amphibians. They also used armoured cars and the method by which they can be distinguished from IJA AFVs is explained in the chapter on vehicles.

JAPANESE NUMBERING

Throughout this book when referring to vehicle types, uniforms and so on, I have used the Japanese system of numbering. This was based on the calendar that began in the year the first Japanese Empire was founded, or in western terms 660 BC. In other words, Japanese years were equivalent to western years plus 660; for example, the Japanese equivalent of the year 1938 was the year 2598, and the war years 1939 to 1945 were 2599 to 2605. Japanese vehicle types, uniforms and so on were numbered using the last two digits of the year of introduction; hence the Type 98 light tank was built in the year 2598 (or 1938). This is complicated enough, but from the year 2601 (1941) the Japanese introduced a new system for numbering tanks, so that instead of a tank built in 2601 being designated Type 01, the nought was dropped and the tank referred to as the Type 1.

As with my other handbooks this is not meant to be an exhaustive treatise on the IJA, but rather a handy reference book for modellers, war-gamers and others. The information comes mainly from a series of wartime US Army manuals and I must thank the US National Archives for allowing me to quote extensively from these references. It is not always easy to cross-reference and verify every single fact – and there are an immense number of facts in this book. As I found out to my cost in the first edition of the *US Army Handbook*, other seemingly reliable references are not always correct. However, I trust this will not be the case in this handbook.

HISTORICAL BACKGROUND

From the twelfth to the nineteenth century the Japanese people had a history of being governed by a military caste – the *Samurai*. They were stoic warriors who held bravery, honour and personal loyalty above life itself, ritual suicide by disembowelment (*seppuku*) being the respected alternative to dishonour or defeat. The *Samurai* dominated the Japanese government until the *Meiji* Restoration of 1868, when Emperor Meiji Tenno launched Japan along western lines. He played an active role in the prosecution of both the Sino-Japanese War (1894–5) and the Russo-Japanese War (1904–5) in which the new 'European-style' army showed itself to be every bit as good as its European equivalent. What made this all the more surprising was that

The Emperor's Birthday Review. Emperor Hirohito, mounted on his favourite white horse 'Snowdrift', reviews his troops on Yoyogi Parade Ground, Tokyo. (IWM: HU 72218)

the majority of the soldiers were ordinary Japanese peasants, who had always been denied the right to bear arms. They proved themselves to be brave, aggressive, obedient and well able to master modern tactics and weapons. Nevertheless, the *Samurai* did not entirely lose their influence, the Choshu clan in particular dominating the armed forces until the 1920s. Yamagata Aritomo, who was from a family of the lowest samurai rank in Choshu, is credited as being the creator of the modern Japanese Army. The Imperial Japanese Army of the early 1900s numbered 380,000 active and reserve troops, plus a second reserve of 50,000, together with 220,000 trained men in the National Army; a further 4,250,000 men were available

Troops marching in Tokyo, carrying banners instead of rifles, but wearing their long bayonets. (IWM: BS 68569)

for induction. Sheer numbers were unimportant in the 1904 war with Russia, because the Russians could easily match them in quantity; much more important was their fighting ability. One contemporary historian described them as possessing hereditary bravery, having 'retained the virtues of the barbarian without the defects of civilization'. The Russians had scant regard for the Japanese soldier at the start of the war, but quickly began to realize their error. The eventual Russian defeat undoubtedly marked the end of the automatic assumption regarding the superiority of European troops, while the bitter fighting and heavy casualties on both sides showed what efficient killing machines were now available on the battlefield.

At the end of the nineteenth century Japan was steadily increasing her trade links with the rest of the world. At the same time she was flexing her military muscles and re-equipping her armed forces with modern weapons. It was not long before her army proved its worth, first against China, then Russia. In the 1894–5 war against China, the IJA had taken Port Arthur from the Chinese, only to see it subsequently acquired by the Russians. From 1900 to 1903 Japan prepared to fight a limited war in Korea and Manchuria, with the aims of curbing growing Russian power and ensuring her own grip upon Korea. The first step would be the capture of Port Arthur (Lushun). Situated on the tip of the Liaotung peninsula in Manchuria, Port Arthur was the Russian Far East Fleet's base and the only ice-free port on the Pacific coast. On 8 February 1904 the Japanese launched a surprise naval attack on the Russian fleet at Port Arthur; they followed it up by declaring war on 10 February and landing their First Army under Gen Baron Yamemoto Kuroki near the port. At the same time their Second Army under Gen Oku began a northern advance through Korea to the Yalu River, in order to cover the Port Arthur operation. Surrounded, the port was besieged throughout 1904, the Russian garrison fending off many Japanese assaults and being subjected to heavy artillery fire – the Japanese employed nineteen 280mm howitzers firing 500lb projectiles over a range of

10,000yd. Eventually the garrison surrendered the port on 2 January 1905, but by then the Japanese had lost 58,000 killed and wounded, plus a further 30,000 sick. Meanwhile, heavy fighting had been taking place in Manchuria where the Russians lost a series of battles, culminating in defeat at Mukden (21 February–10 March 1905), although the Japanese were unable to take advantage and follow up their victory on the battlefield because they had lost so many men. This was the last major land action of the war which ended on 6 September that year. Japan now controlled Formosa, Kwantung Peninsula (the southern tip of Manchuria) and south Sakhalin Island.

In 1910 the Japanese annexed Korea; they would remain in control there until the end of the Second World War. Japan declared war against Germany on 23 August 1914, but was more interested in its own territorial aspirations in China, Korea and the Pacific than in helping the Allies. The IJA was now organized along European lines, with universal male conscription – initially for two, later three years – for all men up to the age of thirty-seven. They saw little fighting in the First World War, except for occupying the Caroline, Mariana and Marshall Islands, and, with British assistance, besieging and capturing the German fortress-port of Tsingato in the Kiaochow colony on 7 November 1914. The IJA of this period wore European uniforms, dark blue in colour and comprising a single-breasted tunic, trousers and peaked cap in which was worn a brass five-pointed star. The main rifle was the Japanese-produced 6.5mm Arisaka Type 38, a Mauser derivative, which they had first adopted in 1905. There was also a carbine version which differed only in barrel length, being just under a foot shorter.

When Yamagata died in 1922, the power of the *Samurai* declined significantly and the heirachy of the Army began to change, taking in a growing number of young men from the middle classes who were interested more in self-advancement than in the ascetic way of life of the warrior. This led in the late 1920s to the emergence of a 'secret society' of dissident officers who plotted a *coup d'etat* to sweep away the old order. This came to a head in 1931, when the Kwantung Army,* then in Manchuria, acting on its own initiative and on the orders of a group of junior officers, seized first the city of Mukden on 18 September, and then the entire province. The senior commanders were not entirely averse to this action because they were happy to see the pressure on China increased and, despite continuing adverse world opinion, they reinforced the Kwantung Army, landing fifteen divisions of the First and Second Armies in China (the force now numbered 64,900 plus a small air element). Their action was condemned by the League of Nations, but the League was unable to compel Japan to withdraw. The following year (1932), they renamed Manchuria 'Manchukuo' and it became a Japanese puppet state. They also attacked Shanghai on 28 March 1932; they received further censure from the League of Nations and withdrew from the city on 24 February 1933.

* The Kwantung Army was in Manchuria by agreement with the Chinese government in order to defend the railway network against the activities of dissident Chinese warlords. Its HQ was at Port Arthur and in September 1931 it numbered some 10,400 men. The 'Manchurian Incident' that precipitated action against the Chinese was the deliberate blowing up, by the Japanese, of a short section of the South Manchurian Railway, which they then blamed upon the Chinese.

IJA on internal security operations in China in the early 1930s, together with a little tankette. (IWM: STT 3302)

Japanese troops taking cover during street fighting in North China. The infantry section is advancing behind a medium tank. (IWM: NYT 68512)

The IJA was soon involved in heavy fighting against Gen Chiang Kai-Shek's 19th Route Army; this lasted for some six weeks until a truce could be arranged. Thereafter, the Japanese campaigns in China were expanded, so that by 1937 they had become a major strategic advance down the Yangtse, resulting in the capture of Chiang Kai-Shek's capital, Nanking. The IJA was still outnumbered ten to one by the Chinese, but both sides suffered heavy casualties as the fighting continued. The lust for power of a handful of fanatical generals from the early 1930s onwards would lead to their involvement in all-out global war, and the campaigns in China can be considered as part of the global build-up to the Second World War.

While their aggression towards China escalated, the Japanese also launched attacks (always classed as 'accidents') against British and American shipping and their property in China. Also in 1939 they made border incursions into the Soviet Union but were swiftly repulsed by the Red Army. Germany was one of her few allies, Japan having signed the Anti-Comintern Pact with Germany in November 1936 (joined by Italy in November 1937), intended to counter the spread of international communism, so the Japanese leaders were very worried by the Russo-German non-aggression pact, but Hitler's spectacular victories in Europe in 1940 'stilled the voice of caution',* and in September that year they signed a new Tripartite Pact with Italy and Germany. They also prevailed upon both Britain and Vichy France to help them in their war against China, the former closing the Burma Road† for six months, while the latter allowed Japanese military forces into northern Indo-China and later let them establish bases in southern Indo-China. The major threat to their expansionist dreams was, of course, the American Pacific Fleet, hence the unprovoked attack on Pearl Harbor.

At the same time as these external conflicts were taking place there was a series of violent incidents in mainland Japan, not only between the Army and the government but also within the Army itself. These centred around the growing feelings of nationalism and expansionist aggression, not dissimilar to the German desire for *Lebensraum* ('living space') which Hitler used as an excuse for expanding the Third Reich. Two factions emerged within the Army with very different ideas on how this expansion of Japan should be achieved: one group was known as the 'Control'

In Manchuria the IJA made maximum use of railways. Here a group of infantry ride on a Sumida Type 93 armoured car which has been adapted for railway use. (Tank Museum: 1863/E2)

---

* *World Armies*, John Keegan. Hitler is also supposed to have secretly told the Japanese that his pact with Russia was a double-bluff and that he would soon invade the Soviet Union.
† The Burma Road was a 350–400-mile-long supply route connecting Burma with China.

(*Tosei-ha*), the other as the 'Imperial Way' (*Kodo-ha*). The *Tosei-ha* believed that the policy should be one of expansion into China only, while the *Kodo-ha* believed in a more wide-ranging policy encompassing the whole of eastern Asia, whether that meant war with Russia or not. In 1936 the court martial of a member of the 'Imperial Way' faction for the murder of Gen Nagata, the head of the department controlling officers' promotions and postings, and a leading member of the 'Control' faction, was the signal for a coup in Tokyo. Nagata had been trying to remove Gen Mazaki, the principal 'Imperial Way' leader and generally endeavouring to minimize their activities; his actions provoked the 'Imperial Way' into retaliation. In the early hours of 26 February 1936, units of the IJA 1st Division, plus some individual supporters from the Imperial Guards Division, went to the houses of selected senior government members to kill them. The prime minister escaped, but two former prime ministers and Mazaki's successor were all murdered. The rebels then barricaded off part of central Tokyo and occupied various public buildings. Eventually they gave themselves up, hoping for a 'show trial' where they could plead their case and win public support. However, this did not happen and the ringleaders were court-martialled and executed in secret.

This all led to a loss of respect for the Army among the civilian population but there was certainly no loss of military power within the government. For example, no fewer than nine of the eleven prime ministers between May 1932 and August 1945 were either generals or admirals. The senior army leaders were now mainly from the 'Control' faction, and would initially follow a policy of expansion within China. At the same time as Japan signed the Anti-Comintern Pact, the military began to rearm and to put the IJA on to a full war footing. The following year the civilian prime minister was removed and replaced with a general, but when he antagonized the rest of the cabinet they agreed for him to be replaced by Prince Konoye, who was confidently expected to support the Army's nationalist outlook.

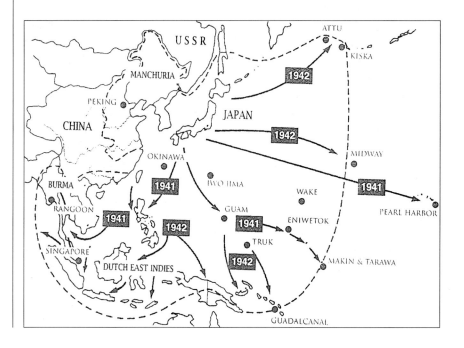

Japanese expansion, 1941–42.

Japanese troops mopping up in Kuala Lumpur, capital of Malaya, which they entered in the late evening of 11 January 1942. (IWM: HU 2776)

Konoye, however, tried to moderate the Army's expansionist policies but with little success and eventually he was replaced by his own war minister, Gen Hideki Tojo, who would remain as both prime minister and army minister until 1944, when the Japanese began to suffer serious military setbacks. In February 1944 Tojo also assumed the office of Army Chief of Staff, but this only infuriated his critics even more. Eventually, in July 1944, he resigned all his offices and withdrew into obscurity.

DAI TOA SEN (GREAT EAST ASIA WAR)

Following 'the Day of Infamy', as President Roosevelt described Japan's pre-emptive strike against the US Pacific Fleet's base on 7 December 1941, Japan embarked upon a series of wide-ranging operations against American, British and Dutch bases in China, Malaya, Burma, the Philippines and the East Indies. What the Japanese called the 'Great East Asia War' – the Japanese term for the Second World War – had thus begun in earnest. In all these campaigns the IJA played a major role, quickly gaining a reputation as a tough, implacable foe, daring in attack and fanatical in defence, invariably showing little inclination to surrender, preferring to die in battle. Most recruits were well suited to army life, being strong, simple and obedient. Those who came from the country – although there were also many from the towns and cities – were also used to a frugal existence and accustomed to carrying heavy loads. They earned a considerable reputation as jungle fighters, which lasted for most of the war. Those from the urban areas were perhaps more bound by their 'soldier's code' of loyalty, valour and the firm belief in the righteousness of their cause, which was the real strength behind their undoubted battlefield prowess. The peacetime standing army had comprised seventeen divisions, plus the Korean, Formosan and Kwantung Armies. By 1941, as will be explained in more detail later, this had grown to thirty-one divisions, mainly created to reinforce those formations fighting in

Lt Gen A. Percival, surrendering in Singapore, 15 February 1942. Just before the surrender, Gen Sir Henry Pownall (Wavell's Chief of Staff) commented: 'From the beginning to the end of this campaign, we have been outmatched by better soldiers.' (IWM: HU 2781)

Lt Gen Taikaishi Sakai leads the triumphant Japanese parade through Victoria, Hong Kong, on 27 December 1941, the day after all fighting had ceased. (IWM: HU 2766)

IJA troops entering Rangoon on 7 March 1942, after it had been abandoned without a fight. (IWM: HU 2774)

Landing on the Australian dependency of Christmas Island, Japanese troops 'Banzai' in a newly occupied enemy artillery position. (IWM: HU 2782)

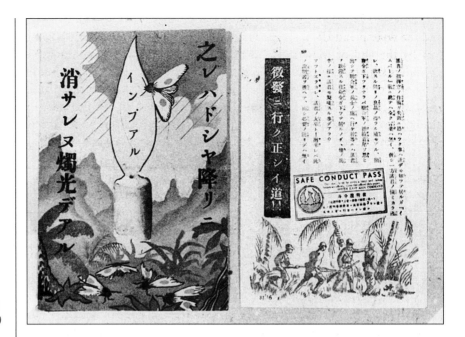

This safe conduct pass was produced by South East Asia Command, but was not often used by IJA troops. (Author's collection)

China. By 1945 the IJA comprised some 191 divisions (mainly infantry), totalling over 2.3 million men. In addition they were supported by the Indian Liberation Army (INLA) and the Free Burma Army, both formed in Japan, which fought alongside the IJA.

The Japanese armed forces enjoyed spectacular successes on land, in the air and at sea between December 1941 and May 1942, ranging over a vast area and taking on the supposedly 'invincible' forces of the colonial powers. Britain, for example, lost Hong Kong, Singapore, Malaya and Burma in quick succession, and the IJA was at the very gates of India by the

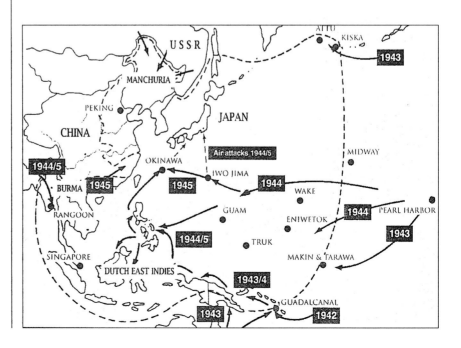

Defeat of Japan, 1942–45.

end of May 1942. The Dutch East Indies had surrendered by March 1942, and the widespread US possessions in the Pacific fared little better, all being lost by the end of May 1942, although isolated parties of indomitable defenders kept up guerrilla activities on some islands. It is surprising that in the whole of these opening campaigns the Japanese only committed a force of some eleven divisions in total; the army that overran Burma, for example, was actually outnumbered by the British garrison there, yet the Japanese outclassed the British troops. Thus was created the myth that they were 'born jungle fighters', mainly through the quality of the troops engaged and the ruthless nature of their operations. After these highly successful opening campaigns, the IJA made no more spectacular advances, needing to keep the main bulk of its forces in China where the Chinese doggedly resisted, gradually wearing down their enemies. However, it was undoubtedly the growing strength of the American and British (including the Commonwealth) armed forces and the massive American industrial potential that would turn Japanese victory into defeat in all areas.

As the war dragged on and defeat began to stare the Japanese in the face, most of the government saw that surrender was the only sensible course, but the generals at the top still thought differently. After the dropping of the atomic bombs and the Russian invasion of Manchuria, the Emperor was now more determined than ever to surrender; this was the last straw for the Minister of War, Gen Korechika Anami, who committed traditional suicide on the night of 13 August 1945. The dissenting generals then surrounded the Emperor's palace and held the Emperor a virtual prisoner, while trying to find and destroy his surrender speech. They were foiled by the general commanding the local operational headquarters, who spoke to the troops in person and won them over to his side. After the surrender the IJA was disarmed and disbanded. Defeat brought an

The IJA surrenders.
Lt Gen Kawada, commander of
31 Division, which attacked
Kohima, hands over his sword to
Maj Gen W.A. Crowther DSO,
at Tharon, north of Moulmein,
in the last week of October 1945.
(IWM: IND 4902)

The Japanese surrender at Singapore: Lord Louis Mountbatten reads the surrender terms to the Japanese before they sign. (IWM: SE 4704)

amazing change of heart within the Japanese people who showed their dislike and distrust for the generals by mounting a massive peace movement and resolving never to fight again. This policy would be maintained for the next five years until the outbreak of the Korean War in 1950, Japan relying on US troops stationed in Japan for their security. The subsequent formation of a 75,000-strong 'National Police Reserve', authorized by Gen Douglas MacArthur as head of the occupation forces, led on to the formation of the National Safety Force (NSF) in 1952 and then to the Ground Self-Defence Force (GSDF). The GSDF would quickly learn 'to walk on eggshells', as one historian put it, because of the strength of anti-war feelings in the country as a whole. For example, it was not until 1992 that the Army obtained permission to serve overseas, contributing troops for a peace-keeping operation in Cambodia.

ARMS AND SERVICES

The division between Arms and Services in the IJA was as follows:

a. Line Branch (*Heika*). From 1940 the following arms were grouped together under the generic term 'Line Branch': Infantry, Cavalry (including tank), Artillery (light – which included field, mountain and horse; medium; heavy; coastal; anti-aircraft), Transport, Chemical Warfare and Air Service. Although this grouping allowed for personnel to be cross-posted between arms, it did not change the basic functions of the component arms.

b. Services (*Kakubu*). These included: Medical; Veterinary; Intendance (cf: US Army Quartermaster Branch); Technical; Judicial and Military Bands.

MOBILIZATION AND CONSCRIPTION

A NATION OF 100 MILLION

In 1939 there were approximately 100 million Japanese citizens, 70 per cent of whom lived on the four main home islands of Honshu, Hokkaido, Shikkou and Kyushu, or on the 3,900 plus smaller islands, which stretched in an arc of some 2,000 miles in length off the eastern coast of the Asiatic mainland. Before the Second World War, during peacetime all male Japanese between the ages of seventeen and forty were subject to service in the armed forces, apart from the seriously disabled and certain criminals. It was possible to postpone service, for example, for educational reasons. Each year, all twenty-year-olds were medically examined and classified in the following manner:

Class A. Candidates had to be in good physical condition, not less than 5ft (1.52m) in height and were thus classified 'Available for active service'.
Class B-1. Taller than 4ft 11in (1.5m) but under the standard of Class A. Also classified 'Available for active service'.
Class B-2. As for B1, but with poorer hearing and eyesight; classified 'Available for 1st Conscript Reserve'.
Class B-3. As for B2, but with even poorer eyesight and physical condition; classified 'Available for 2nd Conscript Reserve'.
Class C. Same height as for B3, but in worse physical condition; also, men between 4ft 9in and 4ft 11in and not suffering from any disabling ailment. Classified 'Assigned to the 2nd National Army'.
Class D. Less than 4ft 9in in height; suffering from certain specific ailments which were not quickly improved by treatment. Classified 'Rejected – unfit for service'.
Class F. Found to be suffering from some temporary ailment and classified 'For re-examination next year'.

From those who were fit for active service (Classes A and B-1), the required numbers would be inducted and given two years' training. The rest of the fit men went into one type of reserve or another, received a limited amount

Regimental colours on show at an IJA camp. As in other armies, unit colours were honoured and protected. When a new regiment was formed, the regimental commander would go to the Imperial Palace to be presented with the colour by the Emperor. (US National Archives)

A unit flag, with 'loyalty' and 'bravery' sayings (kanji) written around the central sun. (The US called this style of 'Rising Sun' flag the 'Meatball Flag'.) (Author's collection)

of training and were available as replacements. Those of a lower medical category were not given any training but put into the 2nd National Army where they were liable to be called up in an emergency. This also happened to all young men between seventeen and nineteen who were not actually inducted into service, but could volunteer for active service (see p. 16).

Once war was declared the system was altered in a number of ways. For example, the call-up age was lowered to nineteen, the upper age limit was raised to forty-five, the length of service rose to three years or more, and reservists in various categories were called up as needed. By 1942 most infantry recruits were receiving only three months' training in Japan before being posted abroad, although more training might well be given in operational areas. As the war progressed other changes were brought in. For example, deferment was cancelled for all students except for a small number of specific types, notably those involved in technical and scientific courses. In 1944 the conscription of Koreans began and, in 1945, of Formosans. Both had been recruited in the past in increasing numbers as civilian labourers for both the Army and the Navy, being used in construction corps, but not receiving any military training. In addition, exemption from military service was broadened to include specialists and skilled technicians in munitions and the aeroplane industry, etc., and the length of peacetime training programmes was cut.

At the time of the Japanese attack on Pearl Harbor the IJA was some 375,000 strong, plus about two million reserves, with roughly 150,000 conscripts being called up every year. After the mobilization which had preceded the attack, the changes outlined above were brought into effect. For example, China became a recognized overseas area where follow-on training could be conducted.

IJA soldier-settlers bow 'Good morning' to each other before going out to work in the fields near their camp in Manchuria, one of the main areas of Japanese expansion prior to the Second World War. (IWM: PIC 68557)

TYPES OF CONSCRIPT

Active Service conscripts (*Genekihei*). These were the men from Classes A and B-1 who were called up for active service for two years as at 1 December of the year in question. They had all been classified physically fit, with the necessary aptitude for the arms or service in which they would serve. Training began soon after induction and continued until the November of the second year. Having completed their two years' active duty, trainees were then assigned to the 1st Conscript Reserve (*Yobieki*) for the next fifteen years and four months. During this period they might be called up for five periods of up to thirty-five days each (or fewer periods if call-ups were over fifty days). They were also subject to an annual inspection muster. After this period they went into the 1st National Army until they reached the age of forty.

Conscript or replacement reservists (*Hojuhei*). These were men from Classes B-2 and B-3, plus those in Classes A and B-1 who were not needed to fill the year's active service quota. They could be called up to serve any period of training of not more than 180 days. After seventeen years and four months, during which time they were subject to the annual inspection muster, they also entered the 1st National Army and remained until they reached the age of forty. This reserve was divided into the 1st and 2nd Conscript Reserves, the distinction between them being purely decided by the physical qualifications of the individuals.

National Army conscripts (*Kokuminhei*). The 2nd National Army was composed mainly of men between the ages of thirty-seven and forty who had served in the 1st Reserve or the Conscript Reserve and who were thus either fully or partly trained. They were given no further training but were subject to call-up in an emergency. Men between seventeen and twenty years of age who were not in the armed forces were also automatically put into the 2nd National Army.

Lonely outposts in Manchuria like this one had to be guarded by conscript soldiers. (IWM: HU 72224)

VOLUNTEERS

There were two classes: the first type consisted of men between seventeen and twenty, over 1.6m (5ft 2.8in) tall, in Class A or B-1 physical condition; the second of conscripts who volunteered for immediate service without waiting to be selected. A special army volunteer system was established for Koreans in 1938 and for Formosans in 1942. There was also an extensive apprentice system to train young volunteers for technical work in the Army and the Navy.

OFFICER RECRUITING

There were two general classifications of officers in the IJA: Regular and Reserve officers. There were, however, three different types of officer, which depended upon their education and background:

1. Regular Commission. These were granted to those men who had either (a) graduated from the Japanese Military Academy or Air Academy as officers of the line branch; (b) graduated from technical or scientific institutions or the Intendance School as officers of the services. Most were selected while still in school, then educated at government expense. University graduates were commissioned as first lieutenants; (c) or were selected warrant officers and NCOs under the age of thirty-eight who received one year courses at the Military Academy, the Air Academy, the Military Police School or other army schools. In peacetime they would not rise above the rank of captain owing to retirement on age.

A line of Japanese tankettes moving through a ceremonial archway during a pre-war parade in Japan. (IWM: STT 875)

Medium tanks on parade in Japan. The tanks were an impressive sight, although the IJA did not take to armoured warfare as well as their German Axis partners did. (IWM: STT 774)

2. Reserve Commission. These were mainly Class A reserve officer candidates who had passed the necessary course. They were drawn from the normal batches of conscripts and held certain educational qualifications. After three months with their units they became eligible for selection, then after a further three months were classified 'A' or 'B', the former being suitable officer material, the latter suitable NCO material. The 'A' candidates then attended a regular course for reserve officer candidates. Once commissioned, they normally went into the reserve from whence they could be called up for active duty in wartime. They thus represented a large proportion of the IJA officers who served during the Second World War.

3. Special Volunteer Commission. Field and company officers from the reserve (and later in the war young reserve officer candidates) could be allowed to volunteer for periods of active service. They might also qualify by examination for a one-year course at the Military Academy after which they became 'special volunteer regular officers' and could rise to the rank of major.

There were basically nine grades of officer rank:

Second Lieutenant	(*Sho-i*)
First Lieutenant	(*Chu-i*)
Captain	(*Tai-i*)
Major	(*Shosa*)
Lieutenant-Colonel	(*Chusa*)
Colonel	(*Taisa*)
Major-General	(*Shosho*)
Lieutenant-General	(*Chujo*)
General	(*Taisho*)

Officers and other ranks wore rank patches on the sides of their tunic and overcoat collars, also on open-necked shirts. These patches were: red cloth with yellow cloth stars for privates; red cloth with a central gold stripe and gilt stars for NCOs; gold with red stripes and gilt stars for officers up to the rank of colonel; general officers' rank patches were all gold with gilt stars. Senior privates and NCOs also wore rank badges on their right arms above the elbow. In combat areas it was common for none of these rank badges to be worn (ditto unit insignia) for security and to prevent the wearer becoming an individual target. Note also that the rank of field-marshal (*Gensui*) was only an honorary one which was given to some generals by the Emperor.

WARRANT OFFICERS (WO) AND NON-COMMISSIONED OFFICERS (NCO)

WOs (*Junshikan*) were normally selected from the NCOs (*Kashikan*) and treated as officers. There were three ranks of NCOs – sergeant major (*Socho*), sergeant (*Gunso*) and corporal (*Gocho*) – and they were in turn selected from the conscripts, i.e. the privates (*Hei*), who were themselves divided into four grades:

Leading Private (i.e. lance-corporal)	(*Heicho*)
Superior Private	(*Jotohei*)

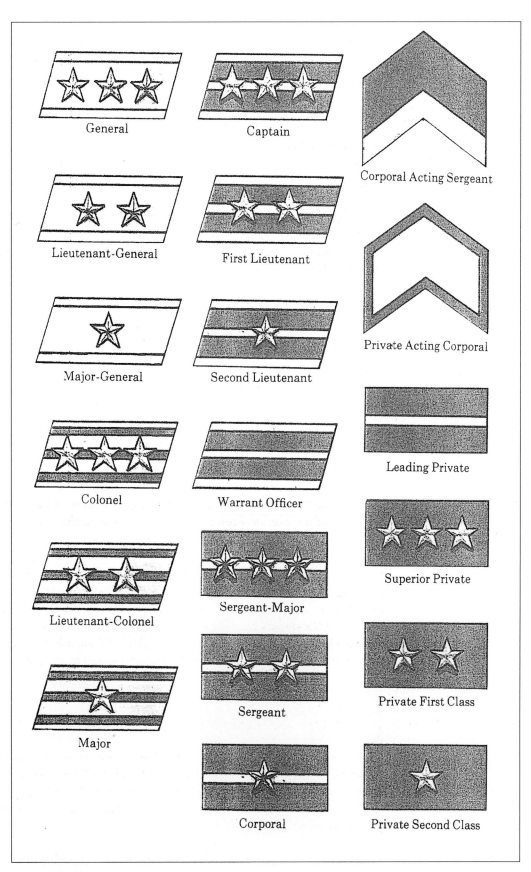

Badges of rank.

First Class Private   (*Ittohei*)
Second Class Private   (*Nitohei*)

They could not volunteer to become NCOs until they had served for three months and then completed a further nine months training with troops. After this they were selected to become NCOs and given a period of training (a year in peacetime, less in wartime) at an NCO school or at one of the Army branch or service schools. NCOs were also selected from Class 'B' reserve officer candidates and Apprentices from various units open to Army Youth Soldiers (see p. 25).

OTHER ARMIES

There were also two other armies which were formed at the instigation of the Japanese, namely the Indian National Army (INA) and the Burmese Independence Army (BIA). The former, the *Azad Hind Fauj*, came into existence in February 1942 and was made up of Indian POWs from Malaya and Singapore. They were persuaded to join by Pritam Singh's Indian Independence League and Maj Fujiwara Iwaichi's 'F Kikan' (part of Japanese Intelligence, the 'F' standing for Fujiwara), who before the war had cultivated the Indian Independence League and who had sent small teams ahead of, or with, the invading Japanese forces into South-East Asia. The 'Minami Kikan' organized the Burmese Independence Army. Later Col Iwakura Hideo's 'Hikari Kikan' (Lightning Organization) assumed the task when Iwakura became Chief of Staff of 28 Army in Burma. The first INA commander was a Sikh captain named Mohan Singh and there were some 20,000 volunteers out of the Indian POWs. However, when Singh became suspicious of Japan's true motives in India, he was arrested and the INA virtually disbanded. It reformed in June 1943 under the command of the Indian revolutionary Subhas Chandra Bose, who

Subhas Chandra Bose, commander of the Indian National Army, is seen here in Berlin, meeting Adolf Hitler in June 1942. On the left is envoy Dr Schmidt. (IWM: HU 40231)

Indian National Army troops surrendered in droves at the first opportunity. These were captured at Mount Popa and now wait to be shipped home to India. (IWM: SE 3827)

Men of the Indian National Army surrendering their weapons after being taken prisoner. They were for the most part unwilling 'volunteers' for the Japanese-inspired INA. (IWM: SE 3830)

Men of the Patriotic Burmese Forces, which were formed to assist the British in April 1945 from defectors who had served unwillingly with the Burmese Independence Army. (IWM: SE 4349)

wanted the force to spearhead the IJA advance into India, predicting that this would lead to a revolution against the British. The Japanese on the other hand wanted to employ the INA piecemeal, attached to Japanese formations, to be used for sabotage and propaganda purposes, or as guides and interpreters. As a compromise, some 7,000 INA were attached to Japanese units during the Imphal offensive of March 1944, while the remainder were used as auxiliaries. Poorly trained, badly equipped and with suspect morale, most of them quickly surrendered without firing a shot. Postwar, some survivors were put on trial and thus became local heroes during the run-up to independence. Bose died in August 1945, after being seriously injured when his plane crashed on take-off in Formosa.

The Burmese Independence Army (BIA) was formed in December 1941. The first leader was Aung San, who had fled to Japan in August 1940 with a nucleus of other Thakins (known as the 'Thirty Comrades'). Some 300 BIA led the Japanese invasion into Burma from Thailand in January 1942. Eventually there were some 1,300 BIA fighting against the retreating British in southern Burma, but they suffered heavy casualties and many deserted. Thereafter, they mainly followed up the IJA, but terrorized the local population and had to be ejected from numerous places by the Japanese military police (*Kempei*). On their return to Japan the BIA was disbanded and reformed as the Burma National Army (BNA) under Aung San, who was now a major-general in the IJA. Initially 3,000 strong, by August 1943, when Japan gave Burma its independence, it had some 10,000 men under Col Bo Ne Win (one of the 'Thirty Comrades'), while Aung San had become Burmese Minister of Defence. They were not allowed to fight alongside the IJA and in April 1945, with clandestine British encouragement, they defected to the Allies in droves; as the 'Patriotic Burmese Forces', they helped to cover IV Corps advance to Rangoon. Immediately postwar, Aung San remained in the forefront of Burmese political life, but was assassinated in July 1947.

TRAINING

Japanese military training was undoubtedly thorough, progressive and modern; however, it was also narrow, arbitrary and inflexible, so that it inhibited original thought and action. This led to leaders being afraid to use their initiative – rather they slavishly followed to the letter all orders from those above.

YOUTH TRAINING

Like their Nazi allies, Japanese children in the 1930s began military indoctrination at an early age. Formal regimentation and training began at about eight years old, when all boys starting in their third year at primary

Military instruction began early in childhood and was continued in middle and higher schools, being given to the students by IJA officers and soldiers. (US National Archives)

Conscripts under basic training in their barracks in Japan, before the issue of their uniforms. (IWM: HU 55367)

A most important part of initial training was rifle practice, learning how to fire the soldier's basic weapon from all positions – standing, kneeling and lying. (IWM: PIC 71353)

school received semi-military training from their teachers. Those students who went on to secondary school, higher school, college or university continued to receive military training, but now from regular army officers. In peacetime this amounted to about two hours a week, together with an annual camp/ manoeuvre period lasting four to six days. Numerous courses with a purely military content were also added to the curriculum at middle schools, higher schools and universities, so that all became, in a sense, military academies for the reserves. Those who had finished their schooling after the compulsory six years at primary school also received military training at special government established Youth Schools (*Seinen Gakko*).

Army Apprentices. Designed to foster the development of potential trained NCOs, especially in the technical fields, army apprentice schools were established for all the

Almost as important as rifle practice was bayonet drill – remember how much was included in all training programmes. The Japanese infantry invariably had their bayonets fixed when on operations. (IWM: HU 72213)

armed services. The Army apprentices, called Army Youth Soldiers (*Rikugun Shonenhei*), came in directly after leaving primary school, thus beginning their apprentice training aged 15–16 years (this was lowered to 14–15 years in 1943). At some point in this training they would be inducted into the Army as young soldiers with the rank of superior private (*Jotohei*) for a period of probation lasting six months, then promoted to corporal. In addition to aviation courses which are not covered here, there were four main types of army apprentice courses:

(a) **Artillery (*Shonen Hohei*).** This entailed two years at the Army Field Artillery School, the Army Heavy Artillery School or the Army Air Defence School;
(b) **Signals (*Shonen Tsuhinhei*).** This entailed two years at the Army Youth Signal School;
(c) **Tank (*Shonen Senshahei*).** This entailed two years at the Army Youth Tank School; and
(d) **Ordnance.** This entailed two years at the Army Ordnance School, similar to the other apprentice courses.

TRAINING FOR CONSCRIPTS

In peacetime, training for active service conscripts (Classes A and B-1) lasted for two years. The following shows the scope of the first year of infantry training.

January–May (5 months). Recruit training, including general military instruction (e.g. drill), section/squad training, bayonet fighting, target

Fencing practice (kendo = the way of the sword) was the traditional Japanese method of practising sword skills without getting badly hurt – although, even with the protective 'armour', the practice bamboo sword (known as a shinai) *could cause nasty bruising. (US National Archives)*

shooting. In the second month there was a five-day endurance march, with bivouacking at night, to toughen up recruits and train them to endure the cold weather.

June–July (2 months). Target shooting, field works construction, platoon and company training, bayonet fighting. Marching up to 20 miles a day with full equipment.

August (1 month). Company and battalion training, field works construction, combat shooting, swimming and bayonet fighting. Marching up to 25 miles a day with full equipment.

October–November (2 months). Battalion and regimental training, combat shooting. Autumn manoeuvres.

Many Japanese soldiers were of peasant stock, and thus were accustomed to hard work and privation. Their initial training was aimed at improving their physical hardihood, by calisthenics, wall-scaling, arduous marches (often in double time and uphill, with full pack and in adverse weather conditions, such as blistering heat or severe cold), open-air bivouacking, bayonet fighting, judo and swimming. Field exercises were both realistic and strenuous, with every effort being made to simulate battle conditions, including the use of live ammunition, which did result sometimes in casualties. Much stress was placed on night operations, with at least one night exercise a week when possible. The regime thus took the recruit's training from the smallest sub-unit through to regimental manoeuvres, culminating in combined exercises. After the end of the first year, a similar programme was followed, but with more time given to specialist training in the conscript's particular branch. This build-up of training, especially for the infantry, produced a tough, well-trained soldier, able to withstand hunger and fatigue for long periods.

Morale. Considerable emphasis was placed upon building up individual and corporate morale, especially via the reading of Emperor Meiji

Cadets at the IJA Military Academy on their passing-out parade. (IWM: HU 72214)

Tenno's* *Imperial Rescript to Soldiers*, which contained his five principles of military ethics – loyalty, courtesy, courage, truthfulness and frugality – expressed as follows:

Loyalty. The soldier should consider loyalty his essential duty. 'Remember that the protection of the state and the maintenance of its power depend upon the strength of its arms. . . . Bear in mind that duty is weightier than a mountain, while death is lighter than a feather.'
Courtesy. The soldier should be strict in observing propriety. 'Inferiors should regard the orders of their superiors as issuing directly from Us [i.e. the Emperor].'
Courage. The soldier should esteem valour. 'Never despise an inferior enemy, or fear a superior, but do one's duty as a soldier or sailor – that is true valour.'
Truthfulness. The soldier should highly value faithfulness and righteousness. 'Faithfulness implies the keeping of one's word, and righteousness the fulfilment of one's duty.'
Frugality. The soldier should make simplicity his aim. 'If you do not make simplicity your aim, you will become effeminate or frivolous and acquire fondness for luxurious and extravagant ways.'†

Undoubtedly all these 'virtues' were stressed and had much to do with the considerable fighting ability and determination of the average Japanese soldier. In addition it was stressed how much dishonour would result, both to the individual and to his family, were he to be taken prisoner by the enemy, not to mention the loss of his pension; in contrast, death in battle meant honour for himself and his family, a pension for them and, if possible, the return to Japan of the soldier's ashes for burial at the national shrine of Yasekuni. 'Fight hard,' the Japanese soldier was told, 'if you are afraid of dying, you will die in battle; if you are not afraid you will not die. . . . Under no circumstances become a straggler or a prisoner of war.

---

* Emperor Mutsuhito Meiji Tenno (1852–1912), during whose reign Japan was transformed from a feudal country into a great world power.
† Quoted in *Japanese Army Handbook, 1939–45* by A.J. Barker.

A class of trainee signallers practising with their morse keys. (IWM: HU 72221)

In case you become helpless, commit suicide nobly.'* Decorations and awards were considered important (see Chapter 8). Despite all this effort, both major and petty crime was not unknown in the IJA, with robbery, rape and trespass all being classed as prevalent offences overseas.

WARTIME TRAINING

The 1st and 2nd Conscript Reserves underwent six months' training only. It was less intensive than that for the active service conscripts, but it did try to cover a similar syllabus, albeit in just a quarter of the time. In peacetime those who had completed their two years of training and were relegated to the 1st Reserve had to undergo further training during their period of liability. However, in wartime this was both impossible and unnecessary. Moreover, conscripts often did the bulk of their training overseas, in China for example, where actual combat experience might be included in their training.

OTHER TRAINING

Officers. Most regular officers who reached the rank of major and above had been to the Japanese Military Academy (*Rikugun Shikan Gakko*). Candidates were selected from those who had graduated from one of the military preparatory schools (*Rikugun Yonen Gakko*) – located at Tokyo, Osaka, Nagoya, Hiroshima, Sendai and Kumamoto – after a three-year

---

* Despite this admonition (quoted in the *Soldier's Guide*), the US Army pamphlet makes the point that, later in the war, there were indications that not all Japanese soldiers were as eager to die as people expected. Heavy casualties, on occasions understandably, had a weakening effect on the morale of survivors.

Newly joined soldiers (in Manchuria) sing the National Anthem (Kimigayo) during their early morning flag-hoisting ceremony to pay homage to the Emperor. (IWM: HU 72216)

An early morning 'Banzai!' to the God Emperor was an essential beginning to each day. (IWM: HU 70945)

course. In certain circumstances, depending upon physical and educational qualifications, other candidates might be chosen from among active service NCOs (under twenty-five) and privates (under twenty-two). Younger applicants between the ages of sixteen and eighteen, if selected, would receive (in peacetime) two years' cadet training at the Junior Military Academy (*Rikugun Yoka Shikan Gakko*) at Asaka in Saitama-Ken, followed by eight months' duty with troops in their chosen branch of service, and finally, a further year and eight months at the Military Academy at Zama. After graduation candidates spent four months on probation with the grade of sergeant-major before receiving their commission. Training at the Military Academy was confined to general military subjects and practical work in the particular branch to which the cadet had been assigned.

Staff training. Regular officers with not more than eight years' commissioned service and at least one year with troops would be selected to attend the General Staff College (*Rikugun Daigakko*) in Tokyo for a three-year course in peacetime. In wartime the course was reduced to one year and was open to officers of units in fighting zones, irrespective of age or grade.

Reserve officers. Class A reserve officer candidates, having completed at least six months with their units, would be selected for various courses at the reserve officer schools. There were nine main ones – seven infantry, one artillery and one for transport – together with special reserve officer candidate schools for cavalry, engineers, signal, medical, veterinary, intendance and certain branches of artillery. Here instruction was normally eleven months but in some cases was reduced to six months. Subjects covered included training regulations and tactical textbooks, plus realistic, if elementary, practical training. Having graduated, candidates served with units on probation for some four months before being commissioned.

NCO training. NCO candidates were trained at one of the four NCO schools, where training was infantry dedicated (apart from some limited artillery and cavalry training at just one of the schools). Candidates in artillery, cavalry, engineers, signals, veterinary, intendance and ordnance were trained at their respective branch and service schools. Special technical courses were also available for NCOs at the Tank, Military Police, Medical and Mechanized Maintenance Schools.

Army Branch Schools. Special technical courses for officers were also run at the branch schools in Japan as follows:

Infantry School near Chiba City
Field Artillery School near Chiba City
Heavy Artillery School at Uraga
Air Defence School in Chiba City
Cavalry School in Chibaken (both horse and mechanized)
Tank School in Chiba (there were two more tank schools in Manchuria)
Engineer School at Matsudo
Signal School at Onomura
Transport School at Tokyo
Military Police School at Tokyo

Tanks moving across flooded fields during an exercise held by the Military Tank Training Institute near Tokyo. (IWM: HU 1211)

Off-duty soldiers playing baseball in Manchuria. (IWM: HU 72215)

Kendo was also taught at the Military Academy. The principles of this Samurai sport were also applied to bayonet practice. Note that the fencing sticks are shaped like rifles. (IWM: PIC 44451)

Army Services Schools. The Army obtained officers for the services by granting commissions to graduates of higher institutions after they had served for two months with troops as probational officers. Most had been chosen beforehand and had their technical education paid for by the Army. The Army services schools were designed to supplement civilian technical training and to adapt the knowledge for military use. The services schools were as follows:

Medical School at Tokyo
Veterinary School at Tokyo
Intendance School at Tokyo
Science School (formerly Artillery and Engineer School) at Tokyo
Ordnance School (formerly Artificer School) at Onomura
Chemical Warfare School in Chibaken
PT and Military Music School at Tokyo
Mechanized Equipment Maintenance School at Tokyo

CHAPTER 4
HIGHER ORGANIZATIONS

The Head of State and Supreme Commander of all the Armed Forces was the Emperor, the 'Imperial Son of Heaven of Great Japan'. During the Second World War it was the shy, unprepossessing Hirohito, who was born in 1901 and was the grandson of the great modernizing Emperor Meiji and son of Crown Prince Yoshihito who was known as Emperor Taisho (1912–26). Hirohito became Emperor in 1936, 'reigning not ruling' as Japanese tradition demanded, but showing his mettle when necessary, the first occasion being when he intervened forcefully in February 1936 to prevent a military insurrection. He remained in the background during Japan's early war successes, although Prime Minister Tojo increasingly sought to involve him when things turned against them, constantly reminding the populace, for example, of the Emperor's divine destiny, which would ensure ultimate victory in the war. Hirohito did exert some influence against the military in support of those who wanted peace and on 15 August 1945, the day after the surrender, he spoke directly to his people on the radio. It was the first time an emperor had *ever* spoken directly to his people! He was named as a war criminal by some Allied countries, including China and Australia, but was nevertheless granted immunity from trial. After the war his role became purely ceremonial, although Gen MacArthur credited him with playing a major part in what he termed 'the spiritual regeneration of Japan'. He renounced the theory of imperial divinity on 1 January 1946 and died in January 1989 after a long illness.

Head of State and Supreme Commander of all the Armed Forces was the Emperor, the 'Imperial Son of Heaven of Great Japan' Hirohito. Shy and unprepossessing, he generally remained in the background during the years of victory, then exerted some influence for peace against the army. Named as a war criminal by China, Australia and New Zealand, he was granted immunity from trial. He died in 1989. (Real War Photos)

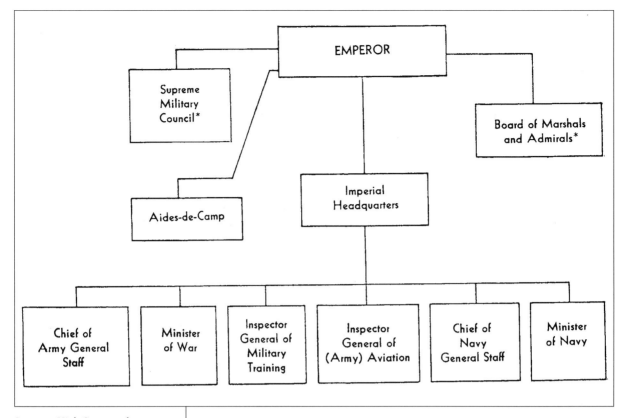

Japanese High Command.
(Source: TM-E 30–480)

HIGH COMMAND

In theory it was the Emperor who declared war, made peace and concluded treaties, but he was of course acting on the advice of his two military councils, the Supreme Military Council and the Board of Marshals and Admirals. In wartime an Imperial General Headquarters was established, with the job of helping the Emperor to exercise supreme command. This consisted of the Chiefs of the Army and Navy General Staffs, the Minister of War and of the Navy, plus a number of others (see drawing).

Underneath this High Command there were four principal agencies who ran the Army: the General Staff (*Sambo Hombu*), the Ministry of War, the Inspectorate General of Military Training and the Inspectorate General of Aviation. (The last of these is not covered in this book.)

The General Staff. Below the Chief of the General Staff (CGS) and the various VCGS, there were five Bureaux: General Affairs, Operations, Intelligence, Transport and Communications, and Historical.

The Ministry of War. This was the administrative, supply and mobilization agency of the Army. At its head was the War Minister, who was a member of the Cabinet and thus provided liaison between the Army and The Diet.* The War Minister had to be a general or lieutenant-general

---

* The Diet, also called the Imperial Diet, was the national legislature of Japan from 1889 to 1947 and comprised two houses with coequal powers.

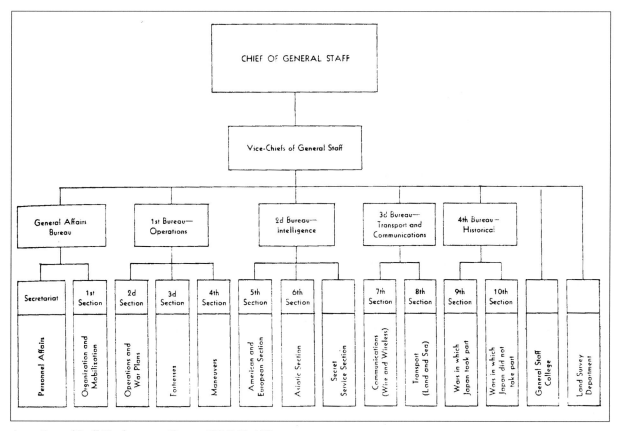

Army General Staff Headquarters. (Source: TM-E 30–480)

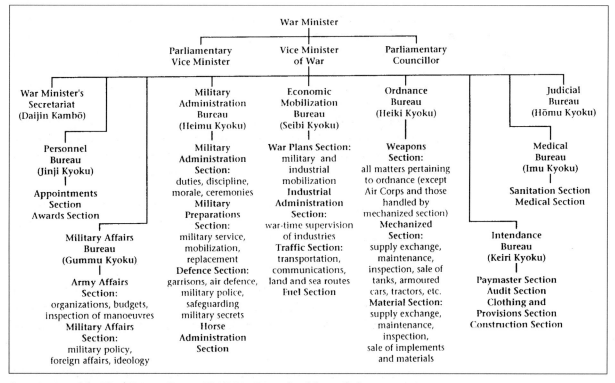

Organization of the War Ministry. (Source: TM-E 30–480, updated from 'Shokan')

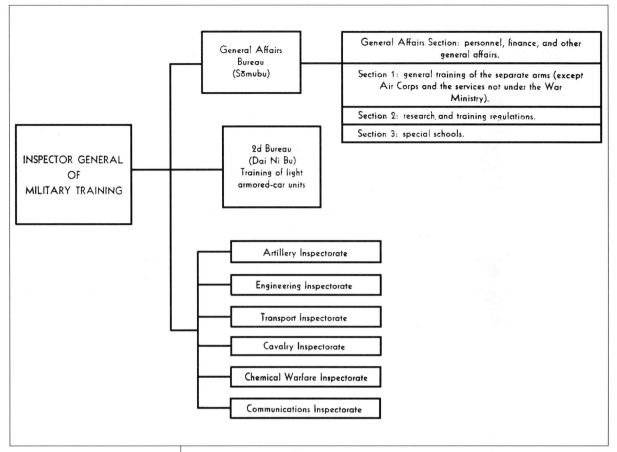

Inspectorate General of Military Training. (Source: TM-E 30–480)

on the active list and was directly responsible to the Emperor. For most of the war this post was held by Gen Hediki Tojo, who was also Prime Minister. The Ministry was divided into a Secretariat, eight Bureaux and several other smaller departments.

The Inspectorate General of Military Training. Last of the 'Big Three', this was devoted to training and comprised two bureaux and several inspectorates, covering technical and tactical training of the separate arms (except aviation) and of the other services not directly under the War Ministry.

TERRITORIAL ORGANIZATIONS

General Defence Headquarters (*Boei Soshireibu*). All units of the Japan Defence Army located in Japan itself, Korea and Formosa (Taiwan) were under the command of the General Defence HQ, created in 1941 and responsible to the Emperor via the Imperial GHQ. As the map of Japan shows, there were four army districts: Eastern, Western, Central and Northern. Below these were divisional districts, further divided into regimental districts which raised recruits for the arms and services.

Gloved hand on sword, this IJA officer is directing the fire of a Type 92 7.7mm heavy machine-gun at the enemy, somewhere in China. (IWM: STT 3306)

Infantry cluster around an emplaced artillery gun, probably a 7.5mm regimental gun. The soldiers all look too clean and tidy to be in action, so it was probably a staged photograph taken for PR purposes. (Tank Museum)

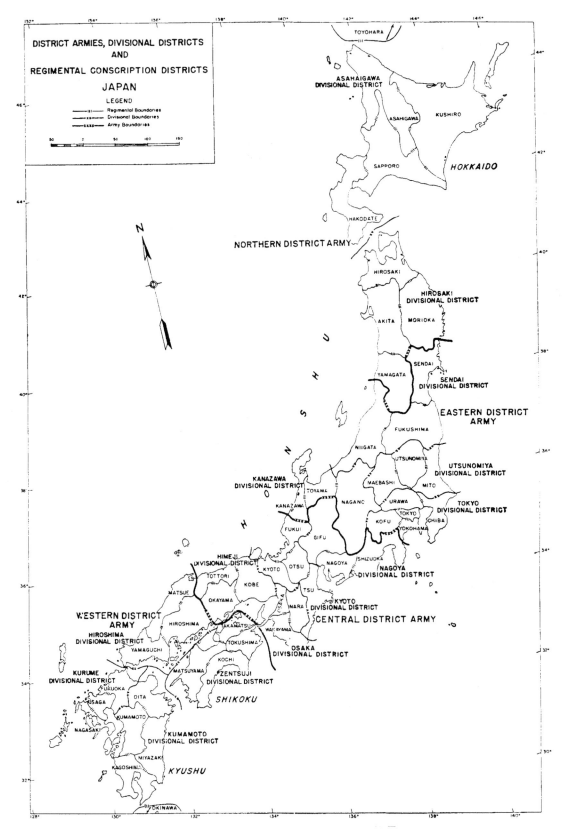

Districts of Japan. (Source: TM-E 30–480)

Army Districts and Divisional Districts (*Shikan*)

Army District	HQ Location	Divisional Districts
Northern	Sapporo	Asahigawa (7), Hirosaki (8)
Eastern	Tokyo	Tokyo (1), Guards,* Sendai (2), Kanazawa (9), Utsunomiya (14)
Central	Osaka	Nagoya (3), Osaka (4), Himeji (10), Kyoto (16)
Western	Fukuoka	Hiroshima (5), Kumamoto (6), Zentsuji (11), Kurume (12)

* The Guards Divisional District HQ was in Tokyo but it drew recruits from all over Japan.

(Source: TM-E 30–480)

Regimental Districts (*Rentaiku*)

Army District	Divisional District	Regimental District (and military affairs districts)
Northern	Asahigawa (7)	Sapporo, Hakedate, Kushiro, Asahigawa, Toyohara (Karafuto)
	Hirosaki (8)	Aomori, Morioka, Akita, Yamagata
Eastern	Tokyo (1)	Tokyo, Kofu, Urawa, Yokohama, Chiba
	Sendai (2)	Sendai, Fukushima, Niigata
	Kanazawa (9)	Kanazawa, Toyama, Nagano
	Utsunomiya (14)	Mito, Utsunomiya, Maebashi
Central	Nagoya (3)	Nagoya, Gifu, Shizuoka
	Osaka (4)	Osaka, Nara, Wakayama
	Himeji (10)	Kobe, Tottori, Okayama
	Kyoto (16)	Kyoto, Tsu, Otsu, Fukui
Western	Hiroshima (5)	Hiroshima, Matsue, Yamaguchi
	Kumamoto (6)	Kumamoto, Oita, Miyazaki, Okinawa, Kagoshima
	Zentsuji (11)	Takamatsu, Matsuyama, Tokushima, Kochi
	Kurume (12)	Fukuoka, Saga, Nagasaki
Korea (HQ Keijo)	Ranan (19)	Ranan, Kanko,
	Keijo (20)	Keijo, Heijo, Taikyu, Koshu
Formosa (HQ Taihoku)		Taihoku, Tainan, Karenko

(Source: TM-E 30–480)

DEPOT DIVISIONS

The Depot Division (*Rusu Shidan*) was primarily a training unit. Its strength varied from 10,000 to 20,000, depending upon the number of conscripts and/or reservists being trained. In peacetime it trained the yearly influx of conscripts, but in wartime it also was responsible for:

(a) equipping and providing refresher training for recalled reservists, using small detachments of the depot division
(b) organizing and equipping new divisional units
(c) providing reinforcments to make up for losses to divisions and other active service units, from the divisional district in which the depot division was located
(d) recruiting and training non-divisional units located in the divisional district
(e) supervising men transferred to the reserve
(f) military training in the district's schools, and
(g) arranging for the return to Japan of casualties and the ashes of the dead.

In some cases a field division which was originally raised in a particular divisional district might return to rest and refit in that district, in which case they might absorb or take over the functions of the depot devision. Since depot divisions were generally organized so as to be able to engage in field exercises and other forms of combined training, its units were capable, after a short period of preparation, to engage in combat, especially in defence of their home areas. For those who consider that the two atomic bombs should never have been dropped on Japan in August 1945, it is worth remembering that this undoubtedly saved the lives of hundreds of thousands of Allied servicemen and those of the Japanese who would have opposed them with the same fanatical courage they had demonstrated so often during the previous four years of war. There were nearly two million Japanese soldiers, organized into fifty-three divisions, in mainland Japan, waiting for the Allied invasion.

Divisional districts used two methods of despatching divisions or other units to operational areas. In an emergency the bulk of the depot division was despatched, made up to full strength with first reservists (*Yobihei*) and conscript reservists (*Hojuhei*), leaving behind just a small cadre for each unit. The division retained the number of the depot division. The depot division was then rebuilt by calling up more reservists and conscripts. The second method was to form the new division around a small nucleus of each unit in the depot division by calling up reservists in large numbers. These reservists then had to be housed in camps or billets near the location of the depot division, but did not occupy the peacetime barracks. Such a division received a new number.

Depot divisions used the name of their main location as well as the number, for example the Nagoya or 3rd Depot Division, and were organized on to the same triangular structure as field divisions, the basic organization being as follows:

A Japanese infantry section advancing down a railway line in China, with their platoon officer carefully watching their progress. Note that he is wearing officer's black marching boots and tall leather gaiters up to the knee. (IWM: STT 9649BB)

This partly ruined bridge near Shanghai provides a perilous pathway for advancing IJA troops. The Type 89 OTSU 13 ton tank was developed by the Japanese from the British Vickers Medium C. (Tank Museum)

Depot Divisional HQ and Staff
Military Affairs Dept (*Heimubu*)
3 × Infantry Regiments (Replacement Units (RU)) (*Hojutai*)
1 × Artillery Regiment (RU)
1 × Cavalry/Reconnaissance Regiment (RU)
1 × Engineer Regiment (RU)
1 × Transport Regiment (RU)
1 × Signal Unit (RU)
1 × Medical Unit (RU)
1 × Hospital
1 × Supply and Repair Depot
1 × Horse Training Centre

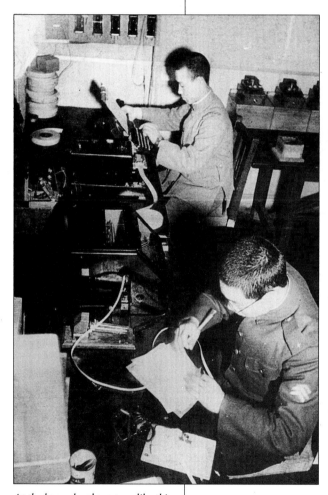

At the larger headquarters, like this one in China, signals personnel would receive messages on teletape machines from higher HQs in Japan. (IWM: HU 72219)

Method of Replacement. Initially, Japanese field units were usually sufficiently high in numbers to be able to provide first reinforcements from within existing establishment. However, once this source was exhausted, two methods were employed:

(a) Direct call on the depot division. This was the preferred system because it ensured that all officer and other rank replacements came from the divisional district. The major disadvantage was that this method took time.

(b) A Field Replacement Unit. This was a specially established unit, located in the theatre of operations and comprising some two infantry battalions, plus attached arms and services. It could rapidly send replacements to a unit to make up casualties quickly, but there was no guarantee that they would come from the same divisional district as the unit being reinforced. They would also vary in skill, ranging from veterans to newly trained conscripts, but it was far quicker than the other method.

Both these methods were employed. On some occasions complete divisions, newly trained, would be assigned on arrival from Japan to a relatively quiet area in an operational theatre (such as the rear areas in China) to gain operational experience. Once this final period of intensive training was completed, the division might provide replacements for units in the theatre, although they were not necessarily from the same divisional district.

C H A P T E R   5

FIELD ORGANIZATIONS

HIGHER ORGANIZATIONS

In the field the IJA was organized into Groups of Armies, Area Armies, Armies and Forces with Special Missions, which initially did not come under the command of any particular army. The basic division into Groups of Armies, under the Chief of the General Staff and his HQ, was as shown below.

(Note: As far as size was concerned, a Group of Armies was equivalent to an Allied 'Theatre of War' so, for example, the IJA 'Kwantung Army' would equate to the British 'Middle East Command'; Area Armies equated to British or US Armies; a Japanese Army would equate to a British or US Corps, being approximately between 50,000 and 150,000 men in size.)

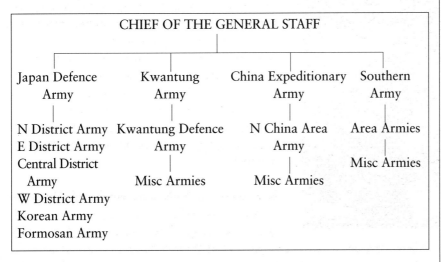

CHIEF OF THE GENERAL STAFF

Japan Defence Army	Kwantung Army	China Expeditionary Army	Southern Army
N District Army	Kwantung Defence Army	N China Area Army	Area Armies
E District Army			
Central District Army	Misc Armies	Misc Armies	Misc Armies
W District Army			
Korean Army			
Formosan Army			

EXAMPLE CONTENT OF AN ARMY

In the South-West Pacific area in early 1943 the IJA 18th Army had a paper strength of 130,000, although this figure was much higher than the actual strength on the ground, owing to casualties, reinforcements en route and detachments. However, it included the following units:

3 × divisions, plus the elements of a fourth
1 × independent mixed brigade
2 × infantry mortar battalions
6 × field artillery battalions
4 × independent field AA artillery companies
6 × independent field searchlight companies
2 × field machine cannon companies
1 × independent anti-tank gun battalion
1 × engineer group
7 × independent engineer regiments
1 × independent engineer company
2 × field road construction units
3 × field duty units
3 × shipping engineer regiments
1 × field MT depot
2 × field transport commands
1 × independent transport regiment
3 × independent MT battalions
6 × independent MT companies
1 × signal unit
2 × fixed radio units
5 × lines of communication hospitals
1 × water purifying unit
2 × debarkation units
2 × anchorages
2 × construction duty companies
3 × land duty companies
5 × sea duty companies
1 × water transport unit
5 × airfield battalions
3 × airfield companies
2 × base forces (naval troops)
1 × field freight depot
1 × field ordnance depot
4 × lines of communication garrison (sector) units

(Source: TM-E 30–480)

TASK FORCES

The Japanese often made use of a flexible system of grouping to make up task forces and combat teams for specific missions. The large number of

The infantry was the basis of the IJA. Here, the elite of the infantry, the Japanese Imperial Guard, march past in Tokyo. Note that they wore a different capbadge, which had a wreath incorporated behind the plain gold star, as worn by the rest of the IJA. (IWM: HU 70944)

Posed for the camera, this group of infantry apparently defending one end of a bridge show not only rifles and bayonets, and an officer with his sword drawn, but also a 50mm grenade discharger and a Model 11 light machine-gun. (IWM: NYT 68777)

Infantry/tank co-operation. All Japanese tanks were used in support of the infantry, like this tiny tankette. They were effective against the tankless Chinese, but no match for US/UK armour. (Tank Museum)

Tankettes towing trailers (for ammunition and stores) crossing a stream in China, via an ad hoc bridge. (Tank Museum)

Type 94 TK tankettes in China crossing a bridge that has just been completed by IJA engineers. (Tank Museum)

independent units that were not specifically part of any particular division assisted them in this task, although they never hesitated to divide or combine units and formations as needed. In the early part of the war well-trained and suitably equipped combat teams were able to advance quickly down through Malaya and the Indies to New Guinea and the Solomons. Later in the war, when they had less time to assemble and organize their forces, troops were frequently thrown into action without the benefit of combined training. For example, in one instance, quoted in the US Army *Handbook on the Japanese Military Forces*, the 6th Independent Anti-tank Battalion was rushed from Manchuria to Guadalcanal in twenty-three days in late 1942 to bolster the task force ordered to take Henderson Field.

There was no uniform type of task force, as the following examples show. In October 1942, to recapture the airfield mentioned above on Guadalcanal, the task force was organized with 2nd Infantry Division as its nucleus and comprised about 25,000 all ranks, heavily armed with artillery (six artillery regiments – one medium, two mountain and three field, plus additional AA, Anti-tank and Mortar battalions). In contrast, the Nankai Task Force in Rabaul in May 1942, designed for an overland campaign against Port Moresby, comprised mainly infantry, with 55th Infantry Division bolstered by another infantry regiment and supporting troops from 5th Infantry Division, but with little artillery support.

IJA infantry advancing through a swamp in the Mayu Peninsula in the Arakan in the autumn of 1943. They all carry 6.5mm Type 38 rifles with the standard 20in bayonet fixed. They have made efforts to camouflage themselves, but the light shirts that two of them are wearing will be easy to spot. (Author's collection)

IJA soldiers operating against Wingate's Chindits in the Shupii mountain range, Burma, March 1943. (Author's collection)

Japanese infantry carefully crossing a wide jungle pathway on the outskirts of a Burmese village, May 1943. (Author's collection)

RAIDING FORCES

These specially organized forces were employed in the South-West Pacific in 1943. For example, in the Buna, Gona and Salamaua areas, the IJA sought to destroy enemy artillery complexes by direct assault using raiding units (*teishintai*), the size and composition of such units depending upon the number of guns in the objective and the type of attack planned. Other raiding units (or flying columns (*betsudotai*) as they were called) operated in China and were highly mobile, with armoured cars, tanks, light artillery and so on in support. They operated over considerable distances, their aim being to disrupt or destroy enemy lines of communication by harassing enemy flanks and rear, destroying roads and railway bridges, carrying out ambushes and surprise attacks, occupying important and advanced positions before the main force had arrived and reconnaissance duties. They could also be called on to assist the main force when it was in a dangerous position.

SPECIAL DEFENCE UNITS

Temporary defensive positions first occupied by assault forces were then assigned to a temporary garrison unit (*shubitai*). However, where the positions were to be more permanent the *shubitai* was replaced by a *keibitai*, which usually contained higher grade service troops as well as garrison troops. There were also two other permanent special defence units (*keibi*): lines of communication garrisons, which were located between the front lines and the main bases to guard those employed in moving personnel and supplies; and observation posts/coast watching stations, whose role was to give advance warning of enemy landing operations or air attacks. Such posts were equipped with radios and, in some cases, with radar.

THE IJA DIVISION

In the IJA there was only one type of division, namely the Infantry Division. However, this did vary in size and strength, depending upon its role and the type of terrain in which it had to operate, so it could be said that there were in fact three categories of division, though there were never any armoured, mechanized, cavalry or airborne divisions as found in the armies of Great Britain, Germany, the USSR or the USA. Some tanks were employed by the Japanese, but they did not embrace armoured warfare in the same manner as the other main combatants of the Second World War. This was deliberate, the Japanese never having shown any interest in mobile armoured warfare, even in the horsed cavalry days; their army had always been dominated by infantry. The cavalry soldier's main task was that of reconnaissance.

The three types of infantry division were: 'A' (*Ko*) – reinforced; 'B' (*Otsu*) – standard; 'C' (*Hei*) – garrison/special. Even this was not strictly adhered to, so a 'B' type standard division might, in a particular set of circumstances, have 'A' strength artillery units. Even the strength of the basic infantry units could be varied when necessary, but the standard 'B' type organization is the main one described in the charts and tables that follow.

The backbone of the Japanese Army was the infantry. This soldier is fully dressed in the M1938 field dress. Note his leather belt, ammunition pouches and other personal items neatly stowed on his person. Note he wears no badges: this was for security reasons in the field. (US National Archives)

Divisional content. The units that made up the standard division consisted of: a Divisional HQ and a divisional signal unit; an infantry group HQ and three infantry regiments (each equivalent to a British brigade); an artillery regiment; a cavalry/reconnaissance regiment; an engineer regiment; a medical unit; field hospitals; a water purification unit; a transport regiment; an ordnance unit and a veterinary unit. The strengthened division would be augmented with additional personnel, vehicles and firepower, such as extra field artillery or mountain artillery, an organic tank unit or perhaps the presence of a chemical warfare/ decontamination unit, depending on circumstances. The extra personnel in the 'teeth arms' would then mean that other units in the division – medical, ordnance, veterinary, etc. – all had to be that much larger. In some cases they were perhaps relics of the original 'square' division (see below) which still existed in northern China and Manchuria. They were not designed for jungle warfare. Special 'C' type divisions were normally smaller units, with fewer infantry – only two infantry regiments instead of three – and thus fewer weapons; they were used for garrison/anti-guerrilla duties, for example, in parts of China.

The IJA used the term 'Intendance' to cover what western armies referred to as the 'Quartermasters Department'.

Square to Triangular. Until 1936 the IJA division had been based on a square organization, with four infantry regiments, the total strength being some 25,000. However, this organization proved ponderous and inflexible, as well as lacking in transport, artillery and automatic weapons. The IJA, like other armies of the period, decided to opt for a triangular organization, which reduced its strength to some 20,000 men. An example organization of the 'B' type standard division is shown in the chart on page 56.

Infantry using ad hoc scaling ladders to climb the walls of Kaifeng in the Henan Province of China, under cover of a smokescreen. (IWM: NYT 68514)

INDEPENDENT BRIGADES

The Japanese often employed independent brigades for special roles. Commanded by a major-general, their strength might vary between 3,000 to 6,000 men, such independent brigades being organized and equipped for their particular task. For example, for garrison/anti-guerrilla duties in China three or four infantry battalions (each of three or four companies), 750–900-strong, would suffice; they were mainly equipped with rifles and other small arms, with small numbers of artillery, engineers and signals in support. They did not need additional powerful weapons such as medium artillery or tanks, as the Chinese Army that faced them was relatively unsophisticated. However, those brigades operating in South-East Asia, the Netherlands East Indies and the central Pacific theatre, where they might meet more sophisticated and better equipped opponents, were at the opposite end of the scale; they were therefore given more firepower (including artillery, mortars and anti-tank weapons), and such brigades could be more than double the size and strength of the others, with perhaps four to eight infantry battalions, an artillery battalion, and so on. An example organization of an independent brigade is given in the chart on page 57.

Independent Regiments. To defend the welter of islands in the Pacific, mixed independent regiments, like mini-brigades, were formed, designed for their special task with, for example, a small artillery, AA or tank sub-unit attached. See the chart on page 61 for an example.

FORTRESS UNITS

Based on fixed coastal artillery units which formed the nucleus, fortress units contained infantry units whose task was to defend the coastal batteries from close-quarter attack. They were often supported by mountain artillery. Such units were located in the Bonin Islands and the Ryukyu Islands,* as well as on the coasts of Japan, Korea, Formosa and Manchuria. Such fortresses were commanded by senior officers, with ranks ranging from colonel up to lieutenant-general, who were responsible to the commander of the army district or army in which the fortress was located. A typical organization consisted of an HQ, one or more heavy artillery battalions (up to a regiment), one or more infantry battalions, construction and port engineers, signals units and AA units. Armament included coastal guns ranging from 4.7in up to 16in. There were some twenty-three of these fortified zones on mainland Japan, Korea, Formosa and Manchuria.

THE STANDARD TRIANGULAR INFANTRY DIVISION

This was the basis of the IJA and its outline organization is shown in the chart on page 56. However, more information about its component parts is given here.

1. Divisional Headquarters

Containing some 300 all ranks, a divisional HQ was commanded by a lieutenant-general, with a colonel of the General Staff as his Chief of Staff. The staff was divided into two sections: the general staff section and the administrative staff section. To the staff were attached five departmental sections, plus ordnance, signals and veterinary detachments.

---

* The Bonin Islands are twenty-seven volcanic islands in the Pacific between Japan and the Marianas; they were annexed by Japan in 1876. There are more than seventy Ryuku Islands, running from the southern tip of Kyushu Island (Japan) to Taiwan. The largest is Okinawa, under Japanese control since 1879.

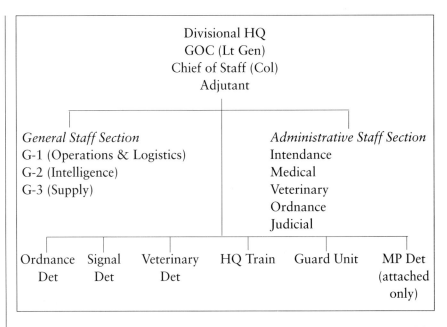

G Staff Section. This comprised some 75 officers and men, supervised by the Chief of Staff, who also coordinated the work of the administrative staff section. In addition, he acted as a link from the GOC to the unit commanders, heads of departments, civil authorities, etc. He thus 'filtered' all questions before they went to the GOC. The G-1 was a lieutenant-colonel who dealt with operations, training and communications. In addition he had a signal officer, a code officer, a gas officer and an ordnance officer as assistants. The G-2 was a major who dealt primarily with intelligence, maps, censorship and mobilization. The G-3 was a captain who dealt with rear services, supplies and lines of communications matters. The adjutant had a captain and a lieutenant to assist him.

A Staff Section. Together with the departmental sections this comprised some 175 officers and men. It was headed by a lieutenant-colonel who dealt with all reports (except those relating to operations) and exercised general supervision of all administrative work. Also in the section were a captain/lieutenant in charge of appointments, promotions, personnel, personal records of officers and NCOs, and administrative details of mobilization; a captain/lieutenant in charge of all matters connected with the departmental services, and for the preparation of administrative orders; and a captain/lieutenant in charge of documents and the secretarial work of the division.

Departmental Sections. The number and rank of the officers employed in these sections varied between divisons; the following is a useful guide.

(a) Intendance – a colonel, three majors and seven or more captains/ lieutenants
(b) Medical – a colonel, two or three other MOs
(c) Veterinary – a lieutenant-colonel, one or two other veterinary officers
(d) Ordnance – a major, two or more captains/lieutenants from the technical service
(e) Judicial (legal) – several officers.

Detachments. Making up the rest of the headquarters were the ordnance, signal, veterinary and guard detachments, together with the drivers of the divisional HQ vehicles.

2. Divisional Signal Unit

Commanded by a captain, its strength was some 250 all ranks and it comprised an HQ, two wire (line) platoons, each of four sections, one radio (wireless) platoon of eight to twelve sections, and one material (equipment) platoon. The size varied according to the number of radio sections, which could be added to or decreased as required. The HQ consisted of the commander (captain) and some twenty NCOs and men. A runner or liaison section might be included. Each wire platoon was divided into four sections, total strength being some fifty all ranks, commanded by a lieutenant or second lieutenant. The radio platoon was over twice as strong, also commanded by a lieutenant or second lieutenant, the number of sections varying from eight to twelve, each with one radio set. The material platoon was divided into two sections, its total strength was thirty-five all ranks. The unit equipment included 32 telephones, 30 miles of insulated wire, 2 ground-to-air radio sets, 8–10 other radio sets, pigeons, dogs, helio lamps, semaphores and ground panels as well as aircraft pick-ups. Personnel were normally armed with rifles.

3. The Infantry Group

The largest element of the division was the infantry group, which was commanded by a major-general and comprised a headquarters, an infantry signal unit (but only in a strengthened division) and three infantry regiments. In some cases there were also tankette companies assigned.

Headquarters. This was composed of 70–100 all ranks, divided into an administrative staff, an HQ guard (with automatic weapons) and a field baggage section. In a standard division there would normally be a small signal unit attached from the divisional signals unit.

Infantry Group Signal Unit. Found only in the strengthened division, this unit was normally commanded by a captain/lieutenant and divided into an HQ, a wire platoon and a radio platoon. Total strength was about 115 men and 24 horses. Its equipment included 12 telephones, 5 light radio sets, 2 switchboards and 11 miles of insulated cable.

Infantry group tankette company. This contained three or four platoons of tankettes, plus a supply train, in total some 80–120 personnel. The seventeen tankettes and trailers were probably used either for recce, because the divisions in which they were found did not have cavalry/reconnaissance regiments, or for moving ammunition with their trailers in forward areas.

Three Infantry Regiments. Commanded by a colonel, each regiment consisted of RHQ (including the regimental supply train), regimental

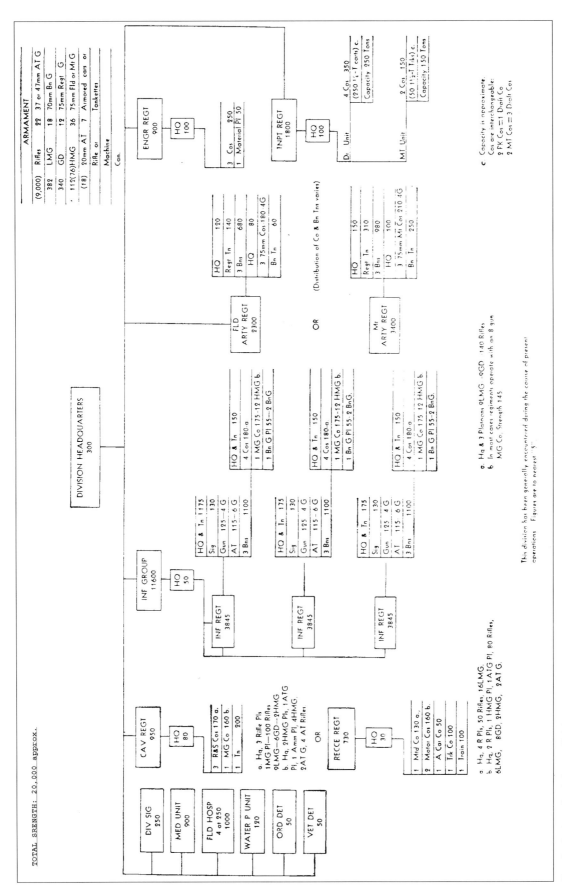

Standard triangular infantry division.

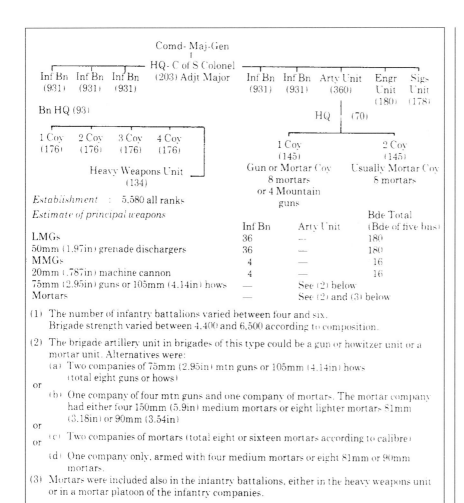

Comd- Maj-Gen

HQ- C of S Colonel
(203) Adjt Major

Inf Bn (931) Inf Bn (931) Inf Bn (931) Inf Bn (931) Inf Bn (931) Arty Unit (360) Engr Unit (180) Sigs Unit (178)

Bn HQ (93)

HQ (70)

1 Coy (176) 2 Coy (176) 3 Coy (176) 4 Coy (176)

Heavy Weapons Unit (134)

1 Coy (145)
Gun or Mortar Coy
8 mortars
or 4 Mountain
guns

2 Coy (145)
Usually Mortar Coy
8 mortars

Establishment : 5,580 all ranks

Estimate of principal weapons

	Inf Bn	Arty Unit	Bde Total (Bde of five bns)
LMGs	36	—	180
50mm (1.97in) grenade dischargers	36	—	180
MMGs	4	—	16
20mm (.787in) machine cannon	4	—	16
75mm (2.95in) guns or 105mm (4.14in) hows	—	See (2) below	
Mortars	—	See (2) and (3) below	

(1) The number of infantry battalions varied between four and six. Brigade strength varied between 4,400 and 6,500 according to composition.

(2) The brigade artillery unit in brigades of this type could be a gun or howitzer unit or a mortar unit. Alternatives were:

    (a) Two companies of 75mm (2.95in) mtn guns or 105mm (4.14in) hows (total eight guns or hows)

or

    (b) One company of four mtn guns and one company of mortars. The mortar company had either four 150mm (5.9in) medium mortars or eight lighter mortars 81mm (3.18in) or 90mm (3.54in)

or

    (c) Two companies of mortars (total eight or sixteen mortars according to calibre)

or

    (d) One company only, armed with four medium mortars or eight 81mm or 90mm mortars.

(3) Mortars were included also in the infantry battalions, either in the heavy weapons unit or in a mortar platoon of the infantry companies.

Organization of a typical Japanese independent infantry brigade. (All ranks strength is shown in parenthesis.)

signal company, a regimental infantry gun unit, a regimental anti-tank gun company, and three infantry battalions, with a pioneer or labour unit attached.

Note: a strengthened regiment could vary between 4,831 and 5,087 all ranks, with 756–1,083 horses and correspondingly more weapons.

Component Parts of the Infantry Regiment.
(a) *Infantry RHQ*. This was composed of some fifty-five officers and men, divided into a staff (administration, code and intelligence, ordnance and intendance sections), an AA section/HQ guard and a colour guard. Details of strengths were:

Officers:		
	Regimental Commander (Col)	1
	Operations/Training officer (Maj)	1
	Adjutant (Maj/Capt)	1
	Colour bearer (Lt)	1
	Code/Intelligence officer	1
	Gas/smoke officer	1
	Ordnance officer	1
	Intendance officer	1
	Medical officers	2
	Veterinary officer	1
	TOTAL =	11*

*Other officers may be added.

Administration:		
	Sergeant Major in charge of personnel records	1
	Sergeant Major in charge of supply	1
	Sergeant Major in charge of arms and equipment	1
	Sergeant Major in charge of orders (liaison)	1
	Runners and Orderlies	6
	Medical Orderlies	2
	Veterinary Orderlies	2
	TOTAL =	14

Code and Intelligence section: 2 NCOs and 8 men
Ordnance section: 1 Ordnance NCO and 6 Technical NCOs
Intendance section: 3 men, including Pay NCO
AA section/HQ guard (with LMG): 1 NCO and 4 men
Colour Guard: 5 men

Regiment Supply Train: divided into a field (baggage) section and an ammunition section. Its transport included 30 one-horse, two-wheeled carts and some 40 packhorses. It carried the regimental baggage plus one day's rations for all regimental units not included in battalions. Kitchen equipment was normally carried in the divisional supply train, but might be attached to regiments on occasions. Frequently all regimental trains were grouped together. The ammunition train, which was also equipped with horses and two-wheeled carts, carried one day's ammunition for the regiment. Strengths were: field (baggage) section: 1 NCO and 39 men; ammunition section: 1 NCO and 80 men; regimental supply train: 121 men (size and strength could vary, especially if the train was motorized).

(b) *Regimental Pioneer (Labour) Unit.* This was generally found in all 'A' Type (reinforced) divisional organizations, with a set composition of six sections and a material section, comprising 100–200 men. Its principal duties were general construction work. When a 'B' Type (standard) division moved into an area where personnel were needed for demolition work or road construction or the like, a labour unit of 4–5 sections was drawn from infantry companies and augmented by a few engineers. In some cases a labour unit of some 250 men might be found in any division but this did not automatically involve an increase in regimental strengths.

(c) *Regimental Signal Company.* The company had a strength of three officers (captains or lieutenants) and 129 men, and was divided into

Company HQ (30 all ranks) and two platoons: no. 1 Line Platoon (29 all ranks) and no. 2 Wireless Platoon (73 all ranks).

Company headquarters consisted of a commanding officer (captain or lieutenant); an administration section comprising a sergeant-major in charge of records, and two NCOs (supply, and arms and equipment respectively); 5 orderlies and 2 medical orderlies; and a runner (liaison) section, consisting of a WO and 18 men.

No. 1 Platoon (Line), commanded by a lieutenant, consisted of four wire sections, each of an NCO and 6 men. No. 2 Platoon (Wireless), also commanded by a lieutenant, consisted of eight radio sections, each of an NCO and 8 men. Their equipment included 12–20 telephone sets, 11–30 miles of insulated wire, 3–5 light radio sets, 2–3 ground-to-air sets, ground-to-air panels, dog sections, pigeon sections and a heliograph.

(d) *Regimental Infantry Gun Company*. With a strength of 122, it comprised Company HQ (25 all ranks); a Firing Unit (66 all ranks) of two gun platoons; and an ammunition platoon (31 all ranks).

Company headquarters consisted of a commanding officer (captain); an administration section comprising a sergeant-major in charge of records, and two NCOs (supply, and arms and equipment respectively); 6 runners and orderlies; 2 medical orderlies; a signal section (an NCO and 6 men) and an observation section (an NCO and 4 men).

The firing unit comprised two gun platoons. Each platoon was commanded by a lieutenant and consisted of two gun sections of an NCO and 15 men. The guns were usually four 75mm infantry guns, although in some divisions two anti-tank guns were substituted for two of the infantry guns, while in others, 81mm mortars were substituted or added. The ammunition platoon consisted of 31 men.
(In the 'A' Type (reinforced) division, the regimental infantry gun company might be replaced by a regimental infantry gun battalion, which had a strength of 364 all ranks and was armed with eight 75mm infantry guns.)

(e) *Regimental Anti-tank Company*. With a total strength of 116 all ranks, it comprised Company HQ (20 all ranks); a Firing Unit (75 all ranks) of three platoons; and an ammunition platoon (21 all ranks).

Company headquarters consisted of a commanding officer (captain); an administration section comprising a sergeant-major in charge of records, and two NCOs in charge of supply, and arms and equipment respectively; 7 runners and orderlies; 2 medical orderlies; and an observation section (an NCO and 6 men).

The firing unit comprised three gun platoons. Each platoon was commanded by a lieutenant and consisted of two gun sections, each of an NCO and 11 men. The guns were usually 37mm anti-tank guns. The ammunition platoon consisted of 21 men.

Sometimes this unit was merged with the infantry gun company, the armament then being two 75mm infantry guns and two 37mm anti-tank guns. The 'A' Type unit was increased in overall strength to about 130 all ranks and its firepower increased to six 37mm anti-tank guns. It was also not a regimental unit in the strengthened division; instead each of the three battalions had its own anti-tank gun company which comprised four 37mm anti-tank guns and had a strength of approximately 100 all ranks.

(f) *Infantry Battalion*. The standard infantry battalion was commanded by a major and comprised an HQ and supply train (147 all ranks), four rifle companies (each 181 all ranks), a machine-gun company (174 all ranks) and a battalion gun platoon (55 all ranks). Its total strength was 1,100 all ranks. Strengthened infantry battalions had, as well as greater manpower and weaponry within companies, additional guns so that the battalion gun platoon became a company of four guns (although the machine-gun company was sometimes reduced in size to eight or even four guns), and an anti-tank gun company was sometimes added. Total strength varied between 1,626 all ranks for a strengthened battalion with an HQ and supply train, four rifle companies (each 262 all ranks) which contained heavy weapons platoons, a machine-gun company of four 7.7mm HMGs, a battalion gun company of four 70mm and an anti-tank company of four 37mm guns; to 1,401 all ranks for the strengthened and modified battalion with fewer men per company (only 205), a machine-gun company of twelve HMGs and a battalion gun company with four 70mm guns and eight 20mm anti-tank guns.

However, the standard battalion comprised:

Battalion headquarters (37 all ranks) included 8 officers. The commanding officer (major) was supported by an adjutant (captain or lieutenant), an ordnance officer, an intendance officer, three medical officers, and a veterinary officer. Additional officers could be added. The administration section (14 men) comprised 4 sergeant majors, in charge of personnel, supplies, arms and equipment, and orders (liaison) respectively; 5 runners and orderlies; 4 medical orderlies; and a veterinary orderly. The other sections were made up as follows: ordnance and intendance section: 2 NCOs and 1 technician; liaison section: 4 men; code and intelligence section: an NCO and 2 men; AA section/HQ Guard: 5 men with one LMG; battalion supply train: 110 men (cf. regimental supply train); field baggage section: an NCO and 49 men; ammunition section: an NCO and 59 men.

The standard rifle company was commanded by a captain and comprised a Company HQ (19 all ranks) and three rifle platoons (each 54 all ranks), with a total strength of 181 all ranks. Company headquarters comprised the company commander (captain), with a WO in charge of personnel, a sergeant major (records), and two NCOs (supply, and arms and equipment) respectively. There were also 10 runners and orderlies (including buglers) and 4 medical orderlies.

Each rifle platoon was commanded by a lieutenant, assisted by a liaison NCO, and consisted of three rifle/LMG sections, each of an NCO and 12 men. There was also a grenade discharger section of 13 men. Equipment included 139 rifles, 9 LMGs and 9 grenade dischargers.

The standard battalion machine-gun company was a twelve 7.7mm HMG company which consisted of an HQ (14 all ranks), a firing unit (138 all ranks) of three platoons, each of 4 HMGs, and an ammunition platoon (22 men), with a total strength of 174 all ranks. Commanded by a captain, company headquarters consisted of a WO in charge of personnel,

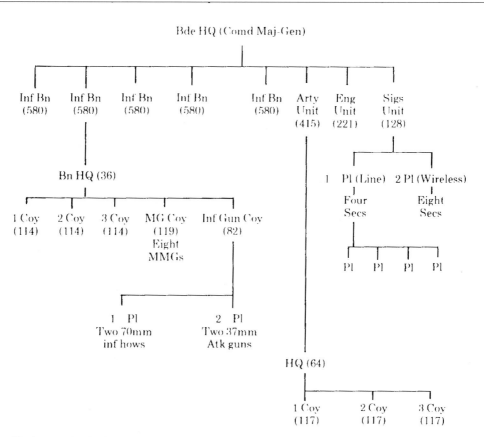

Bde HQ (Comd Maj-Gen)

Inf Bn (580) Inf Bn (580) Inf Bn (580) Inf Bn (580) Inf Bn (580) Arty Unit (415) Eng Unit (221) Sigs Unit (128)

Bn HQ (36)

1 Coy (114) 2 Coy (114) 3 Coy (114) MG Coy (119) Eight MMGs Inf Gun Coy (82)

1 Pl Two 70mm inf hows   2 Pl Two 37mm Atk guns

1 Pl (Line)   2 Pl (Wireless)

Four Secs   Eight Secs

Pl Pl Pl Pl

HQ (64)

1 Coy (117)   2 Coy (117)   3 Coy (117)

Each Arty Coy had four 75mm field or mountain guns or 105mm howitzers.

The total of all ranks in this example was : 3,800

Summary of weapons

	Inf Bn	Arty Unit	Total (five bns)
LMGS	12		60
50mm (1.97in) grenade dischargers	16		80
MMGs (type 92, with AA mount)	8		40
37mm (1.45in) Atk guns	2		10
70mm (2.75in) infantry hows (battalion guns)	2		10
75mm (2.95in) fd or mtn guns or 105mm (4.14in) hows		12	12

Possible additions were a tank unit (92 all ranks), an anti-aircraft company (170 all rank) and extra artillery or anti-aircraft artillery.

Organization of a Japanese independent mixed brigade. (All ranks strength is given in parenthesis.)

a sergeant major (personnel records), two NCOs (supply, and arms and equipment respectively), 6 runners and orderlies, and 3 medical orderlies. The firing unit consisted of three platoons (each of 46 all ranks), each comprising a platoon commander (usually a lieutenant or second lieutenant), a liaison NCO and four gun sections, each of an NCO and 10 men. The ammunition platoon consisted of an NCO and three sections, each of 7 men.

The strength of the battalion machine-gun company could vary and there were both eight-gun and four-gun companies. The eight-gun type was most commonly used during operations in the Pacific theatre.

The battalion gun platoon was a small unit, commanded by a lieutenant or a second lieutenant and only 55 all ranks in strength. It comprised Platoon HQ (10 all ranks) a firing unit (30 men) of two 70mm gun sections and an ammunition section of 15 men. Platoon headquarters comprised the platoon commander, a sergeant major in charge of personnel records, two NCOs (arms and equipment, and observers respectively), 5 runners and orderlies, and a medical orderly. The two firing unit gun sections were identical, each under the command of an NCO, with 2 observers and 12 gunners.

4. Artillery

In the standard division the normal artillery component was a 36-gun regiment of 75mm field artillery, which could be horse-drawn, pack or motorized. Horse-drawn was the most common, comprising an RHQ, three battalions (each three gun companies of two gun platoons, each of two guns, a battalion supply train of three ammunition sections and a baggage section), plus a regimental supply train. Total strength was 2,300 all ranks, with 36 guns, 450 rifles (138 per battalion) and some 2,000 horses. If the regiment was motorized then the strength was reduced to 1,920 all ranks.

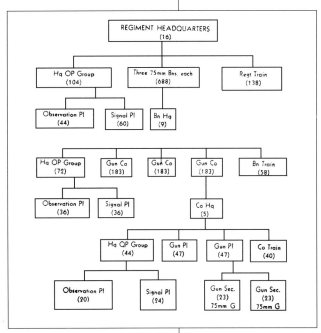

Organization of a field artillery regiment.

Regimental headquarters. Commanded by a colonel or lieutenant-colonel, there were 16 all ranks in each RHQ: the CO, the adjutant and 14 NCOs and men. In addition there was an HQ operational group consisting of an observation platoon and a signal platoon (one wire section and one radio section), which brought the strength of RHQ up to 120 all ranks.

Regimental supply train. Commanded by a captain or a lieutenant, this was divided into three ammunition platoons and a field (baggage) platoon, with a total strength of 140 all ranks.

Field artillery battalion. With a strength of between 680–700 all ranks, this comprised an HQ, three companies and a supply train. Battalion headquarters was commanded by a major, with a battalion staff and an

HQ operational group of an observation platoon, a signal platoon and a machine-gun section for defence, totalling 80 all ranks. The battalion supply train was commanded by a captain or lieutenant, with 60 all ranks, comprising three ammunition sections and a field (baggage) section. There were three gun companies, each commanded by a captain and composed of a company staff, an HQ operational group, two gun platoons (each two sections of 20 men) and a company supply train. Total strength was 180 all ranks with four 75mm field guns.

NB: As the outline organization of the standard division shows, in some standard divisions the artillery component could be a mountain artillery regiment instead of field artillery. Its organization is covered in outline in the next chapter.

5. Cavalry

Each infantry division contained either a cavalry or a reconnaissance regiment. The former consisted of an HQ and supply train, three rifle and sabre companies and a machine-gun company, its total strength being some 950 all ranks.

The *regimental headquarters* consisted of 82 all ranks, divided into a command section (20 all ranks), a signal section (mainly radio) (50 all ranks) and an equipment section (12 all ranks).
Regimental supply train. 200 men.
Rifle and sabre company. Each company contained 170 all ranks (total 510), comprising a company commander, company headquarters (16 all ranks), three rifle and sabre platoons (43 all ranks each), and a machine-gun platoon (24 men).

Each rifle and sabre platoon consisted of a platoon commander, a liaison NCO, three LMG sections, each of an NCO and 10 men, and a grenade discharger section, an NCO and 7 men, with two grenade dischargers. The machine-gun platoon consisted of a platoon commander, a liaison NCO and two LMG sections, each of an NCO and 10 men.

Machine-gun Company. This consisted of 150 all ranks, comprising a company commander, company headquarters (13 all ranks) and two machine-gun platoons (each of 46 all ranks), an anti-tank gun platoon (27 all ranks) and an ammunition platoon (25 all ranks).

Each machine-gun platoon consisted of a platoon commander, a liaison NCO, two machine-gun sections (each an NCO and 10 men) and two 20mm anti-tank rifle sections (each an NCO and 10 men).

The anti-tank platoon consisted of a platoon commander, an observer section and two gun sections (each an NCO and 10 men). Each section was armed with a 37mm anti-tank gun.

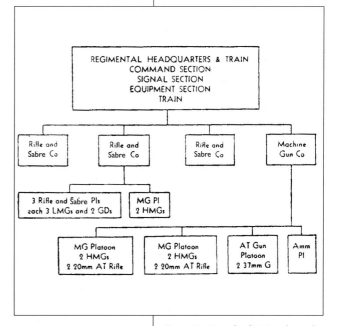

Organization of a divisional cavalry regiment.

The ammunition platoon consisted of a platoon commander and three sections each of 8 men.

Note: As the outline organization of the Standard Division shows, the Cavalry Regiment could be replaced by a Reconnaissance Regiment. Its organization is dealt with in the next chapter, see p. 69.

6. Engineers

Within the standard division there was a small three-company engineer regiment, normally composed of an RHQ, three companies and a materials platoon, with a total strength of 900–1,000 all ranks. Each company of 250 all ranks contained some four platoons (each of four sections) and a materials section (25 men). The regiment was commanded by a lieutenant-colonel, with 4 to 6 other officers and an HQ of 100 all ranks. They were divided into various sections dealing with signals, medical, intendance, ordnance and supply duties. Companies were commanded by captains or lieutenants with an HQ of some 25 men. Platoons were commanded by second lieutenants and had some 50 men in their HQ and four sections. The materials section carried tools and other equipment and was divided into 'Pack' and 'Draught' sections. The regimental materials platoon had an HQ and two sectioms with 50–100 men, with some fifteen trucks and various construction implements.

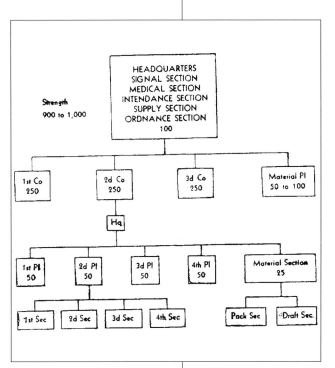

Organization of a divisional engineer regiment.

7. Transport

The divisional transport regiment comprised two battalions which might be draught, pack or motorized, with a total strength of 1,800–2,800 all ranks. Normally one battalion would be draught and one motorized. The former contained three or four companies, each of three platoons of three sections, with 250 single-horse, two-wheeled, transportation carts able to carry some 400–500lb each. The motorized battalion had two or three lorry companies, each of three platoons of three sections, with some 50 vehicles and 150 men per company. There might also be a road maintenance company and/or an armoured car transport company. Pack-horse companies had about 300 pack animals each of which could carry up to 200lb.

8. Medical

Within the standard division, the medical service was considerable. There was a medical unit which collected of the casualties, 3–5 field hospitals where they were treated, plus a water purification unit which was vital in areas where waterborne infectious diseases were prevalent. These units were additional to the MOs who were attached to all arms on the scale of three per battalion-sized unit. Infantry battalion MOs were assisted by two medical service NCOs, and similarly qualified orderlies were attached to sub-units on a scale of one per platoon.

Medical unit. This comprised an HQ and supply train, three collecting companies, each of three stretcher platoons and one ambulance platoon, with a total strength of 700–1,000 all ranks, 180 litters and 45 ambulances. Each company had some 20 litters and 15 ambulances, while the HQ train had extra carts for loading medical supplies, patients' clothing, etc., as well as chemical warfare decontamination material.

Field hospitals. Organized to accommodate 500 patients, each field hospital had a staff of some 250. It could be motorized, pack or draught. Three was the usual number of field hospitals in the standard division, with sometimes a fourth (known as the field reserve hospital) which functioned as a convalescent and evacuation hospital within the lines of communication.*

Water purification unit. Normally some 50–150 personnel, this unit was equipped with material to supply and purify water for the division.

9. Veterinary Unit

The small veterinary unit comprised only 50–100 all ranks. It consisted of a veterinary hospital staff, with individual sections being assigned to various divisional units.

10. Ordnance Unit

This comprised 50–200 all ranks assigned from the technical services.

* This was the area between the divisions and the base areas.

CHAPTER 6

THE COMBAT ARMS

ARMOUR

An impressive display of Japanese tanks, with Type 97 Chi-Ha medium tanks nearest the camera. There also appears to be a command tank SHI-KI in the front row (its frame-type radio aerial around the turret is just visible). (Tank Museum)

By combining the word for battle (*sen*) with the word for wagon (*sha*) the Japanese formed their word for a tank: *sensha*. Despite showing some early interest in tanks during the First World War, which led to the purchase of both British and French models, Japan did not wholeheartedly embrace the philosophy of armoured warfare as did, for example, the Germans and Russians. As a nation, Japan lacked a cavalry tradition –

Japanese light tanks in the Chunking area of central China. The tanks are only Type 97 TE-KE tankettes, but they appear to have caused considerable damage with their 37mm guns. (IWM: HU 2786)

Tank crews of these Type 89 OT-SU medium tanks have dismounted during training for a briefing. The Type 89 weighed 13 tons, had a crew of four and mounted a 57mm gun. (IWM: STT 72)

mounted warriors had played very little part in traditional warfare in mountainous Japan and those horsemen who were employed were used in the main for reconnaissance rather than shock action. Nevertheless they did build several hundred tanks in the early 1930s, becoming for a while one of the world's major tank-building nations (fourth behind the Soviet Union, France and Germany). These tanks were mainly light tankettes, based on the British Carden Loyd carrier, so they were of marginal use on the battlefield. Between 1933 and 1934 they formed four tank regiments in Japan and Manchuria and by the time war began with China in 1937, they had a strong armoured force of some 1,060 tanks, with eight armoured regiments in the field. However, many of these tanks were still the light tankettes or semi-obsolescent models with a poor performance and it is perhaps this which led them to believe that the tank was not a battle-winner.

Although they did form independent armoured units and in their training manuals advocated the theory of using tanks *en masse*, in practice they adopted the French system of dividing their tanks into numerous small units and spreading them throughout their army, purely in support of the dominant infantry arm. These small tank units worked quite well against the Chinese who at the time had no proper anti-tank weapons, let alone any tanks of their own, so the IJA continued to use their tank arm merely as mobile pill-boxes, seldom allowing them to operate independently. This policy would eventually prove disastrous against both American armour in the Pacific and Commonwealth armour in the Far East. By the time they realized their mistake it was far too late in the war and they suffered grievously against such redoubtable AFVs as the ubiquitous American-built Sherman medium tank. Japanese marines were also equipped with AFVs, and once the IJA ceased building amphibious tanks, development of these AFVs was taken over by the Navy.

The Tank Regiment (*Sensha Rentai*)
In designing their AFVs the Japanese had inevitably used the Chinese Army as their yardstick, so even the better tanks they produced in small numbers during the war years were still not up to western standards of firepower, protection and mobility. Their armoured commanders were brave enough, but lacked the knowledge or conviction to be able to use their tanks effectively. The Japanese 14th Tank Regiment, the only one operating in Burma, for example, was no match for XIVth Army's armoured units and found it difficult to carry out even the simplest manoeuvres, losing many tanks as they were pushed southwards. Among the tankettes they left in their wake were some ex-British Stuart light tanks captured from the British 7th Armoured Brigade during the early days of the war in Burma, so they had clearly appreciated the value of better light tanks in the jungle. The largest permanent Japanese armoured unit in the IJA was the tank regiment (*Sensha Rentai*), there being both independent tank regiments and infantry divisional tank units of comparable size. They comprised a headquarters, three tank companies each of four platoons of medium/light tanks and a regimental combat/ammunition supply train of some 80 trucks, with a total strength of 800–850 all ranks, with some 80–95 tanks.

Larger tank formations

Not all IJA armoured commanders were happy with the 'penny packeting' of their armour, citing as an example the considerable defeat which had been inflicted on the IJA by the Red Army armour at Nomonham in Outer Mongolia. Here, in August 1939, after three IJA divisions had made a massive attack on the Soviet forces the previous month, Marshal Zhukov had launched a counter-attack with concentrated tanks, flame-throwers and large numbers of aircraft against a 20–40 mile strip of territory. Lacking heavy tanks and air support, the IJA suffered a major defeat, losing 20,000 men in ten days and having to sue for peace.

This led to some tank regiments being grouped together into tank groups (*Sensha Dan*) comprising 3–4 tank regiments, plus supply and maintenance units, but without supporting arms (infantry, artillery, engineers, and so on) they could not operate independently. There was some evidence of at least one of these groups becoming the nucleus of an armoured division (*Sensha Shidan*) in Manchuria in 1943, but such formations were not used against British, Commonwealth or American armour.

Only strengthened divisions contained organic tank regiments, equipped with light/medium tanks. However, most IJA divisions did have a unit of tankettes, either in an infantry group tankette company or in the reconnaissance regiment (see below). There were also a number of independent tankette companies which had both tankettes and trailers; these were used for supply in forward areas in the Pacific theatre.

Reconnaissance Regiment

The standard infantry division contained either a cavalry regiment or a reconnaissance regiment This was in essence a mechanized cavalry regiment which contained horse troops, motorborne troops, armoured cars and/or light tanks/tankettes. The cavalry company had 130 horsed soldiers, the two motorborne companies comprised some 160 men each, there was an armoured company of seven armoured cars/light tanks/tankettes and a motor truck company of 100 trucks. In total the strength was 730 all ranks. Japanese armoured cars had the added ability of being able to be rewheeled so that they could run on railway lines, which often provided a much better alternative to the roads in some parts of the Far East. Indeed, armoured car-trollies, as they were called, had been used for some time to help protect the railway battalions in Manchuria against guerrillas and bandits.

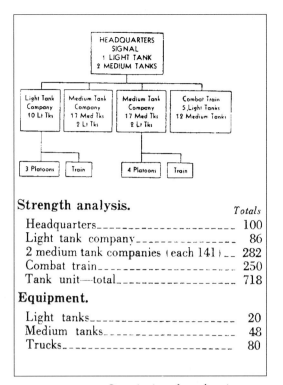

Strength analysis.

	Totals
Headquarters	100
Light tank company	86
2 medium tank companies (each 141)	282
Combat train	250
Tank unit—total	718

Equipment.

Light tanks	20
Medium tanks	48
Trucks	80

Organization of a tank regiment.

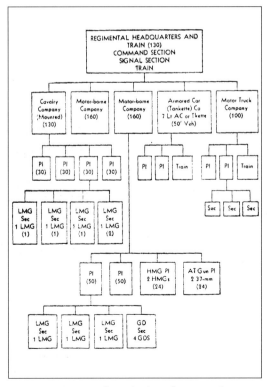

Organization of a reconnaissance regiment.

Cavalry charging across a stream. In addition to some independent cavalry brigades, the IJA used cavalry in some of their reconnaissance regiments in infantry divisions. (IWM: PIC 63771)

Japanese cavalry ride through the triple-arched Chungsan gate leading to Nanking. Cavalry troopers carried a sabre and a carbine (either the Meiji 38 or Meiji 44). (IWM: NYP 57279)

Equipment Totals:

Rifles or carbines	260
LMGs	28
HMGs	4
37mm or 47mm anti-tank guns	4
Grenade dischargers	16
Light armoured cars/tankettes	7
Other vehicles	61
Horses	188

ARTILLERY

Field artillery (*Yahohei*)

Prior to 1914 Japanese industry was not capable of producing artillery, so all guns were purchased from abroad, in particular from Krupp of Germany. During the First World War steps were taken to build foreign weapons – sometimes without bothering to obtain licences – and other foreign guns were modified to suit IJA requirements. The Osaka Arsenal became the principal centre of gun design and manufacture. Postwar it began to produce a comprehensive range of weapons from pack artillery to heavy guns. Two major attributes of Japanese field artillery designs were long range and light weight. In the standard division, the normal artillery component was a 36-gun regiment of 75mm field or mountain

Japanese artillery was lightweight, manoeuvrable and efficient. Here 105mm Type 92 guns carry out counter-battery fire. They were issued at Army level. (Tank Museum)

Horsed artillery struggles to cross a river in China. Horsed batteries were usually the norm for field artillery, although there were some wheeled/tracked gun tractors. (IWM: HU 66703)

artillery, which could be horse-drawn, pack or motorized. Horse-drawn was the most common (see p. 62). There were also a few independent field artillery regiments and battalions.

Mountain artillery (*Sampohei*)

Organized in a similar way to field artillery, mountain (pack) artillery regiments carried all their weapons and equipment on pack animals. Personnel strength was larger than that of the field regiment, totalling some 3,000–3,400 all ranks. The basic weapon was the 75mm mountain gun. There was also an independent mountain artillery regiment, which had only two battalions instead of three, thus its regimental strength was lower (only 2,500 all ranks), and its armament was only 24 guns. It is said that there was also one mountain regiment operating in the South-West Pacific, which was even smaller, because it had left most of its transport in rear areas. It was down to some 1,500 all ranks, had only three guns per company instead of four, and a pioneer section instead of the other gun section.

Medium artillery (*Yasen Juhohei*)

There were several types of medium artillery regiment in the IJA. The most common type comprised an RHQ, two medium battalions (each of three companies of eight horse-drawn/tractor-drawn 'Type 96' 150mm howitzers and a battalion supply train) plus a regimental supply train. Total strength was some 1,500 all ranks for tractor-drawn regiments and 2,300 for horse-drawn. Other medium regiments were equipped throughout with 105mm guns, while others had a mix of 150mm howitzers and 105mm guns.

Heavy artillery (*Yohoei*)

There were two categories of heavy artillery, fixed and mobile. The former was designed for coastal defence and was entirely static, although there were some mobile regiments equipped with tractor-drawn 240mm howitzers or even 300mm mortars.

Anti-aircraft and Anti-tank units

AA units. In the IJA these could be organized into brigades, regiments, battalions or independent companies. Additionally there were other AA units such as searchlight battalions and independent searchlight companies, heavy AA companies, machine-cannon companies, observation units and barrage balloon units. The 18-gun battalion, for example, comprised an HQ, three firing companies and a battalion supply train. Its strength was some 575 all ranks and it was armed with eighteen 75mm AA guns. There was also a 12-gun battalion with a total strength of about 400 all ranks.

Anti-tank units. These independent anti-tank battalions and companies were additional to the normal anti-tank guns in infantry battalions. AA units were also trained to fulfil a dual role. The independent anti-tank battalion had 18 guns (37mm or 47mm), some 500 men and could be motorized, horse-drawn or pack.

Artillery groups

In strengthened divisions there was often an artillery group, which comprised a group HQ, a mixed regiment of field artillery (75mm guns and 105mm howitzers) and a medium artillery battalion of 150mm howitzers. Other independent field/medium artillery or AA units might also be attached. An artillery group was commanded by a major-general or a full colonel. His HQ, which had the task of commanding all organic artillery in the division and providing unified control for any artillery attached, comprised a staff, a small guard, a supply train and sometimes an observation balloon platoon. Total strength was about 160 all ranks.

Miscellaneous

Other artillery units in the IJA included:

(a) Field searchlight battalions: each comprised a battalion HQ and two searchlight companies each consisting of a company HQ and two platoons, containing three sections (each one searchlight and a sound locator). Total strength: 450 all ranks, 12 searchlights, 12 sound locators and 50 vehicles.

(b) Independent mortar regiments and battalions: these were artillery units additional to the infantry mortar units.

(c) Shipping artillery regiments: these units were designed to provide AA (and anti-submarine) protection to troop transports, etc. Regiments had some 2,300 all ranks, broken down as usual through battalion, company, platoon to gun squads, armed with 75mm AA guns, 75mm field guns and 20mm machine-cannons. For example, a small group of army transports might be assigned two field artillery gun squads and two 20mm cannon squads.

(d) Artillery intelligence units: these were equipped for sound-ranging and flash-spotting.

(e) Observation balloon regiments and companies: the latter were, for example, employed during the final assault on Singapore.

Engineers carrying a light steel and kapok assault bridge down to the chosen crossing place. The bridge was made of a light welded steel framework, supported on kapok floats. The decking was made up of 10ft lengths of three-ply boarding about 3ft wide. (IWM: MH 596)

ENGINEERS

Divisional engineers

The engineers found in the divisional engineer regiments were 'maids of all work' whose tasks included constructing tank traps, demolition work and small river-crossing operations. They were not specialists in any particular form of engineering, so the three companies would usually be sub-alloted to the three infantry regiments to fill their normal engineer requirements. Each company carried shovels, pickaxes, felling axes, wire-cutters, hand axes, billhooks, saws, assault boats, rubber boats and some pontoons. If extensive engineering work was needed (such as major bridging work), then specialized engineer units would be attached.

Independent engineer regiments

There were six different types according to their principal function:

Type	Function
'A' KO	Open warfare
'B' OTSU	Defence
'C' HEI	Heavy bridge building
'D' BO	Amphibious landings
'E' TEI	River crossings
'F' KI	Attacking pill-boxes and special firing positions

All these regiments were about 1,000 all ranks each, were equipped with some motor vehicles and armed with rifles and LMGs.

The IJA signallers have set up their wireless station in the corner of a bombed building. The set is a Model 94 Type 2B Transmitter-Receiver. (IWM: HU 72220)

Miscellaneous units

These included independent engineer battalions, companies, field construction units, bridge-building and river-crossing units, and construction-duty companies. In addition there were engineer groups that were administrative units commanded by a major-general or above, designed to supervise engineer activity in a particular theatre.

SIGNALS

IJA signals units could be best described as being simple and flexible. Above divisional level, Army HQs had their own signals section plus a

Signallers erect a wireless aerial at a company or battalion headquarters in some farm buildings in China. Note that they carry Model 38 carbines. (US National Archives)

carrier pigeon section, and signals units to coordinate AA defences and operate fixed radio stations.

AIRBORNE FORCES

The IJA showed an interest in airborne forces from 1940 onwards and a year later had over 14,000 men either in training or fully trained. They were initially assisted by German instructors who played a large part in this initial setting-up, but had little influence over their tactical use. An unusual feature was that airborne formations were sponsored by both the Army and the Navy, the latter being an adjunct to their marine raiding forces.* The army airborne troops were always lightly armed, nevertheless they had some early successes in the war in the Pacific, but their later use was marred by poor planning and preparation, exacerbated by a lack of support. Only one raiding group (5,575 all ranks), comprising a raiding brigade and a raiding flying brigade, was ever fully formed; however, the raiding flying brigade was always short of aircraft.

* The Japanese Navy did have special naval landing forces which were used both in the landing operations in China in 1932 and to occupy various Pacific islands during the Second World War. For example, they seized Wake Island and the Gilbert Islands and spearheaded operations against Java, Ambon and Rabaul, although the bulk of the forces there were IJA. They also occupied a number of outlying bases in the long term. The naval land forces are outside the scope of this book.

Japanese paratroopers being dropped on the Dutch East Indies. (IWM: HU 2767)

This somewhat fanciful photograph purports to show the IJA carrying out an assault landing with infantry and tanks. Although Daihatsu did make landing barges which were used by the engineers, and some were powered by aircraft propeller-type engines, nothing as large as this was ever found, so the photo may be a fake. (IWM: MH 561)

An example organization from 1944 was as shown.

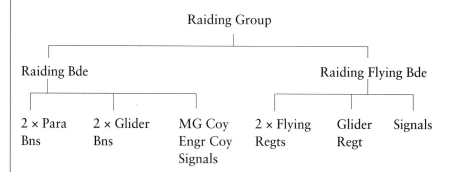

(Each Paratroop/Glider Battalion comprised three rifle companies and a heavy weapons company. Each Flying Regiment was three squadrons.)

Source: *The Airborne Soldier* by John Weeks.

CHEMICAL WARFARE

Some strengthened divisions had an organic decontamination unit which contained gas personnel organized into units of 150–250 men, in three field decontamination platoons, to deal either with affected roads and other areas, or to handle the decontamination of clothing and equipment. Originally, they had a secondary task of producing smoke and this gradually became their main task, although there is some evidence that the IJA did use poison gas against the Chinese.*

* In 1937 the use of mustard gas by the IJA was the subject of a protest to the League of Nations; the following year the Chinese claimed that two of their regiments had been wiped out by poison gas in the Yangtze valley. (Source: *Japanese Army Handbook, 1939–45*, A.J. Barker).

C H A P T E R   7

THE SERVICES

Within the IJA the Services were Intendance, Ordnance (Technical Services), Medical, Veterinary, Judicial (Legal) and Military Band. All these were under the control of the Ministry of War, with lieutenant-generals in command. The IJA considered transport as a 'Teeth Arm' rather than a Service, but for continuity with my other handbooks, I have included it here.

TRANSPORT

In the IJA transport was divided into road transport (including both animal and mountain), railway and water.

Road. The transport regiment was mentioned in the Standard Division (see p. 64), but these regiments in the depot divisions formed the main source of

A well-laden Nissan 180 1½ ton 4 × 2 cargo truck stops beside a (?)Dowa armoured car. This was a local modification of a British Crossley with the dome turret removed and two machine-guns substituted. The Nissan 180 was widely used. (Tank Museum)

On some occasions, when the situation demanded, the IJA would move troops in lorries, although it was more normal for them to march. These jungle-bound troops are detrucking prior to setting off on an operation. (US National Archives)

personnel for the operational divisions and the independent transport regiments. In the field, there were Field Transport Commands (*Yasen Yusobu*) which controlled all independent transport units within an army and were commanded by a major-general. There were also Field Motor Transport Depots (*Yasen Jidoshasho*), commanded by a colonel, lieutenant-colonel or above, which were administrative units used to control all motor transport within an operational area. Finally, at unit level there were:

(a) motor transport regiments: 1,500 all ranks plus 300 vehicles, commanded by a colonel/lieutenant-colonel

(b) independent transport regiments (horsed): 3,000 all ranks with 4 to 8 draught/pack transport companies, commanded by a colonel/lieutenant-colonel

(c) independent motor transport battalions: 800 all ranks, with some 150 x 1½ ton trucks, commanded by a major

(d) independent transport battalions (horsed): 1,700 all ranks with 3 to 4 draught/pack companies, commanded by a major

(e) independent motor transport companies: 175 all ranks, with some 50 lorries commanded by captain/lieutenant

(f) independent transport companies (horsed): 350 all ranks, commanded by a captain/lieutenant, with 200–250 two-wheeled carts with a ¼ ton load capacity, each drawn by one horse

The IJA made maximum use of railways and many of their vehicles could run on both road and rail, like this Sumida Type 93 armoured car and the lorries following. (IWM: STT 1357)

(g) Lines of communication transport supervision detachments which supervised and controlled locally commandeered transport.

Railway. This was divided into railway commands (*Tetsudo Bu*), field railways (*Yasen Tetsudo*), special railways (*Tokusetsu Tetsudo*) and railway transport (*Tetsudo Uso*). All these had HQs commanded by general officers and they commanded, maintained, coordinated and controlled the railways in a particular theatre by means of railway regiments, supply depots, construction and operating units.

For example, railway regiments consisted of some 2,500 all ranks, divided into an HQ, 4 railway battalions (each two companies of four platoons) and a supply depot. Their task was to operate and protect railways. Armoured train units consisted of 500 all ranks including infantry, artillery and engineers, trained to operate armoured trains.

Water. Shipping units were headed by a sea transport HQ in Japan, with branch offices, known as shipping groups, located at the principal base ports in theatres of operations. They controlled a number of shipping engineer regiments and debarkation units, as follows:

(a) Shipping engineer regiments: these were the barge operators of the IJA. They were equipped with landing craft and other items for amphibious operations and the movement of men and supplies. They were commanded by a lieutenant-colonel and comprised some 1,200 all ranks, divided into an HQ and three companies, with some 150–200 landing craft of all types.
(b) Shipping transport commands: like shipping groups, these were located at base ports, but were responsible for all the shipping installations at the bases. They worked closely with the Navy to plan and route sea transport in a given area, also to fuel vessels and store cargoes.

(c) Shipping transport area units: these were responsible for the armament and defence of vessels, thus they controlled AA artillery and shipping signal units, detachments of which were assigned to vessels and convoys.

(d) Anchorage units: these comprised a number of land duty, water duty and construction duty companies, who were responsible for stevedore duties, barge and lighter operations and general engineering, all companies being some 350 all ranks in strength.

(e) Shipping transport battalions: these operated small sailing and motor craft.

INTENDANCE

In some ways this branch resembled elements of the RASC, RAOC, RAPC and ACC all rolled into one, so it was probably more like the US Army Quartermaster Corps than anything else. It was responsible for the 'necessities of life' for the soldier, namely his clothing, rations, personal equipment, pay and buildings, also for the forage for his animals. It came under the control of the Intendance Bureau of the War Ministry and its importance can be gauged by the fact that in 1942 it was estimated that there were 2,700 officers in the Intendance Department, including 20 generals and 630 lieutenant-colonels and colonels. The department was divided under four headings: food, clothing and personal equipment, pay, and accommodation. The Intendance Department maintained main freight depots in Japan, field freight depots in theatres of operations and supply branch field depots which filled the requisitions from divisonal field warehouses. From the last of these, supplies went to regimental distributing centres, from where unit transport collected them. Shortage of transport was one of the main problems and this adversely affected operations. Also commanders were inclined to overestimate the capabilities of their forces and underestimate their supply needs.

Chow line and cook stoves. On occasions the IJA fed centrally in the field. I think this photograph is a good example of 'too many cooks'! (US National Archives)

Food. Undoubtedly there was a wartime myth about the ability of the Japanese soldier to subsist indefinitely on extremely small quantities of food, it being popularly believed that he ate little except rice when in action! Rice was of course a staple part of the ration, comparable with bread or biscuit in European armies, nevertheless the IJA field ration was adequate and reasonably tasty. Cooked dry, the rice had a consistency of a 'sticky mass' which made it easier to eat with chopsticks. To ward off beri-beri some barley was

Soldiers eating, using their mess tins and tinned rations. (See p. 84 for ration scales.) (IWM: HU 72225)

A line of soldier-settlers at a camp in Manchukuo prepare a frugal meal of rice. (IWM: HU 72223)

sometimes mixed in but this was not popular, the alternative being to cook the rice with a few pickled plums; these were a laxative so counteracted the constipating effect of the rice. To make the rice more palatable it was often seasoned with soy-bean sauce (*shoyu*) or its powdered equivalent (*miso*). Other favoured foods included pickled radishes, dried, tinned or pickled octopus, dried bread and vegetables. Preserved food included dried and compressed fish (salmon or tuna) which had to be soaked and salted to make it palatable; all manner of preserved vegetables; canned beef or whale meat; even vitamin tablets. The daily ration varied between 2½–4lb a man, depending on whether it was fresh or preserved. There were two emergency rations: 'A' Ration consisted of 1lb 13oz of rice, 5oz canned fish/meat, a little *miso* and sugar; 'B' Ration was the IJA 'hard tack', issued in three muslin bags each of ½lb of small oval biscuits. It was only to be eaten on the orders of an officer.

There was also another emergency ration which consisted of a cellophane packet of cooked rice, pickled plums, dried fish, salt and sugar, while paratroops were issued with yet another but even lighter to carry 'Iron Ration'.

IJA Ration Scales (weight in oz)

Item	Normal/Fresh Scale	Special/Preserved Scale
Rice/rice and barley	28	
Compressed rice		20
Fresh meat/fish	7.4	
Canned meat/fish		5.3
Fresh vegetables	21.2	
Canned vegetables		4.2
Pickled radish	2.1	
Dried plum		1.6
Shoyu sauce	1.7	
Powdered *miso*		1.1
Bean paste	2.6	
Salt	0.5	0.5
Sugar	1	1
Tea	0.2	0.2
TOTAL	4lb	2lb 2oz

'Living off the land' was allowed and encouraged if circumstances permitted. Fishing, vegetable gardening, local purchase and so on were all encouraged to augment issue rations, the transport of which varied with the nature of the terrain. The *Soldier's Guide to the Japanese Army* quotes an example: in New Guinea a 700-strong IJA battalion carried rations sufficient for twelve days, each man carrying a three-day supply of 'Fresh' rations, plus four days of 'Preserved', while the remaining five days' supplies (2.98 tons) were carried in the battalion supply train. Packaging was generally poor in the early days of the war which resulted in considerable food loss.

Clothing and Equipment. This is covered in some detail in the next chapter, but resupply items were held – as was food – at field freight depots, each being responsible for several divisions.

Other supplies. In addition to food and clothing the Intendance Department issued various 'Daily Articles' to soldiers. Daily Article 'A', issued monthly, included 150 sheets of toilet paper, 10 plain and ten picture postcards, writing paper and envelopes, and a pencil. Daily Article 'B', issued every two months, included: a small hand towel, a loin cloth, soap, tooth powder and a tooth brush. Recreational items, such as chess boards, gramophones and records, were also issued.

Canteens. These were comparable with the British NAAFI or US Army PX, and obtained their stocks from the Intendance Department, which controlled prices so they were kept within the pay of the average soldier. Articles on sale included beer and spirits (sake), cigarettes, sweets, biscuits, tinned fruit, fish and meat, clothing, sewing items, writing materials, washing and shaving gear, prophylactics, etc.

Comfort girls. What was very different to the Allied armies was the Japanese approach to brothels, the alarming VD rate in the Siberian expedition of 1918–20 having convinced them that they had to inaugurate a system of safe brothels, which they did first in China in the 1930s. The 'Comfort Houses' (*Ianjo*) were staffed by 'Comfort Girls' (*Ianfu*), who were mainly prostitutes from Korea, China and Japan, although few of them became *Ianfu* of their own free will. There were also travelling prostitutes (*Karayuki*), who were normally Japanese nationals. Soldiers could be punished if they caught VD instead of using the regularly inspected *Ianjo*. Another reason for this system was to reduce the incidence of rape ('No virgins after the Japanese Army passed by'*), which had adversely affected the IJA's prestige. However, the 'Comfort Houses' had more sinister purposes and the collecting of the 'Comfort Girls' by fair means or foul was run by the dreaded *Kempeitai*, the infamous Japanese military police (see chapter 14).

Pay. Basic pay naturally varied with rank. A general received 550 Yen per month, a Major 170–220 (depending upon grade), a warrant officer 80–110, a Corporal 20 and a 2nd Class Private 6 Yen. Overseas pay was also added depending upon which area they were serving: 'China', 'Thailand & French Indo-China' or 'Other Areas'. This extra money more than doubled most officers' and soldiers' pay and was given to compensate for rising living costs in Japan by ensuring that the soldier's dependents were properly looked after. The extra money made it possible for him to make adequate allotments although these were not compulsory. Extra pay was also given to technicians, musicians and to WOs and NCOs serving in the military police. Pay of higher rank was also given if officers or men

* This was said about the violence which occurred in Nanking and cities in China and is quoted in *Burma, the Longest War* by Louis Allen.

Japanese officers with high-class Geisha 'Comfort Girls'. (Author's collection)

'Comfort Girls.' These Chinese and Malayan girls had been forcibly taken from Penang by the Japanese for their 'Comfort Corps'. The photograph was taken in October 1945, in the Andamans, shortly after their release. (IWM: SE 5226)

performed such duties despite not being promoted. Soldiers were encouraged to save via Post Office Savings Banks. All ranks were issued with pay books and no pay could be drawn without the book being presented and an appropriate entry made in it.

ORDNANCE (TECHNICAL SERVICES)

Prior to 1941, when the technical service (*Gijutsu Bu*) was formed, ordnance duties had been performed by personnel of various branches, mainly artillery and engineers. From 1941 the service included a variety of types of technicians, such as gunsmiths, electricians and saddlers who could be attached to units as required. Their tasks were to carry out repairs on a wide variety of items, but individually they specialized in one skill (e.g. electrician).

Ordnance stores. Ordnance was also responsible for the provision of arms, ammunition, engineer stores and supplies not covered by the Intendance service. They did this in the field from Field Ordnance Depots, located in the principal rear bases, the size of the depots varying according to need, while similar Ordnance depots would be found along the lines of communication.

MEDICAL

We have already covered the medical units in the standard division. Above divisional level there were other medical units which all played their part within the evacuation chain. These included:

(a) casualty clearing stations: these were unassigned units with a strength of some 100 all ranks, who evacuated casualties from divisional field hospitals to lines of communication hospitals
(b) lines of communication hospitals: with a strength of some 250 all ranks, these could accommodate 500–1,000 patients. They were normally found in rear bases or along the lines of communication
(c) army hospitals: these were larger hospitals, situated well behind forward base areas
(d) base hospitals: each home divisional district contained hospitals to meet the requirements of units in peacetime. These, together with other private and government hospitals, were used as base hospitals during wartime.

The Evacuation System. When a soldier was wounded in action he was first attended to by the medical orderly in his platoon who gave him first aid. If necessary, he was then moved to a place where he could be easily found by the stretcher-bearers of the collecting platoons and taken to the first aid station (or dressing station) where supplemental first aid was given and a tag attached to him, giving details of his injury and treatment. Then the casualty was taken to a casualty clearing station (transfer

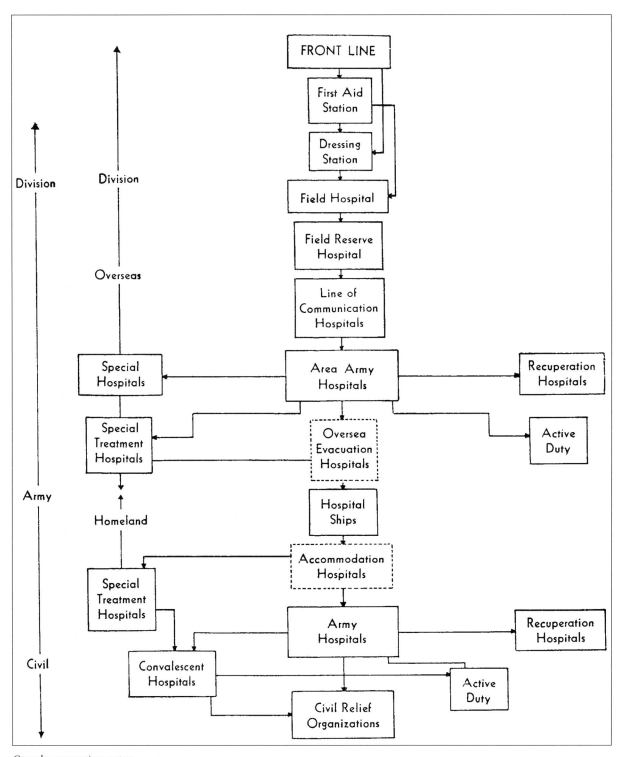

Casualty evacuation system.

station) and evacuated, probably by ambulance, to a field hospital. If seriously wounded, the casualty might be transported by the patient evacuation section of the lines of communication to the lines of communication hospital. If the division was advancing and had moved up its field hospital, then the reserve field hospital of the lines of communication automatically took over the serious cases of the divisional field hospital, continuing treatment until the patient was evacuated to the lines of communication base hospital.

VETERINARY

This was a separate service which functioned under the horse administration section of the military administration bureau of the War Ministry. A veterinary section was attached to the staff of armies, area armies, divisions, etc., while detachments operated with all units which had animals. Veterinary hospitals with a staff of some 150 and capable of handling some 700 sick horses, together with veterinary quarantine hospitals, were located along the lines of communication or in bases.

JUDICIAL

The legal service within the IJA was originally run entirely by civilian judiciary, attached to military units. However, in 1941 these civilians were all commissioned into the Army and continued to perform their legal duties as soldiers.

MILITARY BAND

The military band service provided personnel for all IJA bands. Unlike British Army bandsmen who acted as stretcher-bearers in battle, IJA bandsmen do not appear to have had any other duties.

THE IJA SUPPLY SYSTEM

Before closing this chapter on the Services let us see how it all worked in action. Supplies were shuttled between relay points, the divisional maintenance centre and the field maintenance centre in one of three ways depending on the distance between each. (a) a loaded supply column

On occasions the only power available and/or capable of being used because of the terrain was the muscle-power of Japanese soldiers. (IWM: OEM 3298)

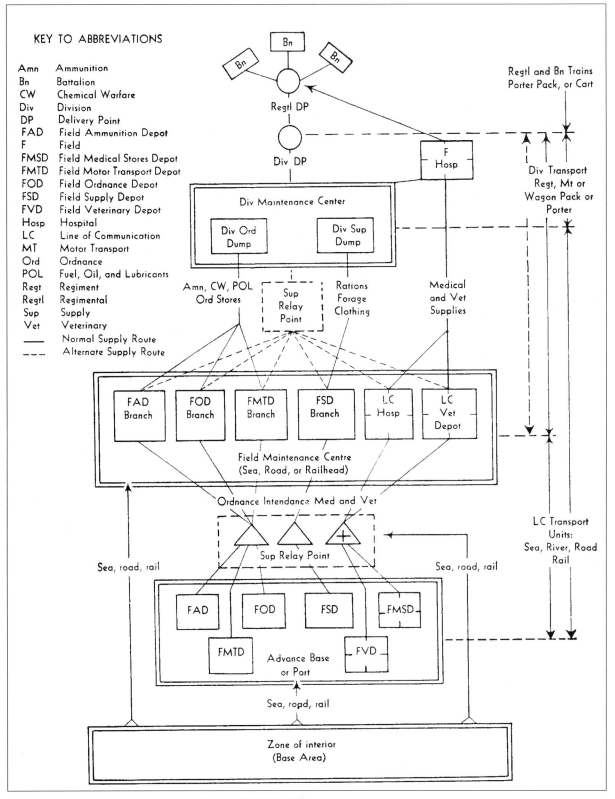

Supply system and communications layout. (Source: TM-E 30–480)

Even camels were used on occasions as pack-animals in desert areas. (IWM: OEM 3300)

moved forward from the supply relay point next closest to the divisional maintenance centre, unloaded its supplies and returned empty to the relay point for reloading; (b) a supply column moved empty from one relay point to the relay point nearest the field maintenance centre (assuming more than one relay point is established between the divisional maintenance centre and the field maintenance centre) loaded up and returned to its original relay point for unloading; (c) a loaded supply column moved from the field maintenance centre directly to the divisional maintenance centre, by-passing the relay points.

When the rate of advance of the force being supplied necessitated the forward movement of one of the depots, this was generally done by pushing forward a branch or advanced section of the main depot and, after the forward branch had been established and was functioning, then the balance of the depot was moved up. Supply relay points were introduced when the type and method of transport between delivery points or terminals had to be changed, or when reserves had to be held in the rear of the field maintenance centre, but forward of the base or advanced base and between the divisional maintenance centre and field maintenance centre. The *Handbook of Japanese Military Forces* quotes an example which occurred during the occupation of Guadalcanal in 1942, where 'the advanced base was Rabaul and a relay point was established on Shortland Island. The Field Maintenance Center was on the northwest coast of Guadalcanal. Supplies were delivered from the advanced base or direct from Japan to either the relay point or the Field Maintenance

Center.' Thus the size of the force, the nature of the campaign, the quantity of stores to be held in reserve and the extent to which permanent maintenance had replaced temporary maintenance all modified the layout of the line of communications.

AN ALLIED APPRAISAL

Towards the end of the war, the British Army assessed Japanese administrative planning and execution. Their report presents a much bleaker picture than perhaps one would imagine from the contents of this chapter, which of course shows what was meant to happen in theory, rather than what actually happened in practice. 'Japanese administrative planning, compared with normal European standards, was very sketchy, and often relied on the capture of some of our supplies or on the ability of their troops to live on the country. The system succeeded up to a point, but the miserable, half-starved specimens of Japanese manhood whom our troops came across during many of the mopping-up phases in the Arakan and Assam, bore gruesome witness to the vital importance of a good supply system. The idea, once prevalent, that the Japanese could live and fight indefinitely on a handful of rice, has been entirely disproved.'*

This aerial view taken in 1942 shows the deficiencies in modern land transport in the IJA. Everything from large trucks to horsedrawn carts and wheelbarrows can be seen being used to move supplies. (IWM: OEM 3259)

Another historian, commenting in the official Australian history of the Second World War, that the majority of Japanese soldiers were urban bred and thus not capable of looking after themselves properly, goes on to say of one encounter that, 'The captured Japanese position was nauseatingly filthy, with an overpowering stench. The habits of some Japanese soldiers in occupation were worse than those of many animals; and this poor sanitary discipline no doubt accounted for the high rate of sickness.'†

* See page 48 of 'Notes from Theatres of War', pamphlet no. 19.
† Quoted in *Jungle Warfare* by J.P. Cross.

CHAPTER 8
THE SOLDIER

'The Japanese soldier is small in stature in comparison with Americans. His average height is 5 feet 3½ inches; his weight, 116 to 120 pounds. His limbs are short and thick. Despite the reputation of the Japanese for quickness and agility, the average soldier even after rigorous training is apt to be awkward. His posture is faulty, and his normal gait shuffling. His teeth usually are poor and often are protruding.' That description from the *Soldier's Guide to the Japanese Army* was clearly written with the aim of helping to destroy the myth of invincibility which had been built up around the IJA during the early war years. However, to be fair, the handbook does go on later to say that in battle the average Japanese

These IJA soldiers were photographed during their advance on Rangoon. They look confident – and with good reason: having invaded from Thailand at the end of January 1942, they would capture Rangoon by 7 March. (IWM: MH 17066)

soldier was '. . . strong and hardy. On the offensive he is determined and willing to sustain sacrificial losses without flinching. When committed to an assault plan, Japanese troops adhere to it unremittingly even when severe casualties would dictate the need for abandonment or modification of the plan. The boldness and courage of the individual Japanese soldier are at their zenith when he is with his fellows, and when his group enjoys advantages of terrain and firepower. He is an expert at camouflage and delights in deceptions and ruses. Japanese troops obey orders well and their training and discipline are well exemplified in night operations. On the defense they are brave and determined; their discipline is good and their fire control excellent. In prepared positions the resistance of Japanese soldiers often has been fanatical in its tenacity.'

While the soldiers were brave, hardy and ferocious, their senior officers suffered from an inability to admit mistakes for fear of losing face. Senior officers gave orders but seldom supervised their implementation, considering it to be beneath their dignity to do so. They often ignored the need for sound logistical planning and continually outran their supply columns, their men having to suffer accordingly. Many officers also suffered from tactical rigidity once they lost the initiative. In his book *Jungle Warfare*, J.P. Cross quotes from a Japanese report, published by Gen Hidemitsu Nakano in New Guinea, concerning Major Takamura (III/102 Bn) who was relieved of his command for incompetence: 'There is still insufficient understanding and zeal in execution. It is a regrettable fact that with the lack of clearness of understanding, there have been many instances of failure to get any practical results. To be specific: there is a lack of quick, reliable transmission of orders; slowness and lack of comprehension in carrying out plans; leaders are lacking in eagerness to serve; they are not strict in their supervision of their subordinates; and there are those whose sense of responsibilty cannot be relied upon. Reports are greatly delayed, some are not straightforward and frank and there have been much carelessness and many mistakes in various investigations; hence opportunities to advance our objective are lost.' Gen Nakano went on to upbraid his senior and middle piece divisional officers for their lack of willpower, poor leadership, prevalent whines, feeble morale, loss of prestige, and lack of attention to detail. In his opinion they had 'forfeited their trust and confidence because of the contradiction of their words and deeds'. If a high commander failed, then he would resort to committing ritual suicide (*seppuku*).

Always ready to die. Loyalty to the Emperor was absolute and the Japanese soldier was, with very few exceptions, always ready to die for his Emperor. As a Japanese commentator put it when describing one action: 'After drinking the *sake* graciously presented to the divisional commander by the Emperor, the unit vowed anew its determination to do or die . . . and demonstrated the unique and peerless spiritual superiority of the Imperial Army. . . . All those who fell severely wounded committed suicide by using hand-grenades and, of the total of 186 men, all except 58 became guardian spirits of their country.' This type of motivation was completely foreign to the Western soldier and made the Japanese soldier all the more difficult to overcome.

An exceptionally smart group of NCOs wearing the M90 full field dress (note the stand-up collar), escorting their regimental flag. (US National Archives)

UNIFORM AND PERSONAL EQUIPMENT

Uniforms

In 1938 the IJA adopted a new khaki combat uniform, the M.98. This was a modified form of the M.90 uniform which had been adopted in 1930, when the need for a comfortable field uniform was first appreciated. It replaced the old mustard-coloured uniform which dated back to 1911 and had been modelled on the dark blue uniform of the Russo-Japanese War, with its uncomfortable 'stand-up' collar. Although the new uniform was issued as quickly as possible, many soldiers continued to wear the old one (M.90) for both fatigues and combat, until they had worn them out, quartermasters being the same the whole world over! The single-breasted M.98 tunic was olive-drab in colour, with a turn-down collar, five buttons down the front and four flapped pockets, those on the breast having buttoned flaps. Trousers were semi-breeches, secured with tapes at waist and ankle. All except mounted troops (who wore leather riding boots or boots and leather gaiters) wore woollen spiral puttees and high pigskin/cowhide boots. Marching boots were unfinished leather outside, with either a hobnailed sole or a rubber sole with rubber cleats. The other universal type of issued footwear were black canvas split-toed 'trainers' (*tabi*) into which a soldier could change when not on duty. Wool or cotton undershirts in grey/white which were worn under tunics had a single breast pocket, and socks were

Officer's field uniform M90 pattern. (US National Archives)

Officer's uniform M98 pattern. (US National Archives)

Good close-up of a tabi – *split-toe 'sneaker'. (US National Archives)*

Tropical and lightweight uniforms:
left – tropical with loose shorts;
centre – lightweight uniform;
right – tropical uniform.
(US National Archives)

heel-less. Field caps were of wool, with a chinstrap and the Army five-pointed star embroidered on the front. In battle a steel helmet was worn, which had webbing ties and incorporated the star insignia. Helmets were made of poor-grade steel and were thus often pierced by enemy fire. It was possible to wear the field cap underneath the steel helmet.

Other dress items. There was a service cap, which had a short black leather peak, a chinstrap, a small crown with red piping and a red felt strip some 1½in wide which encircled the cap, with the metal five-pointed star at the

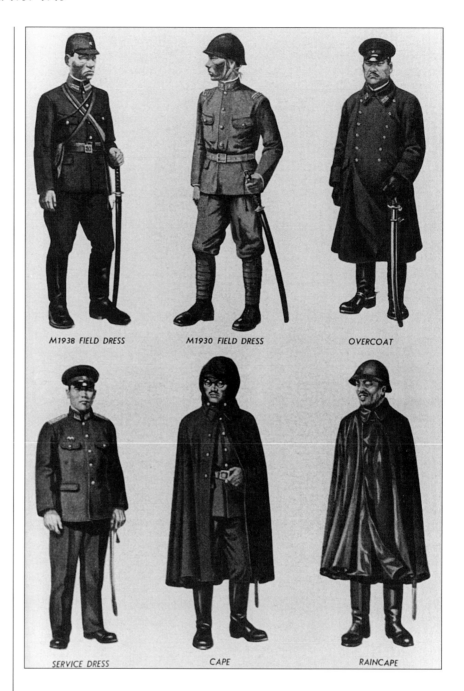

M1938 FIELD DRESS   M1930 FIELD DRESS   OVERCOAT

SERVICE DRESS   CAPE   RAINCAPE

This set of drawings of IJA uniforms appeared in the US TM-E 30–480. J4 = Officers' Uniforms; J5 = NCOs and men; J6 = Winter and Tropical; J7 = Miscellaneous

front. Overcoats, capes and raincoats with hoods were all in olive-drab. (See drawings of the different styles between those worn by officers and other ranks.) Many soldiers wore red-sash *Senninbari* (a 1,000-stitch good luck belt) around their waists under their uniforms.* The breech-clout – an abbreviated loin-cloth – was the most common type of underwear, especially in the tropics, although more conventional pants and vests were issued. Many special types of uniform were issued for various climates. For

---

* *Senninbari* were supposed not only to bring good luck but also to confer courage and make the wearer immune to enemy bullets.

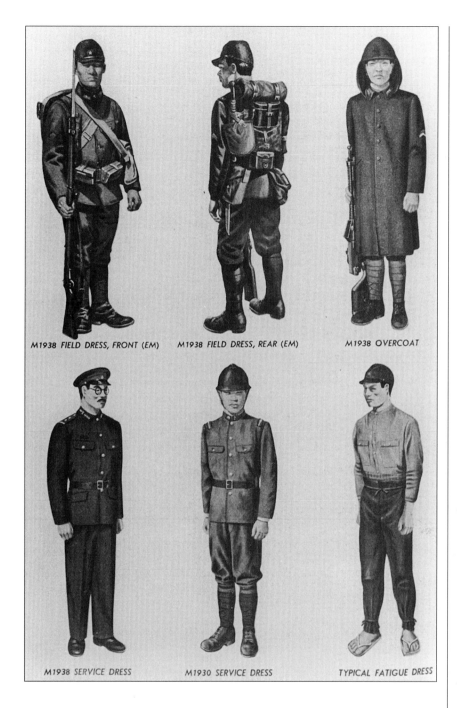

M1938 FIELD DRESS, FRONT (EM)   M1938 FIELD DRESS, REAR (EM)   M1938 OVERCOAT

M1938 SERVICE DRESS   M1930 SERVICE DRESS   TYPICAL FATIGUE DRESS

J5: NCOs and men.

example, special winter clothing had been issued in Manchuria since 1932, and included heavy pile-lined coats and caps. Tropical clothing was still being experimented with, although the summer issue cotton uniform was quite suitable. Lightweight shirts and trousers were sometimes issued, and some tunics were modified with open seams under the armpits for added ventilation. Topees (sun helmets) were quite common; one old-fashioned type looked not unlike a beehive and was made of quilted cotton-covered fibre, the other type was more conventional, like the steel helmet in shape and was made of cork covered with cotton drill.

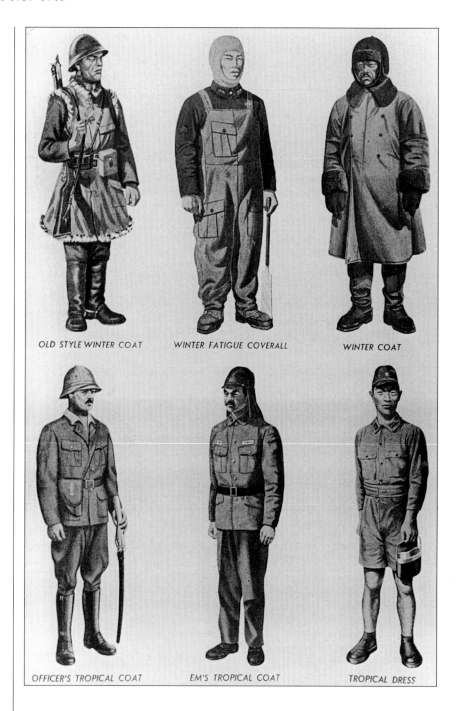

OLD STYLE WINTER COAT   WINTER FATIGUE COVERALL   WINTER COAT

OFFICER'S TROPICAL COAT   EM'S TROPICAL COAT   TROPICAL DRESS

J6: Winter and Tropical.

Officers' uniforms. These were not normally issue clothing, so there was a wide variance in quality, cut and colour. The same applied to their tunics and in many cases these were the old 1930-pattern officer uniform tunic converted by sewing on a turn-down collar over the old stand-up one. Overcoats were double-breasted with belts at the back and a slot for the sword on the left side. At the cuffs were broad brown cloth bands – one (company officers), two (field officers) and three (general officers). WOs wore an intermediate-sized band, while NCOs had a narrow band. Officers wore raincapes with throat fastenings instead of raincoats, and for footwear, riding boots or high boots with black leather gaiters.

RAINCOAT   COTTON FATIGUES   TANK COVERALL

FLYING SUIT   ANTIGAS SUIT   GUARD'S OVERCOAT

J7: Miscellaneous.

Specialized clothing. Personnel in tank units wore cotton fabric overalls, which had a turn-down collar, a single pocket on the left breast and buttons up the front. A special padded tank helmet with earflaps (to accommodate headphones) was also worn with the overalls. Although every Japanese soldier was encouraged to improvise personal camouflage* and did so most cleverly, there were also individual helmet and body camouflage nets, plus

* Some soldiers went so far as to sew loops on thread on to their clothing so that they could attach camouflage materials.

These IJA soldiers are wearing
tropical uniforms and carrying a
wide variety of equipment – but
have no weapons, because they are
prisoners. They were the first
organized Japanese units to
surrender, and belong to 53rd
Infantry Division. They
surrendered on 24 September 1945
to 1/10 Gurkha Rifles, who guard
them in a landing craft as they cross
the Sittang River. (IWM: IND
4873)

IJA officers wearing an interesting
selection of fur-lined winter coats
and fur caps, presumably in
Manchuria. (US National Archives)

A dejected group of IJA officers, all wearing greatcoats with hoods. The reason for their dejection is that they are prisoners of the Chinese and were badly wounded when captured, so unable to commit ritual suicide. (IWM: CHN 488)

special camouflage jackets; snipers were issued with lightweight 'tree-climbers' with spikes, which could be tied to the feet to assist in reaching suitable vantage points. Paratroop smocks were also available; they were a one-piece sleeveless overall garment which was put on over normal uniform and equipment. It reached the knees and had press-stud fastenings.

Individual Equipment

The design of most of the items of individual equipment in use dated back to the First World War, so that, like the German Army, the Japanese used leather for belts, packs, pouches, etc. However, leather became difficult to obtain and was unsuitable both in areas of tropical moisture and in arid deserts, so a large-scale replacement programme was instituted soon after the start of the war with China in 1937. A linoleum-like material of rubberized fabric began to be used for belts, ammunition pouches, instrument cases, holsters, etc., and canvas/cotton duck for bandoliers, packs, etc. Only the officers' equipment tended to remain leather.

Every soldier was issued with the following items:

(a) *Pack*. Made either of cowhide (with the hair still on it) or cotton duck material, it was some 13in square and 5in deep. Attached to the outside there were some 20 tapes which were used to secure the top flap and to

Close-up of infantrymen's packs. Note also the entrenching tools, bayonets, binoculars in carrying case, etc. (US National Archives)

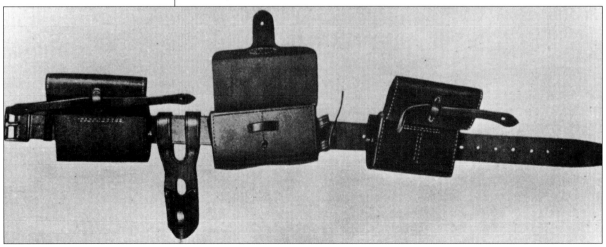

Belt, bayonet frog and ammunition pouches (the smaller ones hold thirty rounds, the larger sixty rounds), worn at the rear. (US National Archives)

This close-up of men of the elite Imperial Guard shows how the front ammunition pouches were worn. (IWM: HU 36524)

bind gear on to the pack's exterior surfaces (e.g. the steel helmet when the field cap was being worn). NCOs had smaller packs and officers even smaller ones made of leather. Inside the soldier carried: *tabi*, a shelter half (4ft 10½in by 2ft 5¼in) with pegs and poles,* spare socks, towel, washing gear, breech-clout, small first aid packet and a sewing kit, together with several days' dry rations. A blanket was fastened in a horseshoe shape around the pack, the shelter half was sometimes rolled and attached across the top, and the soldier's mess tins were strapped on the back. Officers wore their packs on the right hip. Sometimes, instead of a pack, a canvas

* Soldiers also used the shelter half as a poncho, its excellent rain-shedding properties making it preferable to the issue raincoat.

A Japanese tank crewman, standing in front of his tankette. The photograph was found inside the AFV when it was captured by
A Sqn 146 Regiment RAC (Duke of Wellington's Regiment) on the Arakan coast road, 15 March 1945. (RHQ DWR via Bill Norman)

This fascinating photograph shows members of a cavalry unit drying out after being caught in a heavy downpour. Note all the items of clothing and equipment visible in and around the ad hoc shelter, including riding boots, 'tabi' footwear, respirator, water bottle, steel helmets, and so on. Some of the unit horses are in the background. (US National Archives)

holdall was worn on the back, slung across the body and tied over one shoulder. It had light carrying straps at each end, plus two long tapes and several shorter ones, so that it could be rolled, the two long straps forming an 'X' across the chest. It might contain the overcoat, blanket, shelter half, tent poles and pins, plus any other gear, so for all intents and purposes it became a combat pack. In addition, soldiers might carry/wear a variety of bags or sacks, made of cotton duck, leather or a rubberized fabric, in which numerous items (such as extra ammunition or grenades) were carried.

(b) *Mess tins*. These consisted of an oval aluminium container, with one or two tray-like dishes under the cover. Each had handles so that they could be carried, or suspended over cooking fires. The outside container had metal loops on it, to take the strap with which it was fixed to the pack. Officers had similar mess kits, but they were rectangular and often comprised just a container with a lid.

(c) *Water bottle*. Made of aluminium, painted brown and with a flat base, the bottle fitted into a cradle of straps, with one long strap which went over the left shoulder so that the water bottle rested on the right hip. The officer's pattern was similar but had a felt cover and was fitted with a cup. Capacity was either 1 or 2½ pints.

(d) *Ammunition belt and ammunition pouches*. The pouches had a capacity of either six or twelve 5-round clips and were worn on a belt around the waist, with two six-clip pouches in front and one twelve-clip at the rear. They were made of either leather or a rubberized fabric. As the photograph shows, a bayonet frog was also slipped on to the belt, worn on the left hip, and the larger pouch had a small metal/plastic can attached on one side to hold gun oil or grease.

(e) *Entrenching tool*. In line with other armies, all Japanese infantrymen carried an entrenching tool, either a shovel with a short detachable handle, or a pick (on the ratio of 2:1). The blade/pickhead was fixed to the pack, or could be slung over the shoulder by means of a piece of rope.

(f) *Gas mask*. Contained in a canvas carrier, this was very similar to the British equivalent army respirator and was worn in the same way on the chest.

(g) *Miscellaneous*. Officers usually carried leather mapcases, and pistol holsters normally made of leather or rubberized material. All had carrying straps and were carried slung over one shoulder. (NB: Swords are covered under small arms: see p. 126.)

(h) *Tropical equipment*. In the tropics soldiers would be issued with anti-mosquito face/head nets, light cotton mittens, and insect repellent sprays/creams, etc. A tin containing a water purification set (a spoon plus a phial of chemical) was also carried (see p. 195).

(i) *Identity discs*. Oval metal identity discs were worn on a tape around the waist. Generally they showed the wearer's name, arm of service and personal army number. Officers' discs showed arm of service, rank and name.

To summarize, the following was the scale of issue of these items in the IJA:

Helmet, steel	1
Cap, cloth, khaki, peaked	1
Trousers, drill, long, pairs	2
Tunics, drill	2
Shirts, cotton, khaki	2
Underwear, cotton, sets	2
Socks, cotton, pairs	2
Shoes, split-toe, rubber, pairs (*tabi*)	1
Boots, leather, pairs	1
Shelter, half, khaki, waterproof	1
Puttees, pairs	1
Pack	1
Haversack	1
Hold-all, canvas	1
Mess tin	1
Belt, leather	1
Pouches, leather, ammunition	3
Water bottle	1
Gloves, mosquito, pairs	1
Head mask, mosquito	1
Respirator	1
First aid field dressing	1

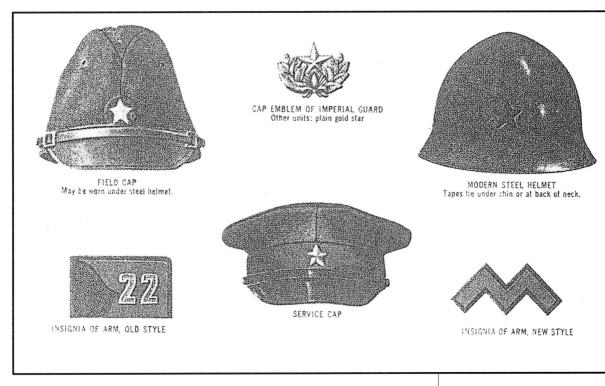

FIELD CAP
May be worn under steel helmet.

CAP EMBLEM OF IMPERIAL GUARD
Other units: plain gold star

MODERN STEEL HELMET
Tapes tie under chin or at back of neck.

INSIGNIA OF ARM, OLD STYLE

SERVICE CAP

INSIGNIA OF ARM, NEW STYLE

Principal types of headgear, cap badges and basic arm of the service. (Source: TM-E 30–480)

BADGES OF RANK AND INSIGNIA

Badges of Rank

The old M.90 tunic had on its stand-up collar coloured patches, badges and numerals; rank was shown by shoulder tabs, and on greatcoats, by various combinations of brown bands on the cuffs (see p. 100). The M.98 tunic with its fold-down collar had the rank insignia transferred to the collar in small compact patches. Regimental numbers and special service badges were worn after the rank badges, as explained below.

The various IJA ranks were mentioned in Chapter 2, showing the badges which were used to represent them on uniforms. It is also worth mentioning here that the commissioned officers' ranks were divided into four classes:

Company officers (*Ikan*)	Second Lieutenant, Lieutenant and Captain
Field officers (*Sakan*)	Major, Lieutenant-Colonel and Colonel
General officers (*Shokan*)	Major-General, Lieutenant-General, and General
Marshal (*Gensui*)	Field Marshal

The Japanese did not use the ranks of Brigadier or Brigadier-General.

Insignia of arm worn on breast of M1938 coat. (Source: TM-E 30–480)

Arm of Service

The IJA did not use arm badges to identify individual divisions, brigades, etc., but they did identify their arms of service by badges, chevrons and numbers.

(a) *Badges.* These were worn on the collar patches on the M.90 uniform and on the collar *after* the rank patch on the M.98 uniform. However, as the colour of the collar patch on the M.90 uniform also identified the service branch, those serving with infantry, cavalry, field artillery, etc., merely wore regimental numbers, so these badges distinguished those serving in specialized units, training establishments, etc. The badges were worn on both sides of the collar, or the badge on one side and the regimental number on the other. During the Second World War, these badges ceased to be worn, being replaced by the coloured chevrons.

(b) *Chevrons.* A small zigzag chevron (like an inverted open 'W') in the arm of service colour was worn by all ranks above the right breast pocket. The main colours were:

Infantry - red, Tanks - red, Cavalry - green, Artillery - yellow, Engineers - burgundy, Medical - dark green, Veterinary - purple, Military Police - black, Legal - white, Intendance - pink,* Transport - dark blue, Army Air - blue.

(c) *Numbers.* The location of the numbers has already been covered. Regimental numbers were in Arabic numerals, while those of specialized units, schools, etc., used Roman numerals.

This IJA officer is wearing the following decorations and medals (left to right): the Imperial Order of the Golden Kite (4th or 5th grade), the Imperial Order of the Double Ray of the Rising Sun with Pawlinia Leaves, Manchurian medal, three campaign or commemoration medals and around the neck, the Imperial Order of the Sacred Treasure (2nd or 3rd Grade). (US National Archive)

Cap Badges

All ranks (apart from the Imperial Guard) wore the five-pointed gold star on their headdress. On the service cap it was made of metal and was set at the front of the red headband; on the field cap it was usually embroidered. All ranks of the Imperial Guard wore a special cap badge, which had a small semi-circular wreath below the star.

Other Headdress Badges

There is evidence of some soldiers wearing special badges to denote their individual unit. For example, the men of the 3rd Company, 214th Infantry

---

* Although the TM-E 30–480 clearly shows the Intendance chevron as coloured pink, other references say light brown.

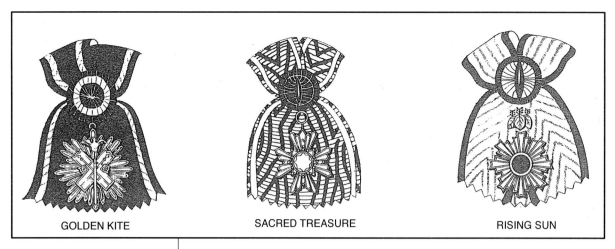

| GOLDEN KITE | SACRED TREASURE | RISING SUN |

Principal Japanese decorations (only First Class shown). (Source: TM-E 30–480)

Regiment, wore 'White Tiger' badges above the stars in their caps. This was the idea of Lt-Col Junosuke Hamada who later commanded the regiment. The 'White Tigers' were a group of young samurai from Wakamatsu, who had fought in the civil war in 1867 and were greatly respected by the Japanese people; Aizu-Wakamatsu was the location of the barracks of the 29th Regiment Home Unit, from which the 214th was formed.

Specialist Badges

As in other armies, qualified specialists were allowed to wear cloth badges on their left upper arm, which showed their trade: artificer, tailor, wheelwright, trumpeter, etc.

DECORATIONS AND MEDALS

Decorations and medals were considered to be most important in developing and maintaining high morale. There were three principal military decorations, although within each decoration there were numerous classes (levels).

(a) *Order of the Golden Kite*. Instituted in 1890, this was open only to military personnel for conspicuous bravery in action. There were seven classes of membership, the top class being open only to officers. In addition to the medal, inclusion in the order carried with it a life pension. Up to the fifth class, the decorations were presented in the field (after appropriate War Ministry Board approval), officers receiving theirs from their divisional commander, other ranks from their commanding officer. It was in the shape of an irregular star in red enamel, edged with gold or silver according to class, upon which is a sort of saltire with two golden rods and sceptres. Over the saltire is a sword, point down, on the guard of which is a golden kite with its wings spread. According to an ancient Japanese legend, a kite hovering in the air had helped to win a victory for one of the early Japanese emperors. The badges of the junior grade were entirely in silver.

(b) *Order of the Rising Sun*. Established in 1875, this was open to both civilian and military personnel who had performed meritorious service. There were eight classes in all, only the lowest two being open to other ranks. Again, there was a life pension included. The decoration has a cabochon garnet in the centre, from which spring thirty-two rays of white enamel edged gold or silver according to class. It hung from a spray of three paulownia flowers (with leaves) enamelled in their proper colours. The chest star consisted of the enamelled badge, without the paulownia leaves, mounted on a similar shaped silver star of eight points.

(c) *Order of the Sacred Treasure*. This Order was instituted in 1888 and was mainly awarded for long service and good conduct, both in peace and war. It had eight classes and again only the two lowest were open to other ranks. The decoration was itself symbolic of the three treasures bequeathed to his successor by the first Emperor of Japan: a mirror, a collar and some swords. The central device consisted of an eight-pointed silver star (the mirror) on a circular ground of blue enamel. This was encircled by an irregular-shaped collar of sixteen rubies from which spring twenty rays of white enamel representing sword blades, edged in gold or silver according to rank.

In all cases, decorations had to be returned to the government after the death of the holder.

These decorations were awarded for bravery, meritorious and exceptional service respectively. However, if the service was not of sufficient distinction to qualify for one of them but was still worthy of recognition, monetary grants and/or diplomas of merit, were awarded. In addition to the three main decorations, campaign medals, good conduct medals, proficiency badges and wound badges were all awarded. Medals were also awarded to the next of kin of soldiers killed in action, as well as to the next of kin of soldiers who died within three years of contracting an illness while serving.

Campaign Medals. Examples of campaign medals include:

(a) Russo-Japanese War (1904–5): green ribbon with a dark yellow stripe, edged in white and with a red centre
(b) War with Germany 1914–15 and 1914–20: equal stripes of dark blue, white and dark blue
(c) Victory Medal 1914–18: usual 'rainbow' pattern of the Allied Victory Medal, but with paler yellow portions
(d) Japanese Red Cross awards: paler red stripe with pale-blue stripes on each side.

PERSONAL WEAPONS

Pistols

Nambu 8mm pistol. Named after its designer, Col Kijiro Nambu, the pistol (*Nambu Kenju*) outwardly resembled the German Luger, but it had

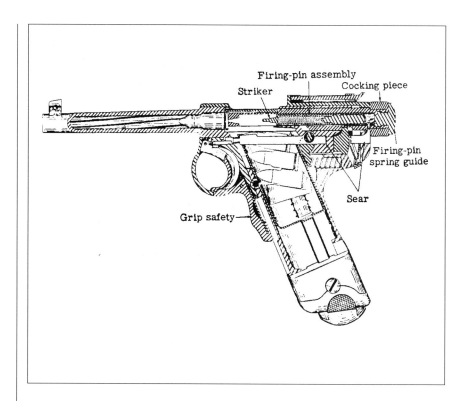

Cross-section of a Nambu 8mm pistol in the firing position.

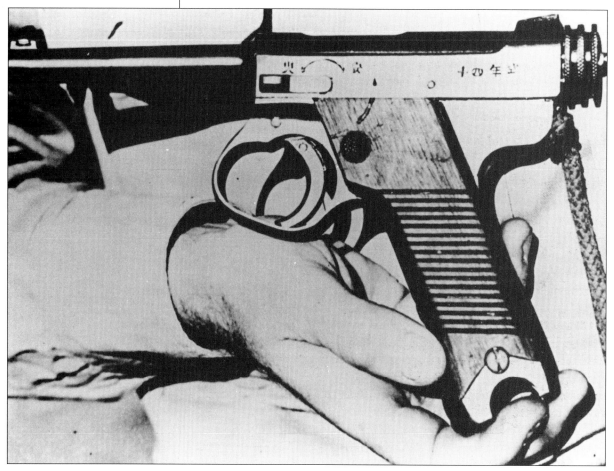

A Model 14 (1925) 8mm Nambu pistol. (Tank Museum)

an entirely different mechanism. The 31oz, 8mm was a semi-automatic, recoil-operated, magazine-fed hand weapon. Its 8-round magazine fitted into the butt, the ammunition being semi-rimmed, bottle-necked case, round-nosed bullets. Its effective range was 50ft (maximum 547yd) and accuracy was increased by using the wooden holster, which had a telescopic section that could be attached to the butt of the pistol as a stock, together with the leaf backsight graduated from 100–500yd. Nevertheless, the leather holster was more normally used.

Model 14 (1925) 8mm pistol. This was developed from the Nambu, which it resembled but the workmanship was not as good. Unlike the Nambu, it did not have a leaf backsight and was not fitted for a shoulder stock. It weighed 2lb, had an 8-round magazine which used the same ammunition as the Nambu, and had the same effective and maximum ranges.

There were two other handguns. The Model 94 (1934) 8mm pistol was inferior to both the other pistols covered here because of its poor manufacture and the bad design of the handgrip. The Model 26 (1893) 9mm six-shot revolver was a copy of the old American Smith & Wesson.

Rifles and Carbines

Model 38 (1905) 6.5mm rifle. This manually operated, clip-loaded, magazine-fed rifle (*Samppachi Shiki Hoheiju* – 38 Model infantry rifle) was commonly called the *Arisaka Sampachi*, after its designer, Arisaka. It was somewhat similar to the US Springfield. It was sturdy but comparatively light (9.4lb) for its length (50.2in – without bayonet, but see below). Its effective range was 400yd, its maximum 2,600yd. Cartridges were semi-rimmed and both ball and tracer were used. The rifle was manufactured in three different lengths: 50.2in, 44.2in and 38in (weight of the latter two being 8.6lb and 7.8lb respectively). It could be fitted with the straight 20in, one-edged bayonet, the Model 30 (1897), which locked firmly on to the muzzle and upper band.

Model 99 (1939) 7.7mm rifle. This replaced the Model 38, being shorter, and of heavier calibre; it was very much an improved version. Its overall length without bayonet was 44in, weight 8.8lb and it fired ball, tracer and armour-piercing ammunition. It had an effective range of 600yd and a maximum range of 3,000yd.

Model 44 (1911) 6.5mm carbine. This carbine was very similar to the Arisaka rifle short model, but it had a permanently attached spiked bayonet that folded under and rested in a slot in the stock when being carried. It weighed 8.75lb, was 38.25in long (bayonet folded) and had a magazine capacity of five rounds. It was normally carried by individual cavalry troopers.

Sniper's rifle. There were two models: the Model 97 (1937) 6.5mm and the Model 99 (1939) 7.7mm. The rifles were fitted with fixed focus telescopic sights which had a ×2.5 magnification, a 10-degree field of

The 6.5mm Type 38 rifle, with the Type 30 bayonet, was known as the Arisaka rifle. These riflemen were in the Yenangyaung oilfields. The light machine-guns are 6.5mm Model 11 (1922) LMGs. (IWM: HU 2778)

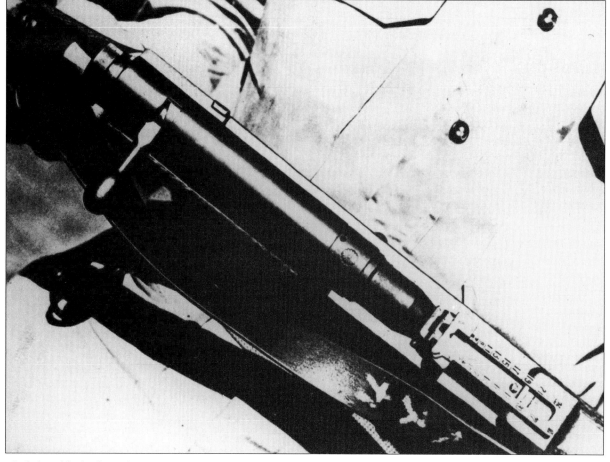

The bolt and leaf sight on the 6.5mm Type 38 (1905) rifle. (Tank Museum)

The soldier nearest the camera in this interesting 'infantry/tank co-operation' photograph appears to be carrying a Type 100 sub-machine carbine. (Tank Museum)

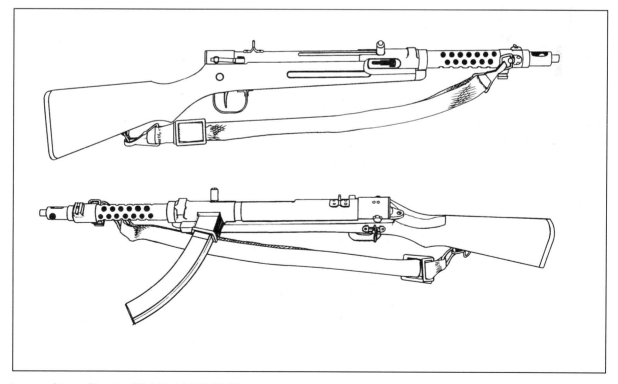

8mm machine carbine simplified Model 100 (1940).

vision and weighed 17oz. In general they were more carefully manufactured than the standard rifles.

Sub-machine-guns. The IJA did not take much interest in SMGs until the early 1940s when they produced the Type 100 8mm *Shiki Kikanshoju* in two versions: one with a folding butt for paratroops and one with a fixed butt. Only some 7,500 of the folding version and 10,000 of the fixed were ever produced so it did not see wide service. Its magazine capacity was thirty rounds and it could be fitted with the normal rifle bayonet. An improved version was produced in 1944, with almost double the rate of fire (800rpm instead of 450).

Grenade launchers. There were two types of grenade launchers used with rifles: a cup type and a spigot type. The cup-type launcher fitted over the muzzle and locked over the front sight of the rifle. It had a short rifled barrel and was an exact copy of the German cup-type launcher (*Schiessbecher*). It fired an armour-piercing grenade which worked on the hollow-charge principle and was a copy of the German rifle grenade *gr.G.Pzgr*. The spigot-type also fitted over the muzzle and locked behind the the front sight of the rifle. Two types of grenades were used in this type of launcher, HE and smoke. The former resembled the Model 91 hand grenade (see below) except that it had a fin assembly and was fired by a special cartridge (fitted with a wooden bullet) which was packed into the fin assembly.

Armour-piercing rifle grenade and cup-type grenade launcher. (Tank Museum)

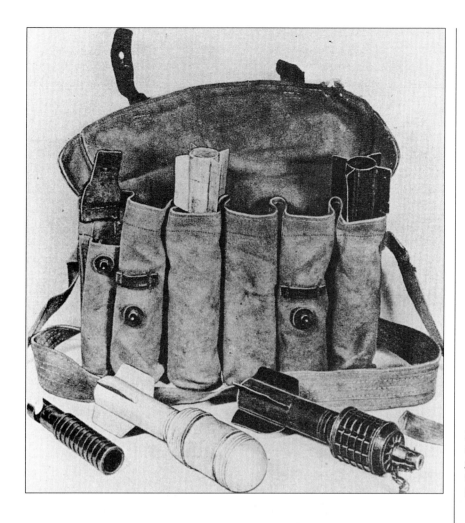

Rifle grenades and accessories. Left to right: a launcher, a smoke grenade and an HE grenade, plus the carrying case in the rear).
(US National Archives)

Grenades

There were numerous types of hand grenade used by the IJA, the most important being as follows:

(a) *Model 91 (1931)*. A cast-iron hand grenade with a serrated black body, brass safety cover and perforated propellant charge container screwed into the base. The firing pin was screwed into the firing-pin holder and when in transit the pin was flush with the top of the holder, so that it did not protrude below. To arm the grenade, the firing pin had to be screwed (with a knife or coin) down into the firing-pin holder as far as it would go. The fuse had a burning time of 8–9 seconds. The grenade weighed 18.8oz, was 1.97in in diameter and 4.95in long (with propellant container). It had a safety pin which had to be removed before throwing or firing in a grenade discharger. Throwing procedure was exactly as outlined for the Model 97 (below).

(b) *Model 97 (1937)*. This was the most widely used hand grenade and looked very like the Model 91. However, it did not have a propelling charge/charge container, so could not be fired from a grenade discharger. It

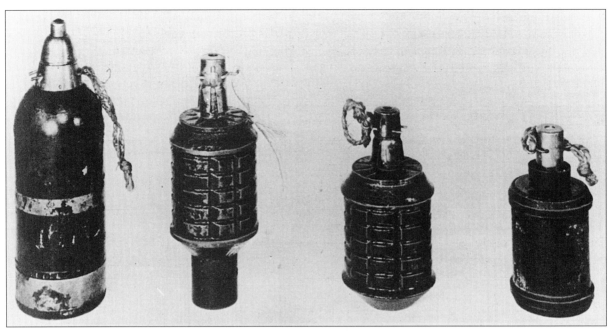

Left to right: Model 89 (1929) shell, Model 91 (1931) hand grenade, Model 97 (1937) hand grenade, Model 99 (1939) KISKA hand grenade. (US National Archives)

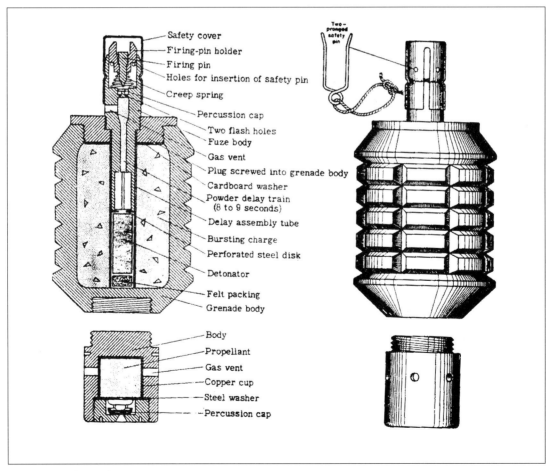

Model 91 hand grenade (1931).

was also made of cast iron and serrated to ensure maximum fragmentation. The fuse delay was only 4–5 seconds and it had a safety pin like the Model 91. It weighed 1lb, was 3.75in long and 1.97in in diameter and was armed as for the Model 91. To throw: grasp the grenade, fuse downwards, and withdraw the safety pin (NB: the firing pin had to be screwed down as on the Model 91); making sure that the safety cover does not fall off, strike the head of the fuse cover against some hard object (such as the heel of a boot or the top of a steel helmet), then throw without any delay as the fuses were 'somewhat erratic'!

(c) *Model 99 (1939)*. Known also as the *Kiska* (named after the island in the Aleutians where it was first encountered by the US Army), it had a smooth body and was smaller than the other models, being 3½in long and 1⅜in in diameter. It weighed approximately 10oz and could be thrown or launched from a discharger. The safety pin was integral with the firing pin holder, so it did not need to be screwed, otherwise the procedure of striking the head on a hard object and then throwing immediately was the same.

Other grenades included a ½kg incendiary grenade, an incendiary stick grenade, a high-explosive stick grenade, a 'Molotov cocktail' incendiary grenade, a frangible glass white smoke grenade and a frangible hydro-cyanic acid grenade.

Grenade Dischargers

In addition to the rifle cup dischargers, there were two types of grenade discharger. They resembled small mortars and could be used to propel small grenades over relatively short distances.

(a) *50mm grenade discharger type 10*. With an overall length of just under 51cm, its small spade base was placed on the ground and the 24cm barrel was then hand-held at an angle of 45 degrees. Range (65–175yd) was varied by means of an adjustable gas port. The Type 91 HE grenade was normally used but smoke, flare and signal grenades were used as well. By 1941 it had largely been replaced by the Type 89. It was given the nickname 'knee mortar', which unfortunately led to numerous broken legs among Allied troops who tried to fire it in this manner.

(b) *50mm grenade discharger type 80*. Coming into service in 1929, seven years after the Type 10, this type differed from its predecessor in being some 10cm longer and having a rifled barrel. Also, instead of having a gas port, it had a movable firing pin which could be shifted up and down the barrel to alter the range. It also had a larger, curved baseplate. The Type 91 grenade could be fired but the more normal projectile used was the Type 89 shell (high explosive, smoke, incendiary, flare and signal types were available) which weighed about 0.8kg. Maximum range was 650yd, which made it a most useful infantry weapon.

Booby Traps and Mines

Booby traps. The Japanese became highly skilled in the use of booby traps and the fragmentation grenades Models 91, 97 and 99 were often used in

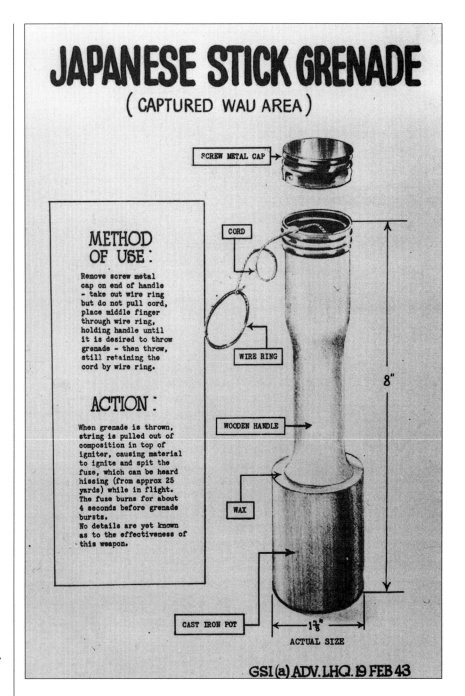

Japanese stick grenade. (IWM: STT 7310)

them, because they all had pull igniters. They would be placed bottom-up inside a tube or piece of bamboo and suspended, so that when the wire was 'tripped', the grenade would fall headfirst and thus detonate. Bangalore torpedoes, normally used to demolish barbed-wire entanglements, were also used in booby traps, the igniter string being tied to a tripwire. In larger booby traps, grenades were used to set off larger explosive devices such as aircraft bombs.

Mines. There were three main IJA mines.

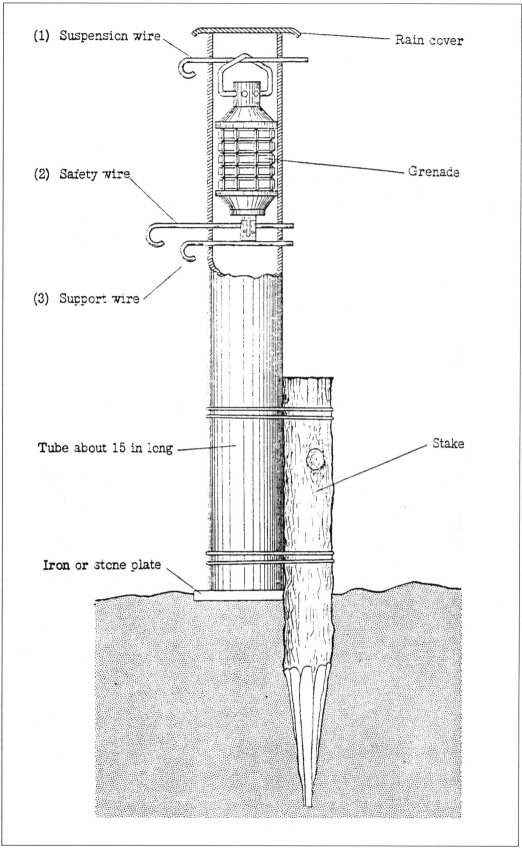

(1) Suspension wire

Rain cover

(2) Safety wire

Grenade

(3) Support wire

Tube about 15 in long

Stake

Iron or stone plate

Method used to construct a booby-trap using a Model 91 hand grenade.

(a) *Model 93 (1933) 'tape-measure' mine*. So-called because it resembled a rolled-up tape measure in a case, this mine was some 6.75in in diameter, 1.75in thick and weighed 3lb. It had four carrying rings which could also be used to tie the mine in place, and a 1½in brass dome at its centre, underneath which was the pressure fuse. Fuses were fitted with shearwires of various strengths, so the fuse might function at any pressure from as low as 7lb up to 200lb. Mines were normally laid in a diagonal pattern about 30in apart.

(b) *Model 99 (1939) anti-tank mine*. Issued to infantry units and often carried by individual soldiers, this was also known as the 'magnetic anti-tank bomb' or 'armour-piercing grenade' because it had four permanent magnets attached to its sides, which held it to a metal target until it detonated. It had to be placed against the tank/iron door of a blockhouse, then the fuse cap had to be given a sharp blow. The 5–6 second fuse delay gave the soldier time to withdraw to safety before the 1½lb of TNT inside the 4.75in diameter mine exploded.

(c) *Model 96 (1936) mine*. This large powerful mine could be used on land or underwater. It had two lead alloy horns that enclosed glass vials of electrolytic fluid; when crushed, the fluid activated a chemical electric fuse which then detonated the mine. It weighed some 106½lb, contained 46lb of explosive, was 10½in high and had a base diameter of 20in.

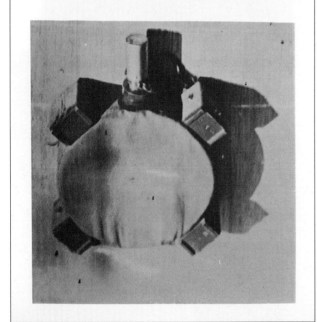

The Model 99 (1939) anti-tank/armour-piercing magnetic mine, sometimes called the 'magnetic anti-tank bomb'. (IWM: STT 7325)

Edged Weapons

Bayonets. I have already mentioned the bayonets used with the various IJA rifles and carbines, the Model 30 (1897) being the mainstay. It is well worth noting the amount of time spent teaching/practising bayonet fighting in the training programmes outlined in an earlier chapter. The IJA placed considerable emphasis on the use of the bayonet, recognizing – as the British Army has always done – that the bayonet could be a most important weapon in individual combat during close quarter fighting in jungle areas, etc. The general issue bayonet had a 15½in blade and was strongly constructed despite its mass-manufacture. Invariably the IJA infantryman carried his rifle with the bayonet fixed when in action.

Sabres. The cavalry sabre was a combination of a European-type hilt with the Japanese cutting blade. It was some 100cm long and weighed 3.13lb.

The Model 93 (1933) anti-personnel/anti-tank mine was known as the 'tape-measure' mine because it looked like a rolled-up tape measure. (IWM: STT 9188)

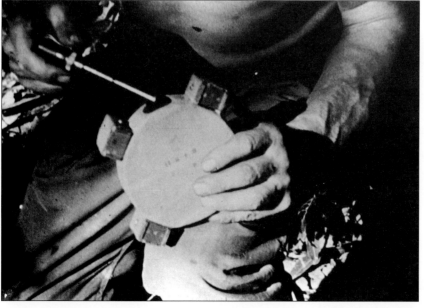

Removing the fuse from a Model 99 mine. (Tank Museum)

The large, very powerful Model 36 (1936) mine could be used both on land and in the sea. It was set off by striking one of the two lead alloy horns. (Tank Museum)

Swords. The sword (*katana*) carried by Japanese officers was not just a badge of rank, nor a hangover from a past age. They were classic weapons, capable of inflicting horrific injuries: they could slice through a man's body from collarbone to waist in one single clean slash. Their ceremonial importance was also well demonstrated during the various surrender ceremonies at the end of the war.

Machine-Guns

In battle, the standard IJA infantry platoon had three rifle sections of an NCO and twelve men, plus a grenade discharger section. There was a Light Machine-Gun (LMG) in each of the three rifle sections and it was the same calibre as the rifle, namely 6.5mm. The two main types are discussed below. The more modern of the two is credited by some military historians with accounting for more Allied casualties in the Pacific and Far East theatres than any other weapon. LMGs were backed up by Heavy Machine-Guns (HMG) in both 6.5mm and 7.7mm calibre; one of the latter (Type 92) was nicknamed 'the Woodpecker' by the Allies because of its unmistakable sound.

6.5mm LMG Type 11. Introduced into service in 1922 and designed by Gen Kijiro Nambu, this gun has many odd features. For example, its feed was via a hopper, using five-round clips of rifle ammunition. Although it was thus

This officer rests his hand on the top of his trusty katana, *which he would use in battle as a fighting weapon. (IWM: STT 9679)*

intended to be able to use the standard rifle ammunition, the complicated mechanism was always going wrong and, eventually, a special reduced charge cartridge had to be produced, which of course negated the whole idea! Also, it could only fire automatic and each round had to be oiled as it was fed in, so it had many drawbacks. Nevertheless it was widely used, especially in China.

6.5mm LMG Type 96. This was the LMG designed to replace the unfortunate Type 11. It entered service in 1936, but production never fully met demand, and both models were in service throughout the war. Introduced in 1936, the Type 96 resembled the Bren LMG in many ways

The 6.5mm light machine-gun Type 11. Known as the Nambu, *it had a strange hopper feed designed so that it could use clips of rifle ammunition, but this proved ineffective. (Tank Museum)*

A Type 11 LMG in action in China, 1942. (IWM: STT 3566)

and was fed by a curved box-type 30-round magazine on top of the gun. One of its more unusual features was that it could be fitted with the normal rifle bayonet (Model 30).

6.5mm HMG Type 3. Although this design went back far beyond the First World War, it was still the standard IJA heavy machine-gun for many years. Designed on the Hotchkiss Model 1900, which it resembled, it was strong and reliable, but lacked hitting power at longer range, which led to its replacement by the 7.7mm Type 92. Its bad features were the need to incorporate an oiling mechanism to coat the cartridges before firing and a 30-round metal strip feed.

7.7mm HMG Type 92. The Japanese realized in the 1930s that they needed a more powerful round for their small arms than the 6.5mm, hence the development of the Model 99 (1939) 7.7mm rifle. Even earlier, in 1932, they produced a heavy machine-gun to fire the new ammunition, which was known as the 92 *Shiki Kikanju*. Apart from the larger calibre of ammunition, it was virtually identical to the Type 3, even to the oiling mechanism and the 30-round metal strip feed.

7.7mm MG Type 99. The best Japanese machine-gun was the Type 99, which came into service in 1939 and was a development of the earlier 6.5mm Type 96. It used a new rimless round (*Shiki* 99), which did not

The elderly heavy machine-gun Type 3 dates from 1914, when the Hotchkiss Model 1900 was modified to 6.5mm calibre for IJA use. (IWM: STT 3143)

A Type 92 7.7mm heavy machine-gun in action in Malaya. (Tank Museum)

Another view of the Type 92 in action. It was called the 'Woodpecker' by the Allied soldiers owing to its unmistakable sound when fired. (IWM: STT 496)

need oiling so the oil dispenser could be omitted, but it could still be fitted with a bayonet. Once again supply could not keep up with demand.

Model	Calibre	Weight in action	Rate of fire	Type of feed
Type 11	6.5mm	10.1kg	500rpm	30-round hopper taking five round clips
Type 96	6.5mm	9.07kg	550rpm	30-round box magazine
Type 3	6.5mm	28.1kg (with tripod 55.3kg)	400–500rpm	30-round metal strips
Type 92	7.7mm	as for Type 3	450–500rpm	as for Type 3
Type 99	7.7mm	10.4kg	850rpm	30-round box magazine

There were other machine-guns including another Type 92 7.7mm which had a round drum magazine and a 13mm Type 93 which was a copy of the French 13.2mm Mitrailleuse Hotchkiss, both of which were mainly

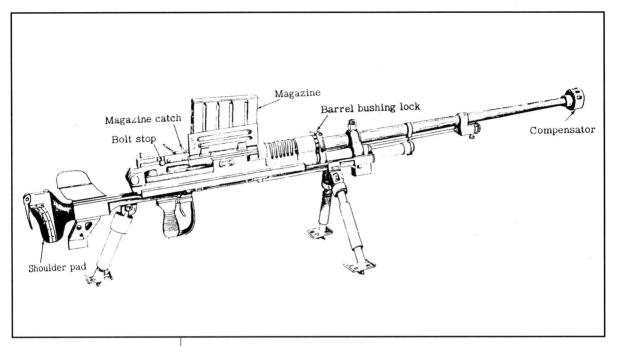

*Type 97 20mm anti-tank rifle
(1937).*

used on AA mountings. The latter fired a useful little lethal projectile up to some 13,000ft, with a muzzle velocity of 2,250ft/sec.

Anti-tank Weapons

In addition to the two anti-tank guns covered in the next chapter and the anti-tank mines already mentioned, there are three other anti-tank weapons which must be covered.

(a) *Type 97 20mm anti-tank rifle.* This very heavy rifle weighed 51.75kg in action and even more in transit, so it needed a crew of 2 to 4 men just to carry it! Recoil was very heavy and penetration poor – just 2.95mm at about 250m, so it compared unfavourably even with the obsolescent British Boyes anti-tank rifle which only weighed a mere 16.56kg and could penetrate 21mm at 300m. It had a semi-automatic feed from a seven-round magazine, but firing it in this mode must have been suicidal!
(b) *Anti-tank rifle grenades.* There were two anti-tank grenades that could be fired from the same internally rifled launcher cup which would fit all IJA rifles: the *Type 2 30mm and 40mm spin-stabilized grenades.*
(c) *'Lunge mine.'* This consisted of a hollow-charge head on the end of a 6ft 4in pole. The head had to be pushed against the side of the tank, so it was a highly dangerous weapon to use!

C H A P T E R 9

WEAPONS

The weapons of the IJA can perhaps best be described as being, like their soldiers, simple, robust and generally effective. They were probably not up to the technical standard of some of the Allied or German weapons, but nevertheless, with the notable exception of their tanks, all were well able to cope with the tasks in hand. They were also generally available in reasonable quantity and this was still the case even towards the end of the war, as the following summary of the weaponry of the Japanese 32nd Army on Okinawa shows (although to be strictly fair there were contributory reasons for this abundance as is explained). This was the last main battle of the war in the Pacific; it lasted from 1 April 1945 until 21 June 1945 and produced one of the heaviest casualty figures for both the IJA (over 110,000 including the commander, Gen Mitsuru Ushijima who committed ritual suicide) and the US (7,000 killed, including Gen Simon Buckner,* Commander US Tenth Army, and some 32,000 wounded). The US official history says: 'The armament of the Japanese on Okinawa was characterized by a high proportion of artillery, mortar, anti-aircraft and automatic weapons in relation to infantry strength. Their supply of automatic weapons was generally in excess of authorized allotments; much of this excess resulted from the distribution of an accumulation of such weapons intended for shipment to the Philippines and elsewhere but prevented by the shortage of shipping and the course of the war from leaving the island. The Japanese also had an abundant supply of ammunition, mines, hand grenades and satchel charges.

'On Okinawa the Japanese possessed artillery of greater quantity, size and variety than had been available to them in any previous Pacific campaign. Utilizing naval coastal guns, they were able to concentrate a total of 287 guns and howitzers of 70mm or larger caliber for the defense of the island. Of this total, 69 pieces could be classified as being medium artillery, including 52 × 150mm howitzers and 12 × 150mm guns. The smaller pieces included 170 guns and howitzers of calibers 70 and 75mm. In addition, 72 × 75mm AA guns and 54 × 20mm machine cannon were available for use in ground missions.

'The principal mortar strength of the 32nd Army was represented by 96 × 81mm mortars and two light mortar battalions. The Japanese also

---

* Gen Buckner was on a visit to the front line on 18 June when he was killed by enemy fire. He was the only American field army commander to die in combat in the Second World War.

The 37mm Type 94 'Infantry Rapid-fire Gun'. This gun started life in the anti-tank role, but could not penetrate US/UK AFVs, so from 1941 it remained in service as an infantry gun. (IWM: STT MH 600)

possessed in greater numbers than had previously been encountered the large 320mm mortars, commonly called spigot mortars; the 1st Artillery Mortar Regiment, reputed to be the only one of its kind in the IJA, was armed with 24 of these. Standard equipment of the ground combat units of the army included about 1,100 × 50mm grenade dischargers (knee mortars).

'To counter American tank strength, the Japanese relied, among other things, on an unusually large number of anti-tank guns, especially the 47mm type. The independent anti-tank units had a total of 52 × 47mm anti-tank guns, while 27 × 37mm anti-tank guns were distributed among the other units of the Army. The entire Japanese tank force, however, consisted of just 14 medium and 13 light tanks, the heaviest weapon of which was the 57mm gun mounted on the medium tanks.

'The 32nd Army relied heavily on a great number of automatic weapons, well emplaced and plentifully supplied with ammunition. Its units possessed a total of 333 heavy and 1,208 light machine guns. In the course of the battle many more were taken from tanks being used as pill-boxes and from wrecked airplanes. The 62nd Division alone wielded nearly half the automatic weapons of the 32nd Army and was by far its most potent unit.'*

* *Okinawa: the last battle*, Historical Division, US Army, 1948.

INFANTRY WEAPONS

I dealt with the smaller infantry weapons and personal arms in the last chapter, so here we will cover infantry guns and mortars.

Infantry Guns

37mm Type 11. This was the Japanese version of the French *Canon d'Infanterie de 37mle 1916* and was produced between 1922 and 1937. It had no wheels and had to be carried into action by four men using poles; weight in action was 93.4kg. It had a maximum range of some 2,400m

The 75mm Type 41 (1908) gun. This was originally the standard pack artillery gun until largely superseded by the Type 94. It was then used as an infantry gun. It is shown here disassembled into pack loads. (IWM: MH 603)

and its high explosive (HE) shell weighed 1.42lb. It was obsolete by 1941 but remained in service as there was nothing to replace it.

37mm Type 94. This gun, known in the IJA as the 'infantry rapid-fire gun', started life in the anti-tank role (see below), until about 1941–42 when it was clearly proving incapable of penetrating Allied armour. From then on it remained in service throughout the rest of the war as a close-support infantry gun. Its 0.49kg HE shell had a maximum range of some 4,570m.

70mm Type 92 Battalion Gun. Despite its old-fashioned appearance, this was a most successful infantry gun, being small and relatively lightweight (213kg in action), yet firing a useful 3.795kg HE round out to a maximum range of 1,375m. It could also fire smoke and shrapnel rounds, and its minimum range was less than 100m, which made it of great use to the infantry for close support. It had a crew of five in action and was usually towed by mules or horses, but could be manhandled fairly easily. It was especially useful in the jungle as it could be accurately fired direct over open sights.

75mm Type 41 Regimental Gun. Initial models built in the Osaka arsenal were a Japanese version of the Krupp M.08 mountain gun and they remained in that role until replaced by the Type 94 (see below), when it was redesignated as an infantry regimental gun. It weighed 545kg, fired a 6.02kg shell and had a maximum range of just over 7,000m. It was normally horse-towed.

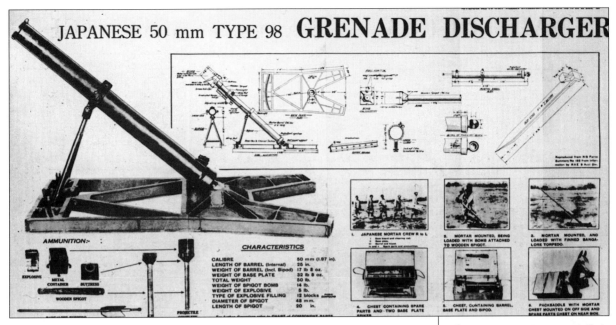

JAPANESE 50 mm TYPE 98 GRENADE DISCHARGER

AMMUNITION:-

EXPLOSIVE · METAL CONTAINER · BUTTRESS · WOODEN SPIGOT · PROJECTILE

CHARACTERISTICS

CALIBRE	50 mm (1.97 in.)
LENGTH OF BARREL (Internal)	25 in.
WEIGHT OF BARREL (incl. Bipod)	17 lb 8 oz.
WEIGHT OF BASE PLATE	32 lb 8 oz.
TOTAL WEIGHT	50 lb.
WEIGHT OF SPIGOT BOMB	14 lb.
WEIGHT OF EXPLOSIVE	5 lb.
TYPE OF EXPLOSIVE FILLING	12 blocks
DIAMETER OF SPIGOT	48 mm.
LENGTH OF SPIGOT	20 in.

The 50mm Type 98 mortar. Called a 'Grenade Discharger' in this US Army drawing, the Type 98 entered service in 1938 and was a specialized demolition mortar which fired either a stick grenade or a Bangalore torpedo. (IWM: STT 7324)

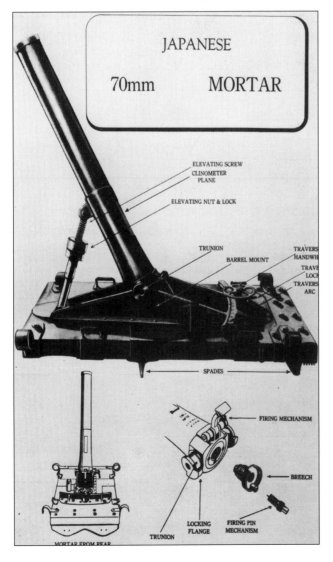

JAPANESE 70mm MORTAR

ELEVATING SCREW · CLINOMETER PLANE · ELEVATING NUT & LOCK · TRUNION · BARREL MOUNT · TRAVERS HANDWH · TRAVE LOCK · TRAVERS ARC · SPADES · FIRING MECHANISM · BREECH · TRUNION · LOCKING FLANGE · FIRING PIN MECHANISM · MORTAR FROM REAR

The 70mm Type 11 mortar. The Japanese called this mortar a 'high angle infantry gun' because of its rifled barrel. (IWM: HU 72212)

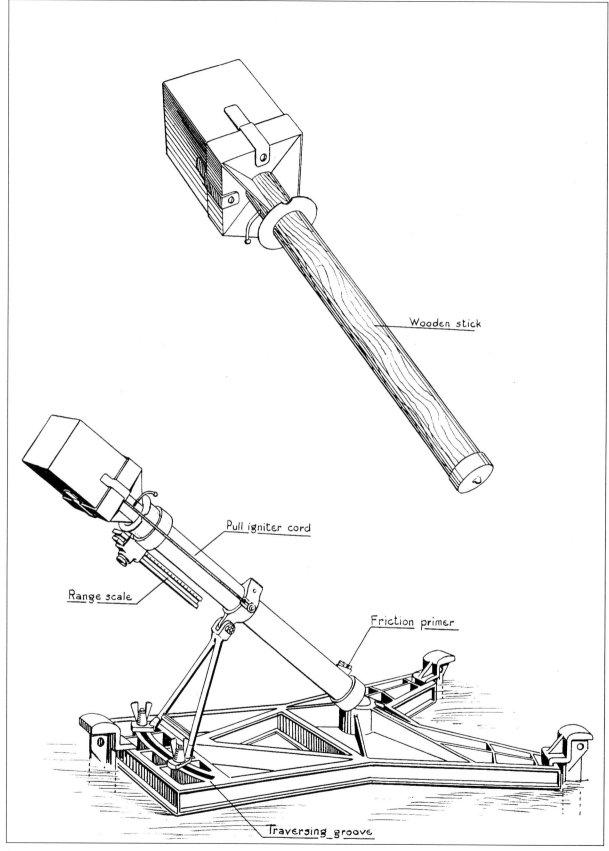

Wooden stick

Pull igniter cord

Range scale

Friction primer

Traversing groove

Japanese 50mm Type 98 mortar (1938).

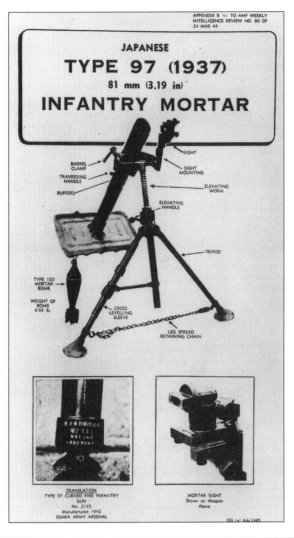

JAPANESE
TYPE 97 (1937)
81 mm (3.19 in)
INFANTRY MORTAR

SIGHT

BARREL
CLAMP

SIGHT
MOUNTING

TRAVERSING
HANDLE

ELEVATING
WORM

BUFFERS

ELEVATING
HANDLE

TRIPOD

TYPE 100
MORTAR
BOMB

WEIGHT OF
BOMB
6.93 lb.

CROSS
LEVELLING
SLEEVE

LEG SPREAD
RETAINING CHAIN

TRANSLATION
TYPE 97 CURVED FIRE INFANTRY
GUN
No. 2145
Manufactured 1942
OSAKA ARMY ARSENAL

MORTAR SIGHT
Shown on Weapon
Above

GSI (a) Adv LHQ

The 81mm Type 97 Mortar. This was the first fully Japanese 81mm mortar and it replaced the Type 3 copy of the Stokes-Brandt mortar. (IWM: STT 7315)

'SMALL'
MORTAR
Type 99

SIGHT BRACKET

FIRE   SAFE

TRAVERSING WHEEL

ELEVATING WHEEL

CROSS LEVELLER

Total Weight
52 lb

12⅜"

BOMB
WEIGHT

6 lb 15 oz

The 81mm Type 99 Mortar. Known as the 'small mortar' because of its barrel length (only 64cm instead of 126cm), it was widely used. (Tank Museum)

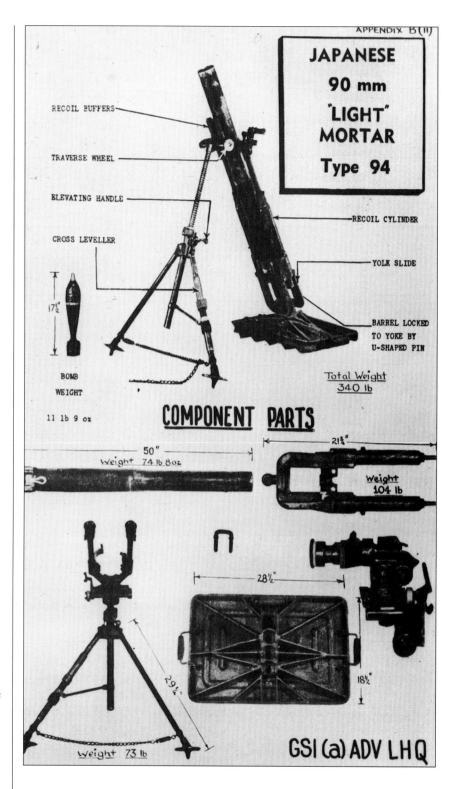

APPENDIX B (II)

JAPANESE 90 mm 'LIGHT' MORTAR Type 94

RECOIL BUFFERS

TRAVERSE WHEEL

ELEVATING HANDLE

CROSS LEVELLER

RECOIL CYLINDER

YOLK SLIDE

BARREL LOCKED TO YOKE BY U-SHAPED PIN

17½"

BOMB WEIGHT

11 lb 9 oz

Total Weight 340 lb

COMPONENT PARTS

50"
Weight 74 lb 8oz

21¼"
Weight 104 lb

28½"

18½"

29¼"

Weight 73 lb

GSI (a) ADV LHQ

The 90mm Type 94 Mortar. Known by the IJA as the 'Kyuyon Shiki Keihakugehiko', it became a static defence weapon when replaced by the lighter Type 97. (IWM: STT 7321)

Mortars

50mm Mortar Type 98. This mortar entered service in 1938. It had a fixed elevation of about 40 degrees, comprised three main parts (baseplate, bipod and barrel) and fired a 10lb stick bomb, which contained an

The 150mm Type 97 Mortar. Largest and heaviest of the conventional Japanese mortars was this heavy bombardment weapon issued in 1937 (shown under the name Type 93 in the US Handbook). (US National Archives)

explosive charge of some 7lb of picric acid in rectangular blocks, while the rectangular body of the bomb was made of sheet metal. Into the base of the body fitted a hardwood stick with a metal cap at the bottom end, which fitted down the barrel of the mortar. The stick bomb produced considerable blast and was very useful supporting attacks against strong points, etc. Range was some 415m. The mortar could also fire a bangalore torpedo, which was used to blow passages through barbed-wire entanglements or to clear paths through minefields, its blast detonating all the mines in its area.

70mm Mortar Type 11. The IJA referred to this mortar as a 'high angle infantry gun' because it had a rifled barrel. Nevertheless, it was loaded via the muzzle, so it rightly appears here under the mortar classification. In service from 1922, its relatively heavy weight – just under 61kg – meant that it was more suited to static warfare. It fired a 2.1kg bomb out to some 1,500m, but was virtually obsolete by 1942.

81mm Mortar Type 97. First issued in 1937, this mortar was a fully Japanese version of the earlier Type 3, which had been a direct copy of the Stokes-Brandt mortar. Weighing just under 66kg, it could fire two types of HE bombs: a 3.27kg to 3,000m and a 6.5kg to 1,200m. It became widely used on all fronts.

81mm Mortar Type 99. Two years later came the shorter and lighter Type 99, which had almost exactly the same performance as the Type 97, but weighed only 23.7kg and had half the barrel length (64cm compared with 126cm). It was widely used and fired the same ammunition as the Type 97.

90mm Mortar Type 94. This 90mm heavy mortar had both a heavy recoil mechanism and breech, so its considerable weight of 155kg limited its

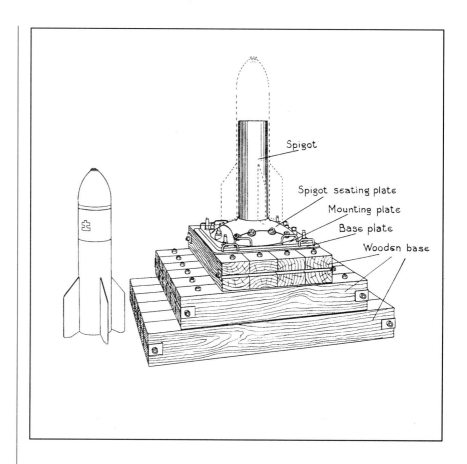

320mm spigot mortar.

The 320mm rocket projectile was fired from the spigot, which was attached to a very substantial wooden base. (Tank Museum)

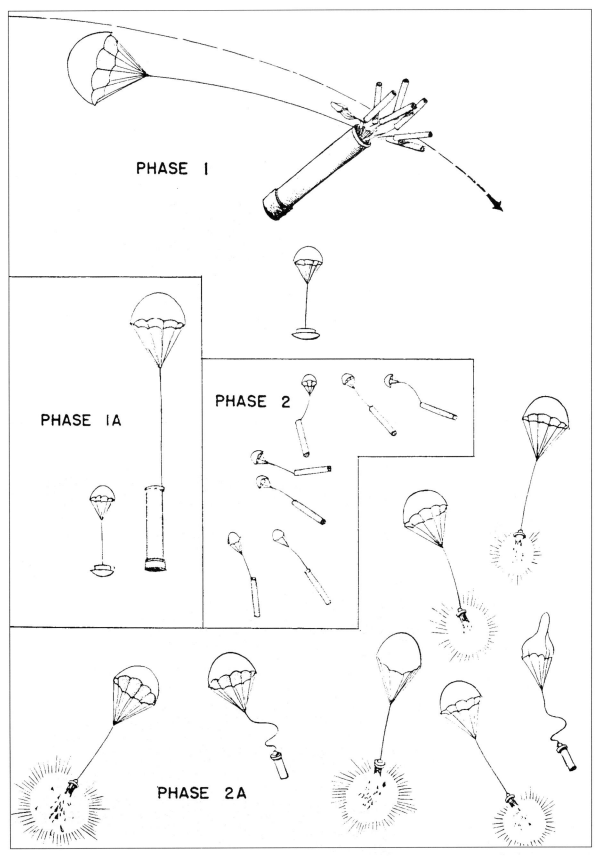

PHASE 1

PHASE 1A

PHASE 2

PHASE 2A

Shell used in the 70mm barrage mortar.

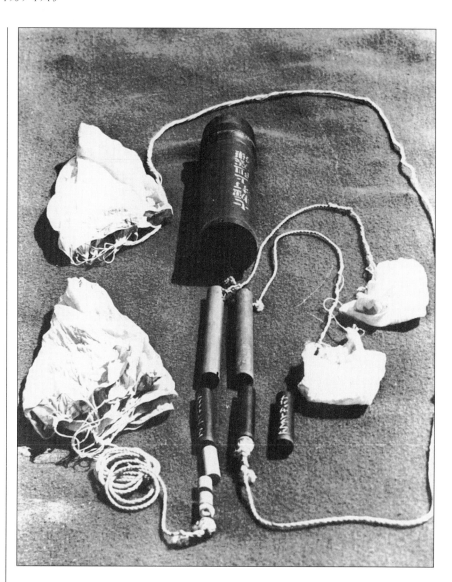

Barrage mortars. This is the shell used in the 70mm barrage mortar, showing some of the parachutes – see the drawing on p. 143 for an explanation of how it worked. (Tank Museum)

mobility. It was therefore largely used for static defence. It fired a bomb weighing 5.22kg and had a range of between 558m and 3,797m. It was replaced by the lighter Type 97.

90mm Mortar Type 97. Entering service in 1937, this was, at 105.8kg, only two-thirds of the weight of its predecessor and thus much more mobile. Its barrel length remained roughly the same (133cm), so the performance was just as good and it fired the same ammunition, and used the same baseplate and bipod as the Type 94.

150mm Mortar Type 97. The largest and heaviest of the conventional Japanese mortars, this came into service in 1937. It was a heavy bombardment weapon with a range of just in excess of 2,000m and a bomb weight of 25.88kg. It was smooth-bored, muzzle-loaded and lanyard fired; in essence, it was little more than an enlarged version of the 81mm mortar.

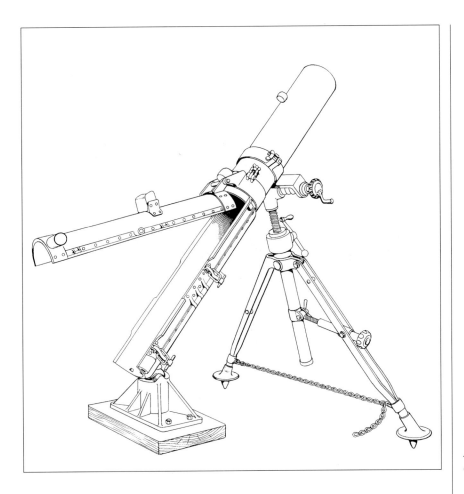

20cm rocket projector Type 4 (1944).

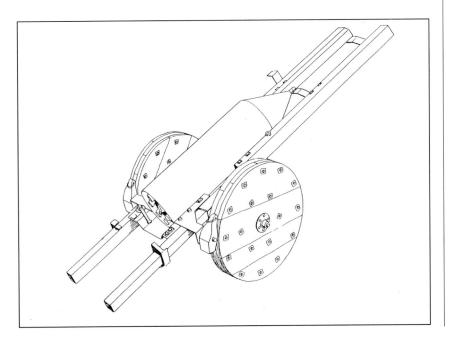

Projector for 45cm high explosive rocket.

Spigot Mortars. The IJA had independent mortar battalions (*Dokunitsu Kyoho Daitai*) equipped with much heavier spigot mortars, such as the 250mm Type 98 which could throw a 700lb bomb some 1,000m, and the 320mm of the 1st Artillery Mortar Regiment – part of the 32nd IJA Army in Okinawa – designed more for demolition work than infantry support. (See p. 142.)

Barrage Mortars. Mention must also be made of the remarkable 70mm and 81mm barrage mortars, whose *raison d'être* was as an anti-aircraft weapon! They consisted of mortar barrels set into wooden baseplates which were fitted with spikes that were driven into the ground to hold them steady. The barrage mortar bomb was then fired by dropping it into the barrel like any conventional mortar. Ignition of the propelling charge subsequently ignited a delay element in the projectile, which, in due course ignited a charge in the projectile. This expelled seven canisters on parachutes, each of which in turn ejected a number of HE shrapnel-filled tubes which exploded to produce a curtain of HE in the sky. The effective vertical range was around 3,000–4,000ft; however, as there was no way of adjusting the time delay on the projectile, the height of the subsequent explosions depended on the angle at which the mortar tube was fired. Each round produced sixteen separate detonations, but as each was under ½oz of explosive, the result was not very effective. As well as HE, the 81mm version could fire a flare projectile.

Rockets

Both the IJA and the Japanese Navy carried out work on the development of various types of ground-based rocket launchers, which fired a variety of rockets from 20cm up to 44.7cm, designed primarily to make up for their lack of heavy artillery. Examples included:

Replacing the 37mm anti-tank gun was the 47mm anti-tank gun Type 1. This was widely used and was the same gun as fitted to their Type 97 medium tank. (Author's collection)

(a) *Type 4 rocket launcher*. This looked very like a large mortar as it used a conventional mortar bipod. It fired a 20cm rocket, which was loaded into the launcher by lifting up part of the barrel casing. The rocket resembled an artillery shell, had a warhead containing some 16kg of explosive and a rocket motor which vented through six venturi tubes at the rear, making the rocket spin. Its maximum range was about 2,750m.

(b) *Type 10 rocket motor*. This rocket looked very like a large mortar bomb with tailfins to keep it stable in flight and weighed a total of some 60kg, of which just under half was HE filling. It was launched from a trough launcher out to a range of about 1,200m. Another version had a larger rocket motor, increasing its range to some 1,800m. Accuracy in both cases was poor.

(c) *44.7cm rocket*. In addition to an improvised 250kg rocket bomb, which was in fact an aerial bomb on to which had been bolted a rocket motor, the Japanese also used a 44.7cm rocket, which, like the projectile used in the Type 4 launcher, had spin stabilization via six venturi at the base of the motor and closely resembled a large artillery shell. It was fired using a 'one-shot' wooden frame launcher, which was normally destroyed during launch. The rocket weighed 683kg in total, of which the propellant weighed 60kg and the explosive 180kg. Its maximum range was some 2,000m. The Americans reported its use against them on Luzon and Iwo Jima.

ARTILLERY

Anti-tank

While the Japanese had anti-tank units equipped with 37mm or 47mm anti-tank guns, they also made no bones about using field artillery, mountain and infantry guns (70mm or 75mm) in the anti-tank role. Hence armour-piercing ammunition was issued for all these three weapons.

The Type 80 20mm machine cannon was light and mobile, and could be brought into action in under three minutes. Its vertical box magazine held twenty rounds. (Tank Museum)

37mm Gun Type 94. (*Kyuyon Shiki Sanjunana Miri Ho*). Introduced in 1934, this small, light, infantry anti-tank/support gun had either wooden-spoked or metal disc wheels, split trails (anchored with spades driven into the earth) and a horizontally sliding breechblock. It could be manhandled over rough terrain, but was more usually towed by horses/mules. Manually loaded, the armour-piercing projectile could only penetrate 24mm of armour at 1,000yd, so, as the war progressed and the IJA found itself up against medium tanks such as Sherman, the Type 94 could not penetrate their armour and rapidly became used more as an infantry gun than for anti-tank work (see pp. 134, 136).

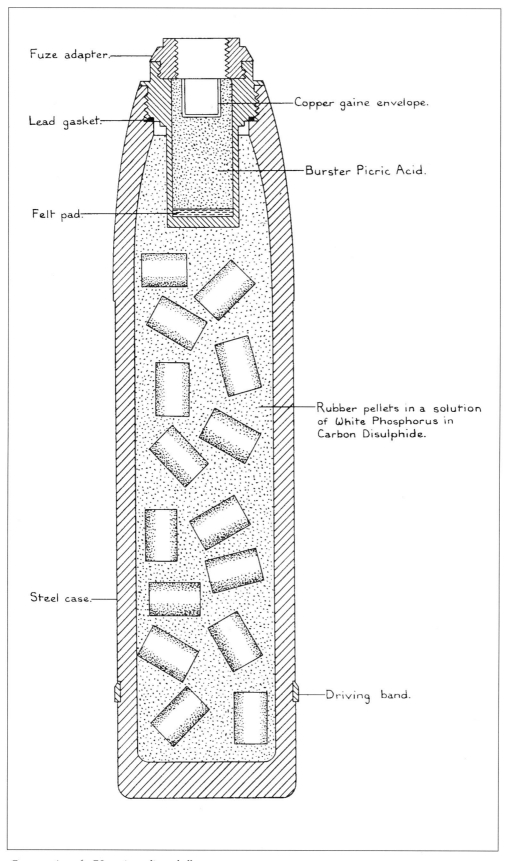

Cross-section of a 75mm incendiary shell.

A dual mounted version of the Type 96 25mm machine cannon in its AA ground role, being used to defend against ground attack aircraft. (It could also be fired in the anti-tank role.) (IWM: MH 605/Tank Museum)

A Type 88 75mm mobile field AA gun in its bunker after being captured. (IWM: NY 8543)

A Type 88 75mm AA gun with the barrel retracted ready for travelling. (Tank Museum)

37mm Anti-tank Gun Type 97. From 1934 onwards, the Japanese built a number of these copies of the German 3.7cm Pak 35/36 under licence. The only alteration was that they added a 'tailwheel' under the rear of the joined trails, to assist in manhandling the gun as it was some 140lb heavier than the Type 94. Sometimes the gunshield was removed to make the gun lighter.

47mm Anti-tank Gun Type 01. Produced by the Osaka Army Arsenal, this first appeared in 1941. It had a disappointing performance, penetrating only 50mm of armour at 500yd, as compared with other nations' designs of the same period. For example, the US Army 37mm M3A1 could penetrate 52.5mm of armour at double the range. It was widely used by the IJA and the same gun was fitted to their Type 97 medium tank.

Model	Weight in action (kg)	Shell weight (kg)	Muzzle velocity (mps)	Max Range (m)
Type 94	370	0.7	700	4,600
Type 97	450	0.9	800	4,000
Type 01	755	1.03	830	7,675

Anti-aircraft Weapons

There was a considerable variety of AA weapons. They included machine-guns; barrage mortars; 20mm and 25mm cannons, both of which were light and mobile; and a range of guns with calibres from 75mm to 127mm. Some of these were dual-purpose naval guns for coastal defensive work, while others, in the 105mm category, were purely AA for home defence in static positions.

Army Type 98 20mm Machine Cannon. This excellent, dual AA/anti-tank weapon was introduced in 1938, although its somewhat archaic-looking gun carriage made it appear much older. It had a cyclic rate of fire of 120rpm, a maximum ceiling of 3,660m and a shell weight of 0.135kg. Feed was via a 20-round vertical box magazine. Light and easily broken down into manageable loads, it was a most useful weapon.

Navy Type 96 25mm Machine Cannon. Although this entered service in the Japanese Navy in 1936, many were diverted for land use, in single, double and triple mountings. With a rate of fire of 190rpm, a maximum effective ceiling of 1,370m and a shell weight of 0.24kg, it could be used in both the AA and anti-tank roles.

Army Type 88 75mm Mobile Field AA Gun. Probably the most widely used IJA AA gun was the Type 88 which entered service in 1928 and consequently was in service with the majority of army AA units when the war began. A large number were later withdrawn from overseas units to defend Japan. It had a maximum effective ceiling of 7,230m, a shell weight of 6.58kg, and all-round traverse on its pedestal mount.

Army Type 14 105mm AA Gun. The other main IJA AA gun was the Type 14, introduced in 1925. It proved to be too cumbersome and unwieldy for mobile use and was relegated to static sites in the defence of the Japanese mainland. Its 16kg shell could be fired to a ceiling of some 10,950m.

Naval Guns. A number of naval guns had a dual role on shore – AA and coastal – with calibres ranging from the 88mm Type 99, through the 100mm Type 98 and the 120mm Type 10, on up to the 127mm Type 89. Their essential details were:

Type 94 75mm pack mountain guns in action. They entered service in 1934 and were a considerable improvement on the Type 41. They could be carried across rough terrain by pack mule or human muscle-power, broken down into requisite loads and reassembled in only about ten minutes. (IWM: STT 3571)

151

The M94 75mm mountain (pack) gun. This was also intended for paratroop use but there are no reports of its use in that role. (IWM: MH 604)

Type	Calibre (mm)	Effective Ceiling (m)	Weight of shell (kg)	Comments
99	88	9,750	9	static pedestal mount
98	100	10,675	13.2	often in twin coastal mountings
10	120	8,235	20.77	still in production in 1944
89	127	7,625	22.96	often in an electric powered armoured turret

Mountain Artillery

Type 94 75mm Mountain (Pack) Gun. Its ancestry was via the 1908 75mm Meiji 41 and the 1917 Meiji 41 (Improved), and it came into service in 1934. It had a better trail, a longer barrel and a sliding breechblock. It could be broken down in just over half an hour into eleven loads (two loads per pack animal) and reassembly took only about ten minutes. It could also be hand carried by 18 to 20 men. With a weight in action of 535kg, it fired a 6.5kg shell out to a range of 8,300m.

Field Artillery

As already mentioned, lightness without loss of range was probably the major characteristic of Japanese field artillery. Models produced since 1930 all had the following:

Type 38 (improved) 75mm field guns in action. These guns were based on the original Krupp design but were extensively modernized. (Tank Museum)

(a) Hydropneumatic recoil mechanisms of the independent type, with the liquid in direct contact with the gas

(b) Spade-plate stabilizers, pintle traverse and three-point suspensions

(c) Horizontal sliding-wedge breechblocks were commonly used

(d) Equilibrators, trunnioning forward of the point of balance and the use of open box or split trails was typical of their design.

Type	Weight in action (kg)	Traverse (degrees)	Elevation (degrees)	Maximum Range (m)	Shell weight (kg)
38 (I)	1,136	7	−8 to +43	11,960	6.6
90	1,400	50	−8 to +43	14,950	6.5
95	1,105	50	−8 to +43	10,950	6.5

Type 38 (Improved) 75mm Field Gun. Based on a Krupp design of the early 1900s and built at the Osaka Arsenal, the original Type 38 guns had been sent back to the arsenal for extensive modernization during the First World War. The result was the Type 38 (Improved) which remained in service during the Second World War, initially being the most widely encountered of all IJA field pieces.

Type 90 75mm Field Gun. Introduced into service in 1930, there were two versions, one with spoked wheels, the other with pneumatic tyres. First used in China in 1940, it resembled the *Schneider Canon de 85mle 1927*.

A Type 91 105mm howitzer. This was a popular and widely used gun, despite its poor finish. (IWM: STT 9517)

Type 95 75mm Field Gun. First produced at the Osaka Arsenal in 1935, this was the Japanese version of the *Schneider 75mle 1933* and was brought in to replace the obsolescent 75mm Cavalry Gun Type 41. It was never produced in larger numbers.

Medium Artillery

There were three 105mm guns and one 105mm howitzer in the range that was initially classed as 'heavy' but was really only 'medium'. These were the Type 38, Type 14 and Type 92 guns and the Type 91 howitzer.

Type	Weight in action (kg)	Traverse (degrees)	Elevation (degrees)	Max Range (m)	Shell wt (kg)
38	3,610	6	–2 to +15	10,050	18
14	3,110	30	–5 to +33	15,000	15.8
92	3,720	36	–5 to +45	18,250	15.8
91	1,495	40	–5 to +45	10,765	15.8

Type 38 105mm Medium Gun. Entering service in the early 1900s, together with 75mm, 120mm and 150mm pieces, all of which were part of the *Meiji* modernization of the IJA, the long-barrelled Type 38 was mainly used in China.

Type 14 105mm Medium Gun. This was the first gun to be built in Japan entirely of Japanese design. It featured the first split trail carriage, was delivered in 1925 and was sometimes called 'the 10cm cannon'. The design was not a great success and only a few were ever produced, being replaced by the Type 92.

Type 92 105mm Medium Gun. This was one of the IJA's most successful guns, having all the right characteristics: good range, a fairly large projectile and light weight. Its main roles were for counter-battery and long-range shooting as it had some 3,000+ metres additional range on other IJA 105s.

Type 91 105mm Medium Howitzer. First produced in 1929, this was not issued to the IJA until 1931. Despite its poor finish it was still a popular gun with a reasonable performance and was the main divisional artillery gun of the war.

Heavy Artillery

As with other types of artillery, those used by the IJA in the Second World War ranged from the Meiji period of the early 1900s, when the Japanese Army had begun to equip itself with modern weapons, up to those produced a few years before the war began. There were four main guns and howitzers in the 150mm class and two larger howitzers which were above that calibre: a 24cm howitzer and a massive 41cm siege mortar.

150mm Type	Gun/ Howitzer	Weight in action (kg)	Traverse (degrees)	Elevation (degrees)	Range Max (m)	Shell weight (kg)
38	Howitzer	2,085	3	0 to +42½	5,960	35.9
4	Howitzer	2,800	6	−5 to +45	9,550	41.7
96	Howitzer	4,135	30	−5 to +75	11,850	31.2
89	Gun	10,400	40	−5 to +43	19,900	45.8

Type 38 150mm Howitzer. A licence-built Krupp-designed howitzer which entered service in 1905. It had a box trail, a short barrel and used a hydro-

The Type 96 150mm howitzer was introduced to replace both the Types 4 and 38 howitzers. (IWM: NYP 32105)

spring recoil system. Obsolete by 1941, it still remained in limited use, but was withdrawn in 1942–43.

Type 4 150mm Howitzer. The Taisho 4 was designed in 1915 to replace the Meiji 38 and was widely used from then on in all theatres, a fair number being captured by the Chinese. It used the same ammunition as the Type 38, together with a separate cartridge case which could accept up to five charge increments, thus nearly doubling its range.

Type 96 150mm Howitzer. This was the replacement for both the Types 4 and 38 and entered service in 1936. However, although it was used on all fronts, it was never produced in suffcient quantity to completely replace the other two howitzers, whose ammunition it could use. Nevertheless, it had an improved range, using new ammunition some 5kg lighter than the old version.

Type 89 150mm Gun. Normally a tractor-drawn weapon used mainly for long-range bombardment, this was employed in both Malaya and the Philippines, then mainly withdrawn for home service. Its main drawback was the time it took to get into action. It also had a split trail and hydropneumatic recoil mechanism.

There were other larger weapons on which information is still scanty and at times conflicting. However, here are details of two examples:

The SO-KI single 20mm AA gun, mounted on a CHI-HA tank chassis. There was also a twin gun version. They were both produced only as prototypes. (Tank Museum)

The HO-NI I mounted a 75mm anti-tank gun on a medium tank (M 2597 CHI-HA) chassis. It was developed in 1942. (Tank Museum)

Most effective was the HO-NI III, which mounted a more powerful 75mm Type 88 anti-tank gun. (Tank Museum)

Most powerful of the SPs was the HO-RO, which mounted a 15cm howitzer, again on the CHI-HA chassis. (IWM: STT 9007)

Type	Calibre (cm)	Weight in action	Range (m)	Shell weight (kg)
Meiji 45	24	Railway gun (35 tons approx)	54,500 (estimated)	181
Siege Howitzer	41	81,280 kg	19,380	997

Self-propelled Artillery

Japan produced a number of satisfactory self-propelled guns: one figure for Mitsubishi Industries' wartime production is some fifty vehicles, based on the Type 97 CHI-HA medium tank. Most common were the HO-NI Marks I, II and III. The first mounted a 75mm gun in a fixed, open-topped turret and was developed in 1942. It weighed 14.6 tons, had a crew of three and was powered by a 170hp V12 diesel engine, giving it a top speed of 25mph and a range of some 130 miles. The Mk II was 1.5 tons heavier, had a crew of five and was armed with a short-barrelled 105mm howitzer. The Mk III was almost identical, but mounted a 75mm Type 88 anti-tank gun and had better armoured protection at the top and rear of the gunshield.

A larger calibre SP was the 15 ton Type 38 HO-RO which mounted a 150mm howitzer, still on the same chassis in a square box-like turret. The howitzer could only elevate 30 degrees and had only 8 degrees of traverse, so its range was limited to 6,000m. The Japanese Navy also built other SPs using the medium tank chassis.

CHAPTER 10

VEHICLES

MOTORCYCLES, BICYCLES AND CARTS

Motorcycles

The IJA used both motorcycles and motor-tricycles, which entered service from 1937 onwards, for solo/sidecar work as despatch riders, also as personnel carriers, convoy escorts and for general liaison.

Solo motorcycle Type 97. Some 18,000 of these robust and reliable motorcycles were issued. It was a copy of the American Harley-Davidson and produced by the Sankyo, Shinagawa Works in Tokyo and later Rikuo (Kurogane). A Sankyo V-twin cylinder, 1196cc engine gave rear-wheel driving via a three-speed gearbox and chain. It had mechanical brakes, a

The Type 97 solo motorcycle. The IJA had some 18,000 of these robust and reliable machines, copied from the American Harley-Davidson. (IWM: STT 9514)

*The Type 97 motorcycle could be
fitted with a sidecar, which, as the
photograph shows, had a mounting
for an LMG. (Tank Museum)*

*The Kurogane 3 × 2 motor-trike
Type 1 (here being driven by a
smiling GI) was used as a
cargo/personnel carrier. (IWM:
STT 8108)*

rigid frame and a tyre size of 4.75 × 18in front and rear. The Type 97 had an unladen weight of 280kg and top speed of some 60mph solo. Military equipment included (fitted as necessary) a rear carry rack or pillion saddle, high level exhaust and, when fitted with a sidecar, mountings for a light machine-gun.

3×2 motor-tricycle Type 1. The Kurogane military version of this trike, originally built in the 1930s as a commercial freight carrier, was known as the *Sanrinsha*. There were a number of models with differing engine sizes, ranging from 350 to 1,000cc, the main type was chain-driven, with a slow-speed, single-cylinder, 4-cycle engine of some 750cc displacement. Steered using girder-type front forks with compression springs, it had leaf-spring rear suspension and disc wheels and weighed some 540kg. It was fitted either as a cargo carrier (box-like chassis) or for carrying personnel.

Bicycles

The Japanese were inveterate users of bicycles, there being over a million in Tokyo alone in the early 1940s. The military model was simple and robust, designed along British lines with front and rear brakes and large wheels. It was used extensively in all theatres. There was also a folding metal hand cart (weight about 100lb) which could be towed behind a bicycle.

The most basic type of transport often used by the Japanese was the handcart. These Japanese sailors are using a variety of wooden and metal handcarts to lug their belongings to the docks in Penang in early September 1945. The metal carts were collapsible, weighed about 100lb and could be pulled by hand or bicycle.

Type 95 4 × 4 scout car, designed by Rikuo and produced under the name 'Kurogane'. They were widely used in Burma. (IWM: STT 8299)

Carts

The IJA used a variety of carts, both hand and horse-drawn. All were of wooden construction with metal bracing. Examples included the 100lb handcart already mentioned; the 350lb transport cart which had a carrying capacity of some 400lb; and the larger 765lb two-horse cart which had a carrying capacity of some 825lb.

CARS, TRUCKS AND TRACTORS

In the late 1920s most civilian cars used in Japan were of foreign design but assembled in Japan,* so they had to use foreign vehicles during the campaign in Manchuria. This all changed in the 1930s when the Motor Car Manufacturing Enterprise Law was brought in, which laid down that 50 per cent of any motor company capital, officials and shareholders had to be Japanese and that they should 'follow any instruction the army might give them'. In 1939 the Foreign Exchange Control Law stopped all assembly of foreign vehicles, by which time the fledgling Japanese motor industry was well established, the leading companies being Nissan (formely DAT), Isuzu, Mitsubishi and Toyota. In 1941/42, they built over

* In his book *World War II Military Vehicles*, G.N. Georgano states that in 1929 American companies assembled about 30,000 cars in Japan, while the native manufacturers built only 437!

This Nissan passenger sedan has been adapted as a mobile workshop. (IWM: STT 9556)

A British soldier inspecting an abandoned Nissan 180 4 × 2 1½ ton cargo truck, one of the most widely used Japanese trucks. (Author's collection)

This Nissan 180 1½ ton truck has been converted into a water truck. (IWM: STT 8112)

An Isuzu TU10 1½ ton 6 × 4 Type 94A truck in a workshop area. They first appeared in 1934 and the chassis was made by various manufacturers. (Tank Museum)

45,000 trucks and buses, half of which went to the armed forces. The IJA also supplemented their vehicle fleet by using captured American and British vehicles. All home-produced motor vehicles had right-hand drive, generally good ground clearance and small turning circles. However, power to weight ratios were not good and vehicles were often overloaded. Japan suffered from a severe shortage of petrol, which led to the design and building of diesel engines.

4 × 4 scout car Type 95. Designed by Rikuo in 1935/36 to meet a specific IJA requirement, this somewhat civilian-looking small scout car was produced under the name *Kurogane* (Kuro = black, Gane = metal). Some 4,775 were built and there was a fair amount of variation. For example, both 2- and 3-seat models were built and there was a pick-up truck variant (cf: British PU truck); four-door models and oversnow models were also built. Basic technical details were: 1,399cc V-twin cylinder, overhead valve, air-cooled petrol engine, producing 33bhp at 3,400rpm. Magneto ignition, dryplate clutch and 3F1R gearbox. Length was 3.55m, weight 1,060kg (laden 1,250kg). They were widely used in the campaigns in Burma and Indo-China.

Staff Cars. All the main manufacturers produced staff cars, both 4 × 4 (Toyota AA and AB, Isuzu PK 10 and Mitsubishi PX33) and 6 × 4 (Isuzu/Sumida K10). They had a strong resemblance to American designs of the 1930s. For example, the Toyota AA was an American-style sedan and the AB a tourer, some versions of which had cut-away mudguards. The larger 6 × 4 car originated in 1933 and shared most of its mechanical

The Toyota KCY/SUKI truck 2 ton 4 × 4 amphibian, which had a boat-like steel hull and used the mechanical components of a truck chassis. (IWM: STT 8106)

components with the TU10 truck (see below), but it owed its styling to a batch of six-wheeled cars which the Hudson Motor Car Company of Detroit had supplied during the Manchurian campaign.

1½ ton Cargo Trucks. Nissan produced two such vehicles: the Nissan 80 in the 1930s, which was modelled on the US Federal COE truck, and the Nissan 180 which took its place and was widely used during the war. Both had six-cylinder, 69bhp 3,670cc engines, driving the rear wheels via a 4-speed gearbox, with hydraulic brakes, rigid axles and leafsprings. Alternative bodies included tankers and fire trucks. The Toyota XB was another truck in this class, some 21,000 being produced between 1942 and 1944, while Isuzu produced a 2 ton 4 x 2 cargo truck, the TX40, which was first built in 1933, but restyled a number of times thereafter and used with special bodywork (e.g., as a small fuel tanker, a fire truck and a searchlight truck). They also built a 6 × 4 TU10 (Type 94A), which was suitable for cross-country work. The chassis were built in various factories and it is said that there were some forty body variants in total. The Isuzu TU10 weighed 3,400kg (5,300kg laden) and had an overall length of 5.43m.

2 ton 4 × 4 Amphibious Truck. The strangest small truck was the Toyota KCY/SUKI, which had a boat-shaped steel hull, fitted with a six-cylinder, 63bhp 3,389cc engine, driving either rear two or all four wheels via a 4-speed gearbox and 2-speed transfer box. Water propulsion was by a propeller driven via a power take-off. It had hydraulic brakes, leafspring suspension, was some 7.81m long and weighed 4,000kg. Just under 200 were built between November 1943 and August 1944.

3 ton 6 × 4 Cargo Type 1. This 4,400kg (laden 9,800kg) load carrier, known as the Isuzu TU23, was introduced into service in 1941 and was powered by a 5,100cc diesel engine, producing 85bhp, driving the rear wheels via a 4-speed gearbox.

7 ton 4 × 2 Cargo Type 2. Also produced by Isuzu was the TB60, a 5,500kg (laden 12,900kg) 7-tonner which entered service in 1941. It was powered by a 8,550cc diesel engine, producing 100bhp and driving the rear wheels via a 5-speed gearbox.

20 ton 6 × 4 Dump Truck. The largest Japanese truck was the Isuzu TH10, which weighed 8,000kg (laden 28,000kg) and had a rear dump body of 12 cubic metres capacity. It was built mainly for the Navy, being used for port construction and other heavy building work.

Trailers. For towing behind their trucks, the IJA used a two-wheel metal trailer with pneumatic tyres. There was also a ¾ ton tracked metal trailer that could be towed behind tankettes (see p. 175) for the transportation of ammunition and supplies in forward areas. It used the same type of track as the tankette, with two bogie wheels and idlers front and rear.

HALF-TRACK AND FULL-TRACK ARTILLERY TRACTORS

Half-tracks. Ikegai, Isuzu and Hino all produced half-tracks, but only the last of the three produced an armoured version. The *Type 98 Ikegai KO-HI* was a 5 ton half-track (prototype: Showa 12 (1937)). It was

A Type 98 Isuzu Tractor 6 ton half-track was brought into service in 1937. Designed as a prime mover for AA guns, it could carry the full gun crew of fifteen men. (Tank Museum)

The carrier armoured half-track Type 1 Hino 2A20/Ho-Ha was used for both gun-towing and carrying mechanized infantry. (Tank Museum)

An artillery tractor and ammunition limber (the field gun is off the photograph). The tractor is an 8 ton, full-track Type 92A, made by Ikegai. The diesel version was designated Type 92B. (Tank Museum)

Another more operational photograph of the 8 ton Ikegai limber, Type 92A. (Tank Museum)

The HO-KI carrier armoured full-track was introduced towards the end of the Second World War. It was designed both as an APC/load carrier and as an artillery tractor. (Tank Museum)

designed as a towing vehicle for AA guns, carrying the crew of up to fifteen men in its capacious 5.67m long body. Weight was 5,700kg and it was powered by a six-cylinder 110bhp diesel engine. It had modified light tank bogies and 36 × 6 wheels at the front. The *Type 98 Isuzu* was a 6 ton half-track also employed as an AA gun tower. It was powered by a six-cylinder 120bhp diesel engine and weighed some 6,000kg. The *Type 1 Hino 2A20 HO-HA* was a 7,000kg armoured half-track with armour some 4–8mm thick and a maximum speed of just over 30mph. It could carry fifteen men and was used both as an APC and for gun-towing.

Full-tracks. There were also three fully tracked artillery tractors: the 4 ton *Type 98 SHI-KE*, the 6 ton *Type 98 Isuzu* and the 8 ton *Type 92A Ikegai* in the IJA. All were designed for towing guns and carrying crews and all were fitted with power winches with capacities of 2.2 tons, 5 tons and 5 tons respectively. Finally, later in the war, a fully tracked armoured APC was developed, known as the *HO-KI*, which could also be used to tow artillery pieces. It weighed some 10,000kg and could also be used for carrying stores. Armour thickness was approximately 6mm.

Vickers Crossley Type 87 armoured cars supporting IJN sailors in a sandbagged emplacement in China. Bought in 1927 from the UK, they were later modified by fitting pneumatic tyres. (IWM: STT 2584)

A mixture of Crossley and naval pattern M2592 armoured cars in a Chinese street. All these armoured cars belonged to the IJN as the flag on the side denoted. (Tank Museum)

Another view of the naval pattern M2592 armoured car, heavily camouflaged with cut greenery. It weighed 6.2 tons and had a crew of six. (Tank Museum)

The Sumida M2953 armoured car could be swiftly adapted for railway use (and vice versa). Note the flanged rims carried on the sides of the car. (Tank Museum)

This is the Sumida M2593 adapted for railway use – the solid rubber tyres are carried on the vehicle's sides. (Tank Museum)

ARMOURED CARS AND ARMOURED RAIL CARS

In their war against China, the Japanese used a number of obsolescent armoured cars which included, for example, the *Type 87*, which was the Indian-pattern Vickers-Crossley six-wheeled armoured car that had been purchased from the British in 1927 and now modernized by fitting pneumatic tyres. Another was the *Sumida Type ARM* which had entered service in 1928 and was based on an Osaka lorry chassis with heavy spoked wheels and solid tyres. More recent were the four- and six-wheel *Osaka Type 92* armoured cars, produced in 1932, the four-wheel version being for the IJA, the six-wheeler for the IJN.*

Most widely used was the *Sumida Type 93 6 × 4*, which was designed so that it could quickly be adapted for rail use by fitting six flanged steel wheels. To change it back to road use, the vehicle was jacked up on four built-in jacks (mounted front and rear), then solid rubber tyres (carried on the hull sides) were fitted and the AFV driven off the track, using short lengths of rail (also carried on the hull) to get it down to the road. The 7½ ton *Type 93* had a crew of six, and mounted a single machine-gun in the turret. However, there were weapon slits on the sides and a small observation hatch towards the rear of the roof of its large body. Armour thickness was up to 16mm, it had top speeds of 37mph on rails and 25mph on roads and was powered by a six-cylinder 100bhp diesel engine. Dimensions were 5.67m long × 1.9m wide × 2.95m high.

TANKS

Tank Production

The Japanese had shown some interest in tanks during the First World War, obtaining a variety of models such as the British Heavy Mk V and the French Renault FT 17. They named the latter *KO-GATA Sensha* (*Sen* = battle, *sha* = wagon). After purchasing various other British and French tanks during the postwar years they began to develop their own light and medium tanks, some of which they used in Manchuria and Shanghai. In 1933 Maj Tomio Hara designed a bellcrank scissors-type suspension, which had paired bogie wheels (two pairs on each side), connected by a single coil-spring mounted horizontally outside the hull. This type of suspension became a feature of many Japanese tanks for the next decade. During the period 1931–38 they built nearly 1,700 tanks which put them into fourth place in the world; however, as we have already seen, they did not see the tank as a battle winner, devoting their heavy industry to the building of warships, AA weapons and aircraft, rather than tanks. Nevertheless, they did still continue to build tanks, reaching peak output in 1942. Later in the war they realized their mistake, but could not then catch up although they did produce some innovative designs, including a number of amphibious models, but by then it was a question of too little too late.

---

* One can distinguish between the IJA and IJN AFVs by the fact that the former used the national flag – the red disc (*Hi-No-Maru*) on a white rectangle – painted somewhere on the vehicle, while the IJN used the rising sun disc with red rays extending all the way to the borders of the white rectangle.

A Type 94 TK tankette, which was produced both in petrol then diesel (prototype only) versions, and was used in all theatres. (Author's collection)

The tiny 3½ ton tankettes could not survive on the battlefield against any meaningful opposition. This is what was left of one Type 94 that was involved in the Japanese counter-attack on Pelelieu airfield, 15 September 1944. (USMC)

The final development in the tankette series was the Type 97 TE-KE. It had more room in the turret, allowing for a 37mm gun to be fitted. (Tank Museum)

Tank Production 1939–45

1939	345
1940	735
1941	1,190
1942	1,290
1943	780
1944	295
1945	130
TOTAL =	4,765

The Japanese classified their tanks into four groups:

Up to 5 tons	Tankettes	(*Choki Sensha*)
5 to 10 tons	Light tanks	(*Ki Sensha*)
10 to 20 tons	Medium tanks	(*Chi Sensha*)
Over 20 tons	Heavy tanks	(*Ju Sensha*)

Tankettes

Japan bought several export models from Vickers, including the Carden-Loyd Mk VI which they used to develop a range of tankettes, the first being the **Type 94**. This was a two-man AFV, weighing 3½ tons and armed with a single 7.7mm machine-gun mounted in a small turret offset to the right. Armour thickness was 4–12mm. It was powered by a front-mounted 32hp petrol engine, was 3.07m long × 1.62m wide × 1.63m high, and had a top speed of 26mph and a range of 120 miles. The Type 94 was later modified, being fitted with a better suspension incorporating a trailing idler, which lengthened the chassis by some 30cm, and thus increased the length of track in contact with the ground which improved the cross-country performance. Some work was also done on a diesel-engined model, but it came to naught. However, it was of great value in developing the engine for

The Amphibious Type 2 KAMI-SHA was one of a number of amphibious light tanks which the Japanese produced to support deep penetrations in areas without adequate roads. However, they soon lost interest. (Tank Museum)

One of the best Japanese tanks was the Type 95 HA-GO light tank; some 1,250 of these 7½ ton three-man tanks were built. Its main problem was the one-man turret. (Tank Museum)

A HA-GO Type 95 moving at speed. Its armament consisted of one 37mm gun and two machine-guns. A later model (not this one) had a modified suspension. (IWM: STT 8031)

the final tankette, the **Type 97 TE-KE**, which was powered by a 65hp diesel. The vehicle weighed over 4½ tons, was 60cm longer than the original Type 94, had a larger turret mounting a 37mm gun, but still only had a two-man crew. It had a top speed of 28mph and a road range of 150 miles.

Light Tanks

At the same time as building tankettes, the Japanese decided to design a three-man light tank, for use in supporting deep penetrations. Also, because of the lack of good roads in the areas of China and the Far East where they were operating, they decided to develop amphibious vehicles. This began in 1931–32 with the **Type 92** light tank and an amphibious version of the same vehicle, known as the **A-I-GO**. The production version of the Type 92 was one of the earliest all-welded AVFs in the world. The running gear that distinguished it from the earlier 1931 prototype comprised six small rubber-tyred bogie wheels, mounted in pairs, with three semi-elliptical springs. Later production models had this suspension replaced by four larger spoked wheels, grouped in pairs with helical coil-springs and bell-cranks – also designed by Maj Tomio Hara. Both models weighed 3½ tons, had a crew of three, mounted one heavy 13mm machine-gun in the hull and one ball-mounted LMG (6.5mm) in the small turret. The 3.77m long AFV had armour only 6mm thick and was powered by a 45hp petrol engine, which gave it a top speed of 21.6mph. Both models were produced in reasonable numbers and both saw service during the Second World War.

The amphibious A-I-GO had a watertight hull, enlarged to give more buoyancy and to allow for the fitting of propellers and floats. Although it did not go into production, much useful information was gained which was used in the design of the next amphibian, the SR-I or I-GO, but again this got no further than prototype stage. The IJA then lost interest in amphibians and turned the project over to the IJN.

The Type 89 OT-SU medium tank still had many features of the Vickers Medium C from which it had been developed. (Tank Museum)

A column of Type 89 OT-SU medium tanks advancing down a jungle road. Its armament was one 57mm gun and two machine-guns. (IWM: STT 869)

*A smiling tank crew 'bomb up'
their medium tank Type 89 OT-SU
with ammunition for its 57mm
main gun. (IWM: STT 487)*

Type 95 HA-GO. One of the best Japanese tanks of the war, this was in production at Mitsubishi from 1935 for a total of seven years, during which 1,250 were built. It mounted a 37mm gun in its offset turret, plus a 7.7mm ball-mounted machine-gun in the turret rear. The suspension was Maj Tomio Hara's bell-crank and helical compression spring design and the 7½ ton tank was powered by a 110bhp diesel engine. The dimensions of HA-GO were: length 4.36m, width 2.05m, height 2.18m, and armour thickness 6–12mm. Developed later from the HA-GO was the KE-NI, which appeared in 1938. This had three pairs of bogie wheels instead of two, better armour and was more streamlined, but it was only ever produced in small numbers, apparently because the crews preferred the HA-GO. Further developments produced the KE-HO light tank Type 5, a four-man, 10 ton tank, armed with a 47mm gun. However, the war ended before it could enter production.

The 15 ton CHI-HA medium tank followed the design lines of the HA-GO light tank, but it had a two-man turret, a more powerful armament (57mm) and thicker armour. (Author's collection)

Best of the CHI-HAs was the SHINTO CHI-HA, which entered service in 1942. It weighed 15.8 tons and had a crew of four men. (Tank Museum)

The command version of the
medium tank was known as the
SHI-KI and is clearly recognizable
by its all-round aerial on the turret.
Presumably the turret gun was a
dummy as it had a 37mm gun in
the hull (it is difficult to see on this
photo). (Tank Museum)

Medium Tanks

Type 89 OT-SU. The Japanese had bought a Vickers Mk C export model in
1927 and two years later developed their first medium tank – the Type 89-
KO (also called the Type 89-A) – which had many of the features of the
original Vickers tank. A second model followed, the Type 89-B, which was
also known as the Type 89 OT-SU. The original Type 89 had been powered
by a petrol engine, but after cold weather trials in Manchuria it was decided
to fit a diesel, the 115hp Mitsubishi being developed specially for the tank. It
was widely used in China and Manchuria where it was sometimes fitted
with an unditching tail (cf: the French First World War Renault FT 17). The
OT-SU continued in service up to 1943, but was by then, outdated.

Type 97 CHI-HA. In 1936 the Japanese launched a programme to build a
successor to the OT-SU and, after a year of trialling various models, the
CHI-HA was chosen for mass production, its thicker armour meeting the
requirement for a heavier tank. It was probably the best Japanese tank of
the war. However, although it performed well enough, it cannot be truly
compared with the Allied mediums such as Sherman and Grant because it
only weighed 15 tons and its armour was only 8–25mm thick. Suspension
was by six roadwheels on each side, paired in three bogies. The rear-
mounted engine drove a long propeller shaft to the gearbox and final drive

The recovery tank SE-RI had a low conical cupola and was a development of the CHI-HA medium tank built by Mitsubishi. It weighed 15.4 tons. Note its simple, rear-mounted lifting jib. (Tank Museum)

This captured Japanese armoured crane appears to be built on the chassis of a light tank/tankette with a six-bogie wheel suspension. (IWM: SE 3696)

A tank bridgelayer on a multiple bogie chassis with eight small bogies, like the CHI-NI experimental medium tank. (Tank Museum)

at the front. The 57mm main armament had vertical trunnions instead of the usual horizontal trunnions; this allowed the gun to be traversed 5 degrees left or right without moving the turret, thus permitting very precise aiming without having to move the turret through small angles. Also produced was the SHI-KI, which was the command version of the CHI-HA, which had an all-round turret aerial and mounted a 37mm or 57mm gun in place of the bow machine-gun, because the turret guns were dummies.

SE-RI Armoured Recovery Vehicle. Another variant of the CHI-HA was the SE-RI ARV. It had a low, conical cupola in place of the normal turret and on the rear decks a small 'A' frame crane, or on some versions, a jib crane. There were several versions of this AFV including some fitted with a flame-thrower, but its main task was to tow disabled tanks and/or to take fitters out to repair them. Not many were made and at least one version had two cranes, mounted fore and aft, with the driver in the middle. The cranes could be fitted with earth-moving buckets and worked using winches and drums of wire rope.

Other versions of the CHI-HA included the Type-G which was a mine-clearing vehicle, fitted with twin flail-drums, and a tank dozer with a front-mounted blade. Attempts were also made to upgun the CHI-HA, replacing the short-barrelled 57mm gun with a high velocity, long-barrelled 47mm. The resulting tank was called the SHINTO CHI-HA.

The HA-TO, built in 1943, mounted a 300mm mortar on its rear decking. The chassis and running gear was the same as for the experimental medium tank Type 4 CHI-TO, with seven large bogie wheels on either side. (Tank Museum)

The heavy tank Type 91 (sometimes also known as the Type 92) was built in the Osaka Arsenal in 1931 and was the third of the multi-turreted heavy tanks built by the Japanese. (Tank Museum)

Tank	Weight (tons)	Crew	Length × Width × Height (m)			Armament	Armour Thickness (mm)	Engine	Top speed (mph)	Range (miles)
Type 89 OT-SU	13	4	4.29	2.13	2.18	1 × 57mm gun 2 × 6.5mm MG	10–17	115bhp diesel	15	100
Type 97 CHI-HA	15	4	5.51	2.33	2.23	1 × 57mm gun 2 × 7.7mm MG	8–25	V–12 170bhp diesel	24	130

Further development continued on medium tanks, with models like the Type 1 CHI-HE (new 47mm gun, redesigned superstructure and welded armour); the Type 2 HO-I (like the CHI-HE but with a 75mm short-barrelled gun); the Type 3 CHI-NU (larger turret with a 75mm Type 3 field gun); the Type 4 CHI-TO (as above but with a longer chassis and larger turret mounting a 75mm Type 4 long-barrelled gun); and the Type 5 CHI-RI (a 37 ton tank with a massive turret mounting a 75mm gun; this was still in development on VJ Day!).

Heavy Tanks

Type 95. The first Japanese heavy tank was known as the Experimental Tank no. 1 and was produced at Osaka Arsenal in 1927, then modified in 1930. The first model was multi-turreted, weighed 20 tons and had a suspension which comprised nineteen small bogie wheels on each side. In 1930 its weight was reduced to 18 tons by various modifications and its armament increased from 57mm to 70mm. Both these models were forerunners of the Type 91 heavy tank, also sometimes called the Type 92, which was also multi-turretted. This was followed by the Type 95, again multi-turretted, with a 37mm gun in the front sub-turret and a 70mm gun in the main turret, plus a ball-mounted machine-gun at the rear. Only four Type 95 tanks were produced before the project was cancelled. Some work was, however, done on a 'super-heavy' which mounted a 100mm gun.

One of the most modern-looking IJA tanks – although it did not get further than the prototype stage – was the Type 4 CHI-TO, which was built in 1944 and mounted a long-barrelled 75mm gun, developed from an AA gun. (Tank Museum)

The amphibious tank Type 3 KA-CHI, seen here both out of the water and in (after capture), weighed nearly 29 tons, mainly because of its large, detachable pontoons. It was developed by the IJN after the IJA lost interest in amphibious vehicles. (Tank Museum)

Amphibious Tanks

Although these were produced by the IJN, they were met by the US Army and USMC in the Pacific theatre, so are worth including here. The Navy produced three main models in about 1942:

(a) **Type 2 KA-MI**. Most successful of the trio, this weighed 9 tons (12½ tons when fitted with sponsons and all waterproofing), was armed with a 37mm gun and two machine-guns. For amphibious operations it was fitted with two detachable sponsons fore and aft, which were dropped once ashore. Water propulsion was via twin propellers and steering via twin rudders.
(b) **Type 3 KA-CHI**. At nearly 29 tons this was larger and heavier than the KA-MI and was based on the CHE-HE medium tank.
(c) **Type 5 TO-KU**. Slightly larger and heavier again, this had a 47mm gun and machine-gun in the hull and a 25mm naval cannon and a second machine-gun in the turret, but it never entered production.

Miscellaneous AFVs

Having already covered the small number of SP guns and APCs found in the IJA, that leaves just two other areas where AFV chassis were used as a mobile weapons platform: trench mortars and AA guns.

The Japanese even resorted on occasions to building wooden mock-ups of tanks – this one was captured by the US 41st Infantry Division on Mindanao, 9 March 1945. (IWM: NYP 61486A)

This strange contraption was intended to cut through wire and also mounted flame-throwers, again on a multiple bogie medium tank chassis. (Tank Museum)

HA-TO 300m mortar. Built in 1943, this had a very large 300mm trench mortar mounted on the open rear deck of a long tank-like chassis with seven large bogie wheels. The engine was mounted in front and there was a centrally placed crew cabin.

SO-KI AA mount. This had either a single or twin 20mm AA cannon mounted on the open-topped chassis of a light tank, while the SA-TO mounted a 20mm cannon on an open-topped medium tank chassis. Finally, there was a never completed project, known as the TA-HA, which mounted twin 37mm AA guns also on medium tank chassis.

ARMOURED TRAINS

As well as the Sumida armoured rail cars, the Japanese used armoured trains to help protect their railways in places like Manchuria. However, they were by no means as elaborate as those used by the USSR. They mainly consisted of armoured freight cars, mounting up to four machine-guns, with travelling space for some twenty fully equipped riflemen. Other freight cars were adapted to carry field guns (up to 75mm) or machine-guns, or were fitted out as command cars. Finally there were flatbed trucks fitted with equipment to repair damaged track. A suitable mixture to deal with whatever the task was in hand would then be drawn by an armoured locomotive.

CHAPTER 11

MISCELLANEOUS EQUIPMENT

ENGINEER EQUIPMENT

IJA engineers were well equipped and also armed with infantry weapons. They were adept at bridge building and bridge demolition, but depended more upon manual labour than mechnical equipment. They were well equipped with explosive devices for both assault and demolition work, and were good at constructing field defences (see photographs in Chapter 12). In short, they were well-equipped, well-trained and well-motivated field engineers. Here is a brief survey of some of their equipment.

Operational Bridging

Assault bridging. Many of the jungle areas in which the IJA operated against the Allies contained a mass of streams and small rivers which had to be crossed, the small ones by wading, the larger ones by using assault bridging of very basic construction. For example, one type, which was used to cross streams up to some 100ft in width, was made of lengths of steel tubing, supported either by bags filled with kapok* or on the shoulders of soldiers standing in the water. The light metal sections, which were joined and locked together, were light enough to be easily carried by infantrymen and could be quickly disassembled when the stream had been crossed.

Pontoon bridging. For heavier bridging the IJA used pontoons of various sizes to support the bridges, one of the smallest being designed to be broken down for carriage on pack-mules. It had two end (bow) sections, each about 4½ft long and three centre sections each 4ft long. The assembled pontoon was some 21ft long and weighed 920lb. Another type – normally vehicle-borne – had two end (bow) sections each some 9ft long and two centre sections each just over 7ft. The resulting 32ft pontoon weighed 1,650lb when assembled. There was an even larger model which also came in four sections and was 45ft long and weighed some 3 tons when assembled.

---

* Kapok, also known as Java Cotton or Ceiba, is fibre obtained from the kapok tree, a large tropical tree of the *Bombacaceae* family. The floss was widely used in water safety equipment, being able to support as much as thirty times its own weight in water.

The most basic type of assault bridge was made from lengths of steel tubing/tree trunks, held up on the shoulders of IJA engineers. This photograph was taken in the Malay Peninsula in 1942. (IWM: AP 71358)

A small infantry pontoon bridge. Each of the pontoon floats could be carried by one man. (US National Archives)

A slightly more robust footbridge, with many more pontoons in place. Note also the collapsible assault boat on the near bank. (IWM: STT 7111)

On the road to Moulmein. These IJA troops are crossing a river by means of a pontoon footbridge which has been built alongside a wrecked railway bridge. Some soldiers have bicycles and there is also a lightweight handcart – or is it a load-carrying trike? (IWM: F 6486)

IJA engineers would, when necessary, build wooden trestle bridges from local timber. These medium tanks are crossing such a bridge while training in June 1941. Note the umpire's white armband. (Tank Museum)

Trestle bridging. Japanese engineers were very adept at constructing wooden trestle bridges, often using local timber lashed together with straw rope. Although the resulting bridge looked flimsy, it was capable of carrying artillery guns and other heavy equipment, but of course could never provide for fully permanent bridging. In some locations, the IJA did use sectionalized steel bridges, but not as often as the Allies did. One such model is described in the US Army *Handbook on Japanese Military Forces* as being 48ft long and weighing 820lb.

Assault Boats and Landing Barges

Assault boats. The simplest form was a collapsible boat which came in two sections, each of which would fold flat on itself and was individually floatable. The wooden frame had braces and all the joints were rubber-bonded. The resulting boat was some 27.2ft long and could hold twenty men. It was estimated that nine such boats could be loaded flat on the back of a 2 ton truck. The boats were either paddled or propelled through the water using lightweight outboard motors. In addition, there were a number of varieties of pneumatic rubber boats used mainly by the engineers which could carry up to ten men. The engineers also employed

Japanese engineers raft a Type 94 medium tank across a wide river. Note also the Model F collapsible assault boats, possibly marking the best route across, on safety duty. (IWM: MH 595)

US Army engineers assemble one type of Japanese folding boat. (IWM: MH 581)

other sectionalized boats, all of which could be broken down into easily transportable loads for pack animals/lorries, dependent upon their size and weight.

Landing barges. The IJA used a variety of landing barges, for supply and evacuation as well as for amphibious assaults, as many as 500 being reported congregated in one port. They were of course vulnerable to Allied air attack in such situations and this grew more the case as the war progressed and the Allies achieved air superiority everywhere. One type, the Daihatsu Model A (Army) was some 49ft long, and powered by a 60–80bhp diesel engine, which gave it a cruising speed of some 6 knots. It could carry 100–120 men on short trips, but only half that number on long hauls. Other loads might be a light tank or a field howitzer. It was normally armed with heavy and light machine-guns, with a vertical armoured shield to protect the coxswain and control gear from direct frontal fire. The metal-hulled barge was developed from standard Japanese fishing boat designs and was, despite its clumsy looks, extremely robust and versatile, its heavy, double-keeled bow and well-protected screw being specially designed to operate in shallow, rocky waters. Miscellaneous other equipment included folding ramps.

US Marines 'acquired' this Japanese KOMATSU tractor on Kolombangra Island in the Central Solomons. Designed for towing purposes it weighed about 3 tons, was just over 8ft long and had four small bogie wheels on each side. (IWM: NYF 9687)

Construction Equipment

IJA engineers used a variety of robust, simple machinery including road-rollers ranging from 9 tons to 18 tons and over, power rock-crushers, concrete mixers, mobile saws, mobile well-drillers and a wide variety of other engineering equipment to assist them in constructing bridges, defence works, roads and airfields. In certain areas they also made extensive use of portable railways, one with a 2ft gauge which used 18ft rails, along which ran light flatcars 6ft long by 4ft wide. These flatcars could be pushed by hand or pulled by small petrol/diesel-driven locomotives.

Electric Power Units

These ranged in size from portable to static, were normally diesel-powered and were widely used. The US handbook quotes that on one island fortress it was found that: 'the power units ranged from 20 to 100KVA, all 2,300 volts, 3-phase, 50 cycle. Underground cables led to intermediate transformer vaults, where the current was stepped down to 11/220 volts for consumption by gun-turret motors and communications equipment. Searchlights were DC type, with motor-generator convertors. A large number of battery-charging panels served to charge batteries for communications equipment.'*

Demolition Equipment

The Japanese were extremely adept with booby traps and similar devices. The same applied to demolition equipment, in particular small charges for assault tasks. They did use plastic explosive (in ¼lb rolls) but mainly employed blocks or cylinders of picric acid, TNT and toluol (toluene) cheddite. Electric detonators were sometimes used, but sensibly the IJA also retained and widely used simple friction-type igniters. Bangalore torpedoes, some 34ft long and weighing 225lb, were also used.

Water Purification Equipment

IJA soldiers in the field were issued with special filters to purify drinking water. Two chemically treated wads (one green/blue and one white) were located inside the plastic body of the filter. One end of a rubber tube, attached at the top of the filter, was placed in the mouth and the untreated water sucked up through the chemically treated wads. When the water started to flow, the tube was placed into a canteen and allowed to siphon through the filter. After five canteens had been filled, the two chemically treated wads had to be replaced. There was also a small water purification kit containing chemicals and a measuring spoon in a flat tin, for use in an emergency, when the water contained large quantities of impurities.

* Quoted from TM-E 30–480.

A GI demonstrating a Japanese flame-thrower. The fuel was in two tanks, with a nitrogen pressure cylinder in between (not visible). The fuel was ignited by means of the flash from a blank cartridge located in the revolving cylinder at the nozzle end of the flame gun. (Tank Museum)

Opposite: The leading soldier crawling in the trench appears to be armed with another type of flame-thrower. The rear soldier is carrying a metal container, perhaps with more fuel? Note also the soldier's waterbottle and carrying case. (Author's collection)

Epidemic Prevention and Water Supply Unit. After the problems caused by the prevalence of cholera during the fighting in Shanghai in 1937 a special unit was formed, comprising seven doctors, a pharmacist, three other officers and some 250 men. They used porcelain microfilters in order to provide clean bacteria-free water. They were equipped with four sets of automatic regeneration filters mounted on trucks (remodelled from fire engines) with a capacity of 30 tons of water an hour; plus eight 90kg filters, carried on horses, which could deal with 720 litres an hour. These filters gave much better water – both in quality and taste – than the old 'alum and chloride of lime' treatment, which then had to be followed by boiling. They also had thirty foldable canvas tanks with aluminium frames and seventy small shoulder-carried water bags.

Flame-throwers

There were two types of flame-thrower: the Type 93 and the Type 100, which weighed 10lb and 8½lb respectively. The fuel unit for both comprised two fuel tanks and a nitrogen pressure cylinder. Both were ignited by the flash from blank cartridges, which were loaded into a 10-shot revolving cylinder at the nozzle end of the flame gun and actuated by an operating handle which controlled the fuel ejection valve. Both had a maximum range of 25–30 yards, a fuel capacity of some 3.25 gallons and, on continuous charge, would last for about 10–12 seconds.

SIGNAL EQUIPMENT

Communications Equipment

Radio communications. The IJA placed great emphasis on wire communications, using cable, and field telephones, although radios were often used initially, before the wire could be laid. They had a wide range of transmitters, receivers and transceivers for both ground and airborne communications. Details of the main types of IJA ground radio equipment is listed in Annex 'C' (see p. 264).

Wire communications. The IJA mainly used three types of cabling:

Wireless operators at work, using morse keys. Everything is so tidy that they must be in a training school! (IWM: HU 72217)

One of the smallest Japanese wireless sets was this Type 66 'Walkie-Talkie' transceiver. (US National Archives)

Two IJA signallers busy up a telegraph pole, connecting cables. The Japanese placed great emphasis on wire communications. (IWM: HU 72222)

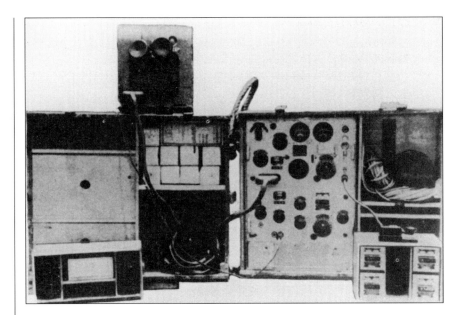

The Model 94 3A no. 36 Transmitter-Receiver relied on a hand generator for its power supply. (US National Archives)

(a) Assault wire: this very thin single conductor, made up of one copper and seven steel strands, with an outer coating of yellow-covered braid, was used for ground return circuits between battalions and forward units.

(b) Seven-strand wire: of larger diameter and higher tensile strength, this wire was made up of three copper and four steel strands, rubber insulated, again with a yellow braid outer coating. This heavier duty wire was normally used between battalions and regiments.

(c) Heavy wire: comprised of two heavy rubber, insulated conductors (one black and one red), with an outer covering of green braid, this was generally used between regiments and divisional headquarters and above, also to airfields.

Cable-laying was done by hand, using various types of wire reel units. For example, one type was carried on the back or pushed along the ground at the side of the layer, using a 'broomstick'-type handle. It held just over 500yd of the larger diameter yellow-braided field wire. Its main drawbacks were that its construction was flimsy and it did not have a crank for easy recovery of the wire once laid. A second, more solidly made reel fitted on the back or chest, held in place by straps, so that the layer still had his hands free. Designed for use in forward areas, it could be fitted with a crank handle for recovery and could be folded up when not in use.

Miscellaneous
(Air/ground panels, signal flags, dogs and pigeons, signal pistols)

A variety of other methods of communication were used, such as ground/air recognition panels, mainly of white material, although in extremis rags, maps or even pieces of paper might be substituted, or soldiers ordered to lie down in the form of panel signals. Small hand flags (one red and one white) were used for signalling using semaphore, while morse code was sent by means of a large red and white flag on a 5ft bamboo pole. Dogs and pigeons were sometimes used for message-carrying purposes. Like every other army, the IJA also used signal pistols which took a 35mm cartridge, or fired coloured pyrotechnics via grenade dischargers. Listed below are details of the main types of such signals (coloured bands were painted on the body and/or a design was embossed so that it could be read in the dark by touch):

Signal	Coloured band
Black smoke, parachute	one wide black band
White star, parachute	one wide white band
White star	one narrow white band
White star, double	two narrow white bands
White star, triple	three narrow white bands
Orange smoke, parachute	one wide yellow band
Green star, parachute	one wide green band
Green star, single	one narrow green band
Green star, double	two narrow green bands
Red star, parachute	one wide red band
Red star, triple	three narrow red bands

(Source: TM-E 30–480)

The Model 97 35mm signal pistol, which dated from 1937, was well made of good grade steel, weighed just under 2lb and was nearly 10in long. Normally single-barrelled, some three-barrelled models were supposed to exist.

CHEMICAL WARFARE EQUIPMENT

Defensive Equipment

Gasmasks have already been mentioned (see p. 108). There were in fact two models, the Type 95 and 99 (the latter had a smaller canister), both of which gave good protection against common types of war gases and closely resembled the British service respirator, being worn on the soldier's chest in much the same manner as in the British Army. Accessories included a packet of anti-fogging discs (in a small plastic box) used to cover the eyepieces in freezing temperatures, a container for anti-freeze liquid (applied to the inlet valve of the mask when the temperature dropped below freezing point), a hinged clamp for closing the air hose and a special cleaning rag. These were all carried in the gasmask haversack, while a can of decontaminant powder was carried separately in a small cloth bag with carrying straps. Both lightweight and heavyweight protective clothing,

These two young soldiers are wearing their gasmasks in the 'ready' position on the chest, which was exactly the same as for the British Army service respirator of the Second World War. The satchel contained the gasmask and other items. (US National Archives)

designed to be worn over existing uniforms, was available, the former being made either of rubberized silk with a cellophane interlining, or casein-coated rubberized silk.

Various types of decontaminating agents were issued for use after gas attacks by tear gases and vomiting gases, blister gases, and blister and vomiting gases. However, their effectiveness was not known. Gas detector kits were also issued.

Offensive Equipment

The Japanese marked their offensive gas munitions using a colour banding code, which covered all the toxic gases, under the term 'special smoke'. This code was listed in TM-E 30–480 as follows:

Type of Agent	*Colour of Band*
Choking gases	Blue
Tear gases	Green
Blister gases	Yellow
Vomiting gases	Red
Blood and nerve poisons	Brown
Screening smoke	White

Japanese troops wearing respirators during mopping-up operations in Shanghai shortly before the beleaguered city fell in November 1937. Whether they were wearing the respirators because they had used gas against the Chinese is not known. They were certainly capable of doing so during the war and had manufactured a variety of offensive weapons, but did not use them. (IWM: NYP 57278)

Chemical projectiles, such as chemical aerial bombs, were painted grey, with a red band on the nose (indicating filled), followed by a blue band (indicating special handling needed because of its chemical content), then a band coloured as above denoting content. (This band was twice as wide as the others.) A narrow yellow band indicated an HE burster charge, while a narrow white one showed that the projectile was made of steel. Both the 81mm and 90mm mortars were believed to have chemical munitions in addition to the 150mm mortar, whilst 105mm and 150mm shells were thought to have alternative chemical fillings. The 75mm field gun could fire both a blister gas shell (weight: 12.5lb) and a vomiting gas shell (weight: 13.25lb).

The IJA infantry had both frangible white smoke grenades and frangible hydrocyanic (poison) grenades which were spherical flat-bottomed glass flasks, some 3in in diameter, packed in sawdust (plus a neutralizing agent in the case of the latter), inside a cylindrical metal container some 5.25in high and 5.5in in diameter. Also in their chemical arsenal were gas and smoke candles which could be used static (the outer container was fitted with a metal spike which was driven into the ground to maintain the candle at the desired angle) or be hand-thrown. A match-head fuse was struck on a scratcher block which then set off the propellant charge, expelling the inner container (the projectile) which carried the main charge. This was then set off by a delay fuse ignited by the propellant charge. Finally, there were both smoke grenades and incendiary grenades.

GLIDERS

Despite the inability of Japanese industry to make gliders in any quantity, the Japanese did produce a number of different designs and apparently could never make up their minds which one they really wanted! Specifications were issued in 1941, but none was flying in any numbers before 1944. The situation was further bedevilled by the IJA and IJN both pursuing separate development, which led to much duplication. By 1944, when gliders were at last available in any quantity, the idea of airborne assault had long been shelved.

The first model built was the Ku-1, a high-wing twin-boom glider, with a 16.8m wingspan and a payload of ten men (2 crew and 8) or 590kg of cargo. It had a fixed, two-wheel undercarriage. The best design was the Ku-7, known by the Japanese as the *Manzuru* (Crane) – the Allies called it 'Buzzard'. It resembled the German Gotha 242 and could just about carry an 8 ton light tank, or more easily 32 men or a 75mm gun plus towing vehicle. Its specifications were: wingspan – 34.7m; weight (empty) – 4,536kg; payload – 7,462kg. Lack of suitable towing aircraft led to the fitting of two engines, turning it into a slow but successful transport plane. About fifty Ku-7s were built; most were converted to power, but few were actually used in service.

TACTICS

'The Japanese, in their tactical writings and training manuals, emphasize that a simple plan carried out with power, determination, and speed will disrupt the plans of hostile forces and lead to a quick and decisive Japanese success. The stated aim of every Japanese military action is annihilation of the opposing force, with the achievement of surprise a goal toward which all Japanese commanders constantly strive.'*

Since the start of the 'Manchurian incident', the Japanese Army had fought in virtually every type of terrain and climatic condition possible, and they had learned their tactical philosophy the hard way. Initially their swift action policy certainly paid off, making both the British and American forces look old-fashioned and pedestrian. These tactics were based on the conviction that the Japanese infantrymen were the best in the world no matter where they fought, and this unshakeable faith in their own ability was certainly successful. They were convinced that nothing could compare with offensive action, that they must manoeuvre quickly, close with the enemy, and then exploit the alleged superiority of their soldiers in hand-to-hand combat. The preferred form of offensive manoeuvre was envelopment: after bringing some pressure on the front of an enemy position, the main effort would be directed against one or both flanks. Frontal attacks were avoided wherever possible, except when the commander felt that he would give the enemy too much time to strengthen their position or augment their force if he resorted to envelopment.

The Attack

Speed was of the essence, especially in the initial confrontation, when low-level commanders were given a surprising amount of freedom so as to be able to seize the initiative and, for example, occupy vital ground swiftly before the enemy could react. The meeting engagement was broken down into four steps:

(a) As soon as contact was made the march columns† broke up into smaller ones, ideally outside the range of enemy artillery.

---

* Quoted from *Soldier's Guide to the Japanese Army*.
† A division normally advanced in two, sometimes three, columns, with the divisional commander controlling the right-hand column and its advance guard, while the left-hand column was under the command of the senior officer in that group. Supply trains would follow behind, with part of the transport regiment at the front, then unit supply trains, then the rest of the transport regiment.

A typical coastal defensive strongpoint, with bunkers and pill-boxes defending a coastal battery. This shows just how intricate many Japanese defensive positions were. (US National Archives)

(b) These smaller columns then moved forward to the Start Line and deployed.

(c) The advance began at 'H' hour, with small squads/sections moving forward.

(d) The attackers then deployed even further so as to allow individual firing to take place during the last few hundred yards of the assault.

Control of the attacking forces was decentralized so that speed remained of the essence, although the highest echelon commander still laid down fundamental items such as the order of march and final details of the overall attack, timings, etc. This meant that the enemy was often attacked almost immediately after first contact and before they had had time to complete their own offensive or defensive arrangements. The Japanese commanders normally selected the least likely avenue of attack – often deliberately choosing to negotiate terrain that the enemy commander would have considered impassable and so would not be defending in any strength. When there were strong defensive obstacles to be negotiated – such as thick barbed-wire entanglements – special assault teams were detailed to cut paths for the attacking echelons. The teams comprised six men: a commander, two men to cut the wire, one to provide covering fire and two more as replacements. These teams were part of a 'working party' which was established in every infantry battalion, usually some twenty strong, and commanded by a sergeant major. The Japanese infantry attacked with great boldness and usually with complete disregard for casualties. Infiltration, envelopment and pursuit were all carried out with speed, despite bad weather or difficult terrain or any other hindrance.

Ruses

The Japanese also made full use of deception and ruses to alarm the enemy and destroy his morale. These might consist of shouting, using fireworks, barking dogs, moving vehicles and haphazard shooting to conceal manoeuvres, cause distractions and thoroughly disturb the defenders. Also they would use English words, false flags, civilian dress or enemy uniforms in order to conceal and confuse. They had no compunction about flouting the normal recognized rules of warfare. For example, they would pretend to surrender or use a flag of truce in order to get close to the enemy, then unexpectedly open fire. However, as these deceptions became increasingly well known their effectiveness declined and often led to harsh retaliatory action being taken upon the perpetrators.

Gen Bill Slim's XIVth Army HQ considered the Japanese use of ruses was so important that they compiled a list of them which was published as an appendix to *Notes from Theatres of War no. 19: Burma 1943/44.* Details are repeated in Annex 'A' to this chapter.

Night Attacks

This was a favourite tactical manoeuvre. 'As a captured Japanese officer is reported to have remarked, "You Europeans march all day, prepare all night and at dawn launch an attack with tired troops. We Japanese allow our troops to rest all day while we reconnoitre your positions exactly. Then that night we attack with fresh troops."'* Night attacks were used in a variety of situations:

(a) to extend or complete successful daylight attacks
(b) to seize important terrain features, the possession of which would facilitate further operations
(c) to confuse or distract local forces from their preparations for a major assault.

They were happy to accept all the problems which a night attack presented (such as the decline in co-operation between arms, difficulties in maintaining direction, the magnifying of mistakes and confusion) in order to obtain the obvious tactical advantage of a night operation. They favoured attacks just after dusk or before daylight. The assault phase usually took place within two hours of crossing the Start Line. Thorough reconnaissance was considered to be an essential prequisite, and limited objectives (ideally clear terrain features) were normally selected on narrow frontages. The assault would be made by two echelons, the second passing through the first in the final phase. For example, at battalion level, the two echelons would each have consisted of two rifle companies (except that one of the two companies in the second echelon would be minus one platoon, which was held in reserve for immediate counter-attack purposes, or to attack the flanks). Great care would be taken in the approach to

* Taken from *Soldier's Guide to the Japanese Army.*

enemy positions so as to get as close as possible without detection, thus enemy artillery and mortar fire could then not be laid down without endangering their own troops. They would also try to approach using dead ground and ideally assaulting up a slope in order to avoid silhouetting the attacking troops.

At battalion level, patrols were sent ahead to cover the assigned sector and these would be followed up by an advanced group whose task was to deal with any enemy troops not dealt with by the patrols. On the line of march, some heavy weapons were usually located behind each company, so that they could be rapidly brought up to defend captured objectives, while a reserve of at least platoon strength was maintained against emergencies. Night attacks were often made by single companies or even platoons, using the same principles, with a small recce patrol (5 to 10 men) being sent ahead and forward look-out points being established, followed by more patrols to draw enemy fire and delineate the extent of their positions. Soon after last light on the night of the attack, another patrol would be sent out to lay out the line of approach, normally following easily recognizable features. On the approach march the company advanced in a line of columns with squads in close formation, plus patrols to give all-round protection. Using maximum stealth, the company would approach their objective until they were within rushing distance. When the company deployed, rifle sections in each platoon formed a single line; when they reached the enemy wire the leading section would cut it, then pass through and automatically turn left, the second section then went through the cut and turned right, while the third section and the heavy machine-gun occupied the space between the other two.

The Pursuit

Units always had to be ready for quick and determined pursuit of the enemy, the aim being to destroy them by pinning them down by direct pressure, while enveloping one or both flanks. If the enemy was seen to be initiating a daylight withdrawal then frontal pressure would be immediately stepped up and, at the same time, pursuit groups would be formed from reserves and sent to turn the enemy flanks and fall upon his rear. However, if the enemy did succeed in disengaging (usually at night) then the IJA commander would renew the frontal attack at first light, then push through the hostile line of resistance as quickly as possible. Reserves would be sent against the flanks to turn them, but they would be prepared to charge in hot pursuit operations if the frontal assault had in the meantime succeeded.

The Defence

Although the Japanese did not like to consider defence – and only did so as a passing phase, they naturally trained to achieve a successful defence, and, as the war progressed, they showed how adept they were at defensive warfare, being prepared to hold until the last round and the last man. Stress was laid upon the utilization of terrain features, and the need to dig anti-tank obstacles was fully appreciated and practised. Defensive

Beach obstacles. These concrete tetrahedrons would be placed on reef-free beaches, interspersed with waterproofed mines. (US National Archives)

This close-up of a typical Japanese bunker on a Pacific island shows how solidly constructed they were, using local materials, with several layers of logs to provide good cover from air/ground attack. (US National Archives)

Another view of a Japanese bunker, this time in the jungle, again showing how well constructed they were despite the fact that they used local resources, such as timber. (IWM: IND 3233)

positions were normally organized in two lines: an advance/outpost line and a main line of resistance, the former being tasked to conduct proper reconnaissance so as to determine the direction, strength and tactical intentions of the enemy, thus preventing the main line from being surprised. When the enemy launched an attack, the advance line had to delay enemy progress for as long as possible before falling back upon the main line. The advance line was a series of strongpoints rather than a continuous line, the intervening spaces being covered by artillery and anti-tank gun fire. In a divisional defensive position, the advance line would normally comprise one or two battalions. In some cases a third line would be organized between the other two so as to force the advancing enemy to commit his forces prematurely. The main line of defence was normally divided into two sectors (three on a broader front). The infantry battalion frontage was normally from 800 to 2,000 yards. However, if the front was very broad then battalions would be allocated a frontage of 3,000 yards and would probably then opt for battalion centres of resistance with all-round defence. Normal depth of the main line of resistance was from 700 to 1,500 yards, with automatic and anti-tank weapons sited in depth in this zone.

Sometimes other materials would be used. This hexagonal steel pillbox was found on Betio, Tarawa, where it was being used as a command post. (US National Archives)

Counter-attacks

The Japanese were swift to initiate counter-attacks whenever they were forced on to the defensive, firmly believing that the fundamental purpose of the defence was merely a means by which to wait for the moment when the attacker's forces were sufficiently disorganized and off guard that quick and decisive counter-action could be delivered. In any defensive plan, immediate counter-attack forces were allocated and orders for their use worked out in advance. Japanese counter-attacks were normally directed at the flanks of the enemy and were usually quick and violent. Heavy mortar fire was initially laid down and this might well be so intense as to make the enemy abandon his newly won positions. Major counter-attacks might well develop from a series of small-scale local attacks by small groups of 8 to 10 men each, although coordination of such efforts was difficult and there were examples of units being cut to pieces because of their excessive eagerness to counter-attack too soon.

Delaying Actions and Withdrawals

The IJA used mobile forces, equipped with automatic weapons and artillery, to fight a delaying action, occupying a series of successive lines of resistance, with the aim of maintaining contact with the enemy yet avoiding decisive combat. When hostile pressure became too great to avoid a withdrawal and disengagement of the main force in daylight, then a local covering force would be constituted from the reserves and set up to cover the flanks of the line of withdrawal.

Additionally, a covering force would be organized, also from the reserves, behind which the main force would form into march columns for the rearward move. By night, a thin 'shell' of infantry, with heavy support from automatic weapons and artillery, would be left behind to serve as a cover, its members being expected to fight to the death, although the artillery would withdraw just before daylight so that the guns were not lost.

Defensive Positions

The amazing ability of the Japanese to construct fixed defensive positions became more and more apparent as the war progressed and the IJA was forced on to the defensive all over the Pacific. Where possible, their installations were made strong enough to withstand both heavy artillery fire and air attack. Each position was also capable of all-round defence and great care was taken to ensure the most effective use of all available firepower. Machine-gun posts, pill-boxes, bunkers and other strongpoints would all be integrated into a defensive network within which each position was covered by fire from adjacent ones, so that they could be regained by swift counter-attacks. The Japanese soldiers were masters of the art of personal camouflage and this applied equally to their defensive positions, which would also have facilities for protracted occupation with the storage of ammunition, food and water (ideally from an assured local supply), and properly protected sleeping and rest areas. As their textbooks stressed: 'Even the smallest unit will prepare deeply entrenched and strong positions against the expected attack', but they went on to caution 'it is important not to adhere blindly to set forms in construction work, but to adapt such work to fit the tactical situation'.* Some examples of this work is shown in the photographs in this chapter.

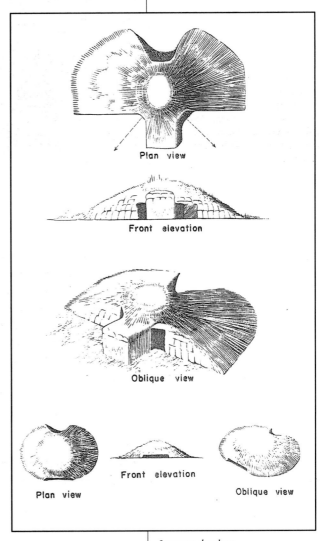

Japanese bunkers.

Jungle Warfare

Initial Japanese success in jungle warfare in the early phases of the war was largely due to the fact that the troops involved had been specially trained and prepared for such warfare. In close jungle terrain, their lack of tanks, motor vehicles and heavy artillery mattered less than if they had been fighting in open country, and the individual soldier's ability to 'live off the land' compensated for any weaknesses in their supply system.

Naturally they adapted their normal tactical doctrine to suit the conditions, emphasizing the need for adequate reconnaissance, all-round security and the importance of effective patrolling both in the offence and defence. Envelopment was still the favoured tactic, although point penetration was used if the

* Taken from *Soldier's Guide to the Japanese Army.*

In some locations, the Japanese dug in their tanks, thus sacrificing the prime characteristic of mobility, but undoubtedly creating very tough 'pill-boxes'. In these three photographs USMC tankers inspect a Type 97 medium tank CHI-HA, which was dug in on Tinian. (Author's collection)

circumstances fitted. Recce was normally conducted by small parties (5 to 10 men) of hand-picked, specially trained troops, equipped with compasses, portable radios and mapping equipment. They would make contact with the enemy, then endeavour to map out his position(s). When advancing in the jungle, Japanese troops moved along trails in single file. Where no trails existed then a 'chopping group' would precede the column, to cut through the dense foliage. A normal rate of march was just over half a mile every two hours, some 4 to 6 miles being covered in a day. The speed of movement was also governed by the speed at which any heavy weapons could be moved, and engineers could deal with any formidable natural or artificial obstacles. Movement direction was by map and compass, the former being reasonably accurate.

Advance guards. Any body of troops moving in the jungle – or in any other terrain for that matter – was led by an advance guard. (For example, a battalion-sized force would be preceded by a company-sized advance guard, a company by a platoon and so on.) If contact was made with the enemy, the advance guard commander immediately informed the commander of the main body, then tried to deal with the enemy. If this was impossible, then they would deploy and endeavour to locate the enemy's heavy weapons positions, their flanks, etc., because the main force would meanwhile be moving to deploy and attack, deep in the enemy flanks or rear. In close terrain especially, the Japanese would always try to utilize infiltration tactics, probing and disrupting enemy positions, using patrols armed with LMGs and grenades, wriggling through seemingly impenetrable jungle to get around the enemy and deep into his rear areas. Such patrols would be self-sufficient, equipped with compact rations so as to be able to sustain themselves,* and so that they could, when necessary,

---

* Such 'compact rations' would consist of rice, condensed foods and vitamin tablets: see p. 82.

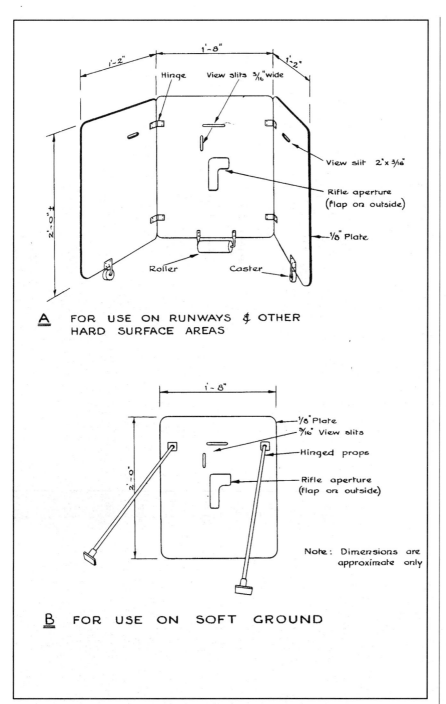

A   FOR USE ON RUNWAYS & OTHER
    HARD SURFACE AREAS

B   FOR USE ON SOFT GROUND

Snipers' shields.

Opposite: *The Japanese would
often take dogs with them to act as
sentries, although it is more likely
that this one – being helped on to a
Sumida railcar – was a pet. (Tank
Museum)*

dig in on reaching suitable positions in the rear areas and stay there causing maximum disruption. They would use infantry support weapons with daring and site machine-guns well forward – usually in pairs – although the restricted fields of fire in the jungle did reduce their effectiveness. Battalion and regimental guns, including anti-tank guns when not needed for their primary role, would be sited well forward and used against enemy heavy machine-guns and other support weapons.

Snipers. Each IJA infantry section normally had two men assigned to sniping missions. Their task was to distract the enemy from his main tactical effort and destroy his morale. Their cunning and patience were legendary: for example, snipers were known to have lain in wait for three whole days without firing a shot. When they did fire, they gave no regard to the fact that they might killed immediately by retaliatory fire. Skilled in the art of camouflage, they selected their positions with great care, but were not always good marksmen at ranges over 50 yards.

Defence in the jungle. Defensive lines were expected to 'bend' under enemy pressure, then to be able to deliver a hard and unexpected counterblow so as to regain the initiative. Sometimes the IJA used forward and main defensive positions, the former being used to prevent the main positions being subjected to surprise attacks. When contact was made, they would either withdraw back to the main positions or remain hidden so as to be able to harass the enemy; snipers were often employed in such a tactic. At the main position, the defenders would try to gain tactical surprise by withholding fire until the very last possible moment – on occasions this was as close as 10 yards. However, if the attacking force was a large one, then it would be fired on from about 50 yards, automatic weapons being sited well forward and thus able to open fire as soon as enemy entered their fields of fire. Great volumes of automatic fire were delivered and supplemented by grenade dischargers, mortars, etc. Some automatic weapons might remain silent if not immediately threatened, ready to open surprise fire later. As always the Japanese soldiers were brave, extremely stubborn and well disciplined in all forms of jungle warfare.

Tactical Weaknesses

The major IJA tactical weaknesses were the result of their inability to appreciate the nature of mobile warfare, so they underestimated the role of the tank and used their artillery poorly on a number of occasions. Generally their artillery concentraions before an attack were weak in both intensity and duration, and thus failed to achieve adequate neutralization of hostile targets. For example, their counter-battery fire was ineffective; indeed, they often had to resort to sending in raiding parties to deal with enemy artillery in jungle areas. Commanders appeared preoccupied with the use of every piece of their artillery in direct support of the infantry – and often in a piecemeal fashion (as they also did with tanks) at the expense of other equally important tasks. Nevertheless, their artillery was imbued with the same offensive spirit as the rest of the IJA, emphasizing speed of movement and surprise, so it is strange that they took such little interest in self-propelled guns.

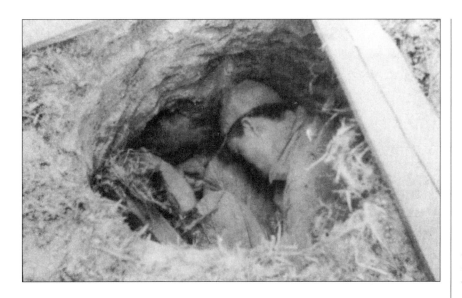

This is how many Japanese soldiers ended up, dying in their foxholes, because they would never surrender. (Author's collection)

Tanks were considered to be exclusively infantry support weapons. Despite training their tank crews to appreciate how successful tank action could be, they then proceeded to ignore its advantages and to restrict tanks to the speed of the walking soldier. Perhaps this was due to their past lack of a proper cavalry tradition. When there was a tank vs. tank action, then the results were inevitable as Bryan Perrett explains in his book *Tank Tracks to Rangoon*: 'On the few occasions that Japanese and Allied armour met, it was apparent that Japanese vehicle commanders would react in one of two ways; either they would panic, running hither and thither in an attempt to escape or they would remain absolutely immobile assuming the role of a pill-box until destroyed.' Perrett goes on to explain that in mitigation, the Japanese tanks were generally excessively outnumbered – because of their obsession with 'penny-packeting' their armour all over the battlefield – nevertheless, they could, by 'good minor tactics, have extracted a higher price for their destruction, had they possessed any instinct for the game'.

Strengths and Weaknesses

The official Australian history gave this summary of the IJA: 'The tactics and equipment, the strengths and weaknesses of the Japanese Army in 1941 were products of the long war in China against stubborn soldiers lightly armed and generally ill-led, but cunning guerrillas fighting in terrain which presented immense difficulties to the movements of mechanized forces. Hence, largely, came the Japanese skill in landing operations and road-making and bridging; their changing organization and tendency towards forming ad hoc forces; their relatively light equipment and reliance on mortars and small guns rather than on the standard field-gun, and on light tanks; their emphasis on envelopment tactics; partly also their development of a large and grimly efficient corps of military police (*Kempeitai*) possessing wide powers and trained to employ those powers ruthlessly.'*

---

* Quoted in *The War with Japan* by Charles Bateson.

ANNEX 'A'

JAPANESE RUSES COMPILED BY HQ. XIVTH ARMY

Foreword by the Army Commander

'Here is a list of ruses the Jap has used against us up to now. He is not very imaginative and in everything he does he goes on repeating himself; so he will probably try them against you again. Be ready and don't be had for a mug.

'You are cleverer than the Jap, you've got more imagination, and you are better than he is in the jungle. Don't be content merely to laugh at his clumsy ruses; think up some hot ones of your own and put them over on him. Don't make his mistake of doing the same thing in the same way too often. Keep him guessing and he'll soon get the jitters.'

Use of British and Indian Languages

On many fronts, the Japanese have used the language of the troops opposing them with the object of persuading them to act on false orders, encouraging them to surrender, or pin-pointing their positions. Although the enemy's accent is often bad, it has sometimes been good enough to deceive our troops. Some typical examples are given in the following paragraphs.

(a) The enemy has been heard to call out in English. 'Where is the CO?' or shout an order such as 'No. 1 Section, cease fire.'
(b) In Burma, the names of units, as well as the names of officers and men, have often been called out in Urdu with the intention of confusing our troops.
(c) At night, a voice has been heard to shout in English, 'No. 1 Section, by the right – advance,' which is followed by a burst of fire but no movement; or a voice may call out in bad Urdu, 'Do number section, hamla kya,' at which there is a burst of fire from the enemy, but again no movement.
(d) During an attack by Bengali-speaking troops, a voice was heard calling out to them in their own language, 'Don't shoot, we are (naming the battalion concerned). Where are you?' (The answer was a burst of automatic fire.)

Use of Wounded and Dead Bodies as Decoys

The Japanese sometimes leave the bodies of British and Indian soldiers, who have become casualties in previous attacks, lying on tracks or in front of their positions, and covered by machine-guns. When our troops make attempts to recover the bodies heavy fire is opened at close range. Bodies have also been seen propped up against trees or in front of the enemy's positions, apparently with the object of discovering other advancing troops. Again, a party of Japanese once lay up near one of our wounded in the hope of ambushing any troops who went out to rescue him.

Use of Dummies

In the Chin Hills and elsewhere Japanese positions have been manned by dummy figures with dummy weapons, with the twofold object of drawing our fire or giving a false impression of their own strength. The dummies, dressed in correct uniform with steel helmets, are often very realistic.

Use of Animals

(a) The Japanese sometimes tether dogs near their positions. They beat and maltreat the animals so that they bark and howl whenever they hear anyone approaching, and thus give the enemy warning of the presence of our patrols.

(b) Small enemy patrols have advanced towards our positions driving cows before them. On one occasion they were heard striking a wooden clapper which they removed from the neck of a cow.

(c) In Northern Burma two Japanese were once seen driving a mule ahead of them with long bamboo poles. They were advancing up a little-used jungle track and the mule's lot clearly was to spring any booby traps that might have been laid on the path.

Use of Noise

(a) In all theatres the Japanese have made much use of noise to deceive and demoralize our troops. For example, bullets that explode on impact have been fired over the heads of our troops (the sound of explosions coming from behind and from the flanks is apt to deceive inexperienced troops into thinking they have been surrounded).

(b) To give the impression of greater firepower, the Japanese have been known to imitate the noise of machine-guns either with wooden rattles or by beating two bamboo sticks together.

(c) Chinese crackers thrown into our positions at night, mortar bombs bursting with a loud explosion, and rattling rifle bolts are some of the devices that have been employed to give an impression of strength and lower the morale of our troops in the hope of causing them to withdraw prematurely.

(d) From the SW Pacific it has been reported that the Japanese have kept absolute silence while they have been moving forward to take up their positions, but that when they have reached their objective they have made as much noise as they could in order to suggest that they are a larger force than they actually were. Similarly, enemy troops making a frontal advance have created a noise in order to cover the silent move towards the flank of the main attacking force.

Use of Uniforms and Civilian Clothing

(a) Japanese patrols have been seen wearing British uniforms and Gurkha-style hats with the object of deceiving our troops into believing that they are friendly patrols.

(b) During attempts to infiltrate through our positions the enemy have sometimes adopted the dress of the local villagers, and in Burma, Japanese have been seen wearing *lungis* (loincloths) and the yellow robes of priests.

Use of Our Own Troops as Decoys

(a) In New Guinea, Japanese advancing against our positions would sometimes turn and flee when they met machine-gun fire. With their usual cry of 'After the bastards', the Australians would rush forward with bayonets fixed. Almost immediately the fleeing Japanese threw themselves to the ground and the Australians ran into withering machine-gun fire from the Japanese rear.

(b) The enemy once made an attempt to draw our troops into the same trap in the Chin Hills, when Japanese were seen running away during an attack, shouting and screaming and displaying every sign of panic. But our troops were wise to the ruse and resisted the temptation to walk into a possible ambush.

(c) Another trick which the Japanese often attempted was to cut our signal lines and then set an ambush for the repair party, or wait for it with snipers. (The enemy is not the only one to carry out this form of ambush, and on several occasions our troops have used the same method to ensnare him.)

(d) The Japanese take infinite pains to encourage their enemy to disclose the locations of their artillery and machine-gun positions. Besides their usual tactics of firing Verey lights, flashing lamps, creating noises near our positions, and firing indiscriminate bursts from machine-guns, they are sometimes prepared to risk casualties in order to draw our fire.

Civilians Forcibly Employed to Allay Suspicion

Quite apart from the use of 'Fifth Columnists', the Japanese do not hesitate to compel the local population to help them. They often employ villagers as guides, and in the Arakan natives have been posted on tracks to watch and give warning of the approach of our patrols. Again, civilians have been forced to drive private cars to bridges that we have prepared for demolition so that Japanese hidden in the cars could shoot up the troops guarding them. During the 1942 campaign in Burma the enemy carried out moves in daylight covered by Burmans whom they compelled to drive bullock carts in which Japanese and their arms were concealed.

Deception with Artillery Fire

When our troops have been advancing supported by a creeping artillery barrage, the Japanese have more than once put down artillery fire immediately in front of or among our troops with the object of creating the impression that our shells were falling short. The intention here is to destroy the confidence of our troops in their own artillery, and discourage them from pressing home their attack.

Booby Traps and Decoys

(a) Besides using the usual rattling tin cans and laying trip-wires across paths and in front of positions, the Japanese show considerable ingenuity in planning boobytraps and decoys. Articles of equipment and clothing found in areas frequented by our patrols, or where the enemy has been contacted, may be so wired that they will detonate a grenade when they are touched; or a fallen tree may be so placed across a road or jungle path that it will explode a mine when it is removed.

(b) Sometimes a number of empty cartridge cases or articles of equipment have been left strewn about on a track with the object of tempting our troops to remove them and thus disclose to the enemy the fact that we have recently passed through the area. Alternatively, this ruse is used to encourage our troops to halt and gather around the spot where the articles are found and, in doing so, provide the target for an ambush.

(c) While searches were being made for enemy documents in the SW Pacific area, it was discovered that the Japanese were using a new type of booby trap with buried documents. A hole, partly filled in, was found to contain three haversacks full of documents and underneath them, mortar bombs, set to explode if they were struck by a spade or heavy instrument.

Deceit

(a) The enemy often uses small parties of men to move about his area and show themselves from time to time in order to confuse our observers and present a picture of greater strength than he actually possesses. This ruse is often adopted to create the impression that all his dug positions are occupied, whereas in fact he had not the resources to man more than a few of them.

(b) Pretending to surrender, Japanese have approached our positions with both hands above their heads and, when only a short distance away, have tossed a grenade towards our troops from each raised hand. Similarly, they have used the white flag of truce to enable them to approach close to our forces in safety.

(c) In order to draw our artillery fire the Japanese have sometimes sent patrols to light fires in an area some distance from their own positions. The smoke rising from these fires, by giving the impression that enemy troops are located in that area, encourages our artillery to open fire and disclose their positions.

Use of Civilians to Give Warning of Patrols

(a) When our patrols have reached certain villages on the west bank of the Chindwin they have noticed that some of the villagers have immediately moved down to the river and made a pretence of washing red *lungis*, which they then place on the bank to dry. The villagers have been ordered by the Japanese to do this 'washing' in order to give warning to their OPs on the east bank of the presence of our patrols. After the patrols have left the area of the village, the information is conveyed to the east bank by a display of white clothing.

(b) In the Arakan, villagers have been placed by the Japanese in front of their posts to act as sentries and give warning of the approach of British patrols. They have been forced to co-operate in this way under threat of reprisals against their families.

False Orders Issued by Wireless

In the Arakan, false orders have been issued by wireless. One of our units, which had been ordered to move to a certain area, received a bogus wireless message which cancelled the first instruction and ordered it to proceed to an entirely different area. In the main, however, the Japanese seldom attempted to pass false orders; their aim was chiefly to cause delay to our communications and confusion among our operators.

PERSONALITIES

This chapter is just a cross-section of the Japanese senior military posts and is not exhaustive. Only a brief mention of their careers is possible, including just their main achievements in the Second World War.

Anami, General Korechika. Born in the Oita prefecture in February 1887, he graduated from the military academy into the infantry in 1906. Described by Mark Boatner in his *Biographical Dictionary of WWII* as being 'a sleek, burly officer, easy going and convivial, but dedicated and loyal', he was also said to be 'the most perfect example of the samurai ideal'. A major-general since 1935, he was promoted to command the 109th Division in China in 1938, then appointed vice minister for war in October 1939, but in April 1941 took command of the 11th Army in China. Promoted to full general in May 1943, he was charged in October 1943 with dealing with Gen MacArthur's offensive, by organizing a counter-offensive in conjunction with the IJN. He was, however, unable to reinforce the garrisons on either New Guinea or the Solomons and could do little but exhort his isolated troops to fight on against impossible odds. He had moved his HQ to Menado on the Celebes, but after the loss of Leyte in December 1944 he was recalled by the Emperor. He advocated an honourable surrender, but without success. Inspector General of Army Aviation until April 1945, he was then made war minister in the Suzuki government. He refused to accept the Allied demand for unconditional surrender even after the atomic bombs had been dropped and the USSR had invaded Manchuria, wanting instead to fight on. He was invited to join an attempted coup by rebel army officers but refused. Early on 15 August 1945, having been told of the radio broadcast of the Emperor's surrender announcement, which he had tried to prevent, he took his own life by *seppuku*.*

Araki, General Baron Sadao. Born in May 1877, Araki was described as 'the epitome of Japanese militarism'. Fiery and idealistic, he commanded the 1st Infantry Regiment of the Imperial Guards in the Russo-Japanese war of 1904–05. He was the leading army expert on Russian affairs and principal advocate of attacking Russia again. An ardent imperialist and leader of the 'Imperial Way' faction, he retired from active duty (ostensibly on the grounds of ill-health) in 1936, after his clique lost out to the 'Control Group', and became minister of education. However, he retained

---

* Gen Anami refused to accept a 'coup de grace': after opening his abdomen, he lived for nearly an hour until given a fatal injection.

much of his militaristic outlook, advocating a tough foreign policy. Arrested as a Class 'A' war criminal and found guilty of waging an aggressive war against China, he was sentenced to life imprisonment in 1946. Released on health grounds in 1955, he died in 1967.

Hiroo, 2nd Lieutenant Onoda. Most famous of those Japanese soldiers who held out after the war had ended, Hiroo continued to follow his commanding officer's orders to carry on fighting guerrilla actions on Lubang Island in the Philippines, until 1974. His former CO had to be flown in from Japan to order him to surrender!

Gen Masaka Honda. Renowned for his kindness to the private soldiers, his army got into difficulties in Burma and finally had to surrender. (Richard Fuller)

Honda, General Masaka. Born in Iida in the Nagano prefecture in 1889, he graduated from the military academy in 1910 into the 4th Regiment of Imperial Guards Division. After heading the 20th Army in Manchuria, he took command of the newly forming 33rd Army in Burma in April 1944. Gen Mutaguchi's 15th Army was attacking towards Imphal and Honda's task was to protect his rear from the Chinese. When Mutaguchi's 'March on India' was halted, Honda was ordered to hold a line from Lashio to Mandalay, but had to deploy his forces further north (Mogaung and Myitkyina) in order to delay Allied efforts to reopen the Burma road. His army was threatened with annihilation when the British captured the Japanese supply base at Meiktila. However, Honda managed to cut them off, but the British held out on air supply and their subsequent advance took Rangoon. Honda's HQ was nearly captured near Pyawbe, and the 33rd Army reduced to only some 8,000 men. On 19 April 1945 his HQ was again attacked and destroyed, this time by enemy tanks, but Honda escaped on foot. After further delaying tactics, he finally surrendered on 25 August, formally presenting his sword to GOC 17th Indian Division at Thaton, Burma, on 25 October 1945. He commanded all Japanese POWs in Burma from 1945 until repatriation. He died on 17 July 1964. Gen Honda was described as: 'Attractive to women. Loved fishing and sake. Did not gamble. Fairly academic and conducted his personal life and career with "studied correctness". Renowned for his kindness to the private soldiers. Unusually for a man of his rank, he told filthy stories even to private soldiers (probably to boost morale).'*

Honma (also spelt Homma), General Masaharu. Born in Sado Island, in November 1887, tall for a Japanese (nearly 5ft 10in), clean cut, artistic and

* Quoted from *Shokan – Hirohito's Samurai* by Richard Fuller.

highly intelligent, he was noted for his long association with the British Army which began when he was attached to the East Lancashire Regiment during the First World War and won a Military Cross. He became fluent in English, both written and spoken. A lieutenant-general by 1938, he commanded the 27th Division around Tientsin and went on to command the Formosan Army. Then, in November 1941 he was put in command of the forces to take the Philippines which he succeeded in doing but not within the 50 days which had been specified (he took a further three months) and needed reinforcements to take Bataan. The CGS was infuriated and Honma was nearly sacked. He further upset the top brass by preventing his troops from running amok after their victory and also for quashing anti-American propaganda. He was finally recalled in August 1942 because of his continuing liberal attitude, and transferred to the reserve list. Later he became minister of information. Charged with war crimes – such as the Bataan death march – he was sentenced to death and shot on 3 April 1946. In 1952 his name was cleared and he was removed from the list of war criminals by the then Japanese government.

Gen Masaharu Honma. An Anglophile, he won the MC during the First World War and infuriated the top brass by his liberal attitude. (Richard Fuller)

Hyakutake, General Seikichi (Haruyoshi). Bespectacled and scholarly-looking, he was born in 1888 and commissioned in 1909 into the infantry, but later became a signals expert, being the head of the signal school in 1937 and Inspector General of Signal Training in 1940, when he was promoted lieutenant-general. In May 1942 he was made commander of the 17th Army, controlling the wide area of New Guinea, Dutch East Indies, Guam and the Solomons. He was ordered to retake Guadalcanal and Tulagi in August 1942, but failed, owing to underestimating the American troops and using too many costly *Banzai* head-on charges. His operations continued to prove unsuccessful, mainly because of the American build-up as compared with his own continuing lack of supplies and the heavy casualties caused by his poor handling of operations. (One action at Bloody Ridge in September 1942 was described as a 'masterpiece of mismanaged ferocity'.*) His last command was Bougainville, which he held, eventually being forced back to the southern tip of the island, where he remained until the end of the war, despite being replaced after suffering from paralysis of his left side. He returned to Japan in early 1946 and died a year later, in March 1947.

Imamura, General Hitoshi (Kinichi). Born in the Miyagi Prefecture in 1888 and commissioned into the infantry in 1907, he also had a long association with the British Army in Europe and India from the First World War onwards. He became

---

* Quoted from 'West Point Atlas' in Mark Boatner's *Biographical Dictionary of World War II*.

one of the IJA's top generals, commanding first the 23rd Army in China in June 1941, then the 16th Army for the invasion of Java and the Dutch East Indies. During the invasion of Java in March 1942, his own ship was sunk (in error) and he had to be rescued from the water. He took the surrender of all Allied forces there on 9 March and adopted a liberal policy towards the locals (including the release of Indonesian nationalist leader Achmed Sukarno); however, this was frowned upon by Gen Terauchi, commander of the Southern Army. Imamura was promoted to full general in May 1943, and thereafter he fought a losing campaign against increasing Allied superiority all over the region, until he was left with a force of just 70,000 around Rabaul, which was then ordered to surrender by the Emperor. He signed the surrender of all Japanese forces in New Guinea, New Britain, New Ireland, Bougainville and the adjacent islands. He was found guilty of war crimes, but was released in 1954 and died in 1968.

Kawabe, General Masakazu (Shozo). Born in 1886, he was commissioned into the 35th Infantry in 1907. Small, even by Japanese standards, and emaciated-looking, he is best remembered for his actions in Burma, where he took command of the Burma Area Army in March 1943. He was sacked after the failure of Mutaguchi's 'March on India', and sent home to command the Central District Army Command, being promoted to full general in March 1945. He died in 1965.

Gen Renya Mutaguchi. He conceived Operation U-GO, the 'invasion' of India, which went badly, losing one-third of his original force. (Richard Fuller)

Kimura, General Heitaro (Hyotaro). Born in 1888 and commissioned into the artillery in 1908, Kimura was quiet and unsoldierlike in many respects. He spent most of the war in Japan, but in September 1944 he was put in command of the Burma Area Army (*vice* Kawabe) and handled them well during the subsequent withdrawal, but was forced to abandon Rangoon. He was a delegate at the formal surrender to Mountbatten in Singapore on 12 September 1945. Classed as a war criminal for condoning atrocities committed by his troops and other war crimes, he was hanged in December 1948.

Kuribayashi, General Tadamichi. Born in 1885, he graduated into the cavalry in 1914, and in February–March 1945 he commanded the 109th Division, plus other troops (including some tanks) and 7,000 sailors, in their spirited defence of the Bonin Islands (including Iwo Jima and Chichi Jima). He decided to concentrate his defence around Mount Suribachi and to leave the beaches undefended. Eventually it took 110,000 US Marines to capture the 8 square miles of the island and to do so they had to kill nearly all of the 22,000-strong garrison. In one day alone five Medals of Honor were awarded and more than one-third of the Marine forces were killed or wounded. Kuribayashi committed suicide by *seppuku* on 27 March 1945 and was promoted to full general posthumously.

Mutaguchi, General Renya. Brash and impetuous, he was born in the Saga Prefecture in 1888. He was commissioned into the infantry in 1910. He was, as a regimental commander, directly involved in the 'Marco Polo Bridge Incident' of 7 July 1937, which led directly to the Sino-Japanese war. Commander of the 18th Division in China in 1941, he was, with part of his division, transferred to the 25th Army for the invasion of Malaya in December 1941. He was wounded while crossing the Singapore Strait in February 1942 and his division was transferred to Burma where he conceived Operation U-GO – the 'March on India' – which went disastrously wrong. Eventually, he had to admit defeat and withdraw all his divisions, losing over one-third of his original force of 150,000, many through sickness. Replaced and sent back to Tokyo, he was retired in December 1944 and died in 1966. He had a reputation for personal bravery and followed the Samurai code of *Bushido*.*

Nishimura, General Takuma. Commander of the 2nd Imperial Guards Division, he took part in the invasion of Malaya, first invading Siam on 8 December 1941, then crossing into Malaya. His division crossed the Perak River and advanced down the west coast, taking Ipoh on 26 December 1941. Regarded by some as 'petulant and unco-operative' (see Fuller's *Shokan*), he had a long-standing feud with Gen Yamashita and continued to flout orders, in particular during the capture of Singapore, deliberately, for example, delaying the final attack. He was sent home in disgrace in April 1942 and retired. However, he was later tried as a war criminal for the beheading of 200 wounded Allied POWs at the Muar River and the execution of several thousand Chinese civilians at Singapore; he was subsequently hanged (although some reports say he was given life imprisonment).

Sakai, General Takashi (Tsutomu). Commander of the 23rd Army in December 1941, he was ordered to capture Hong Kong in ten days, but stiff resistance slowed progress, so it was not completed until the British garrison surrendered on 25 December 1941. He became Governor-General until January 1942.

Sugiyama, Field Marshal Hajime. Born in 1880, he was commissioned into the infantry in 1901. Described as being a leading 'hawk', he constantly advocated war as being the only solution to Japan's problems. He was the IJA

FM Hajime Sugiyama. A leading hawk and one-time C-in-C, he fell foul of Tojo, but became war minister when the latter resigned. (IWM: MH 10253)

---

* *Bushido*, literally the 'Way of the Warrior', namely the maintenance of martial spirit, including athletic and military skills as well as fearlessness in battle. Frugal living, kindness and honesty were also highly regarded, but most important was the supreme obligation to the Samurai's lord with the Emperor replacing the feudal *daimyo*.

FM Count Hisaichi Terauchi. An inept strategist, he was to have a disastrous effect on his brilliant subordinate Yamashita. (Richard Fuller)

Chief of Staff for most of the war, having been a leading member of Tojo's Control Faction. After the Marco Polo Bridge incident, he advocated all-out war, stating 'Crush the Chinese in three months and they will sue for peace' (see Boatner, p. 549). He later assured the Emperor that Malaya and the Philippines could be captured in five months, then opposed the Japanese withdrawal from Guadalcanal and Buna, seemingly believing that the Japanese martial spirit could overcome any obstacle. Although promoted to field marshal in 1943, he was relieved of office in February 1944, Tojo taking over his post as an additional task. After Tojo's resignation, Sugiyama became war minister, then was put in command of all IJA forces for the defence of mainland Japan. He committed suicide, when Japan surrendered, by shooting himself.

Tanaka, General Shinichi (Sumichi). Born in 1893 in Hokkaido, he was commissioned into the infantry in 1939. Described as a 'plump comfortable-looking officer with a toupee', he was both impulsive and hot-headed (see Boatner, p. 555). In March 1943 he succeeded Mutaguchi in Burma as commander of the 18th Division and did well, displaying considerable skill and making the most of his limited resources. Eventually, after he was driven back by Stilwell's Chinese and American forces, he was virtually abandoned by Honda. Replaced in early September, he became Chief of Staff of the Burma Area Army and held that post until being wounded in May 1945.

Terauchi, Field Marshal Count Hisaichi (Juichi). Born in 1879, he was the son of a field marshal, and closely related to the Emperor. Suave and aristocratic, he was commissioned into the infantry in 1900. Promoted to full general in 1935, while he was commanding the Formosan Army, he was a member of the Control Faction, and thus did well under Tojo, becoming commander of the North China Area Army, then of the Southern Army in November 1941. He moved his HQ to Singapore after its capture and was promoted to field marshal in June 1943. Unfortunately for the IJA he proved to be an inept strategist and made many mistakes which had disastrous effects upon the campaigns of his brilliant subordinate Yamashita. He moved his HQ to Saigon, suffered a stroke in April 1945 and, later, after the Emperor's surrender, he succeeded in getting his subordinates to lay down their arms. Initially unable to move because of his ill-health, he eventually was taken (on Mountbatten's orders) to a bungalow at Regam near Johore Baru in Malaya, where he died on 12 June 1946.

Teshima, General Fusataro. Commissioned into the infantry in December 1910, he was a lieutenant-general and provost-marshal in August 1940; next he commanded the 3rd Division in China and took part in operations around Changsha. Later he commanded the Imperial Guards Division, then the 2nd Army in Manchuria, when in early 1942 he and his army were transferred to the area just north of Australia. On Japan's surrender, he signed for all Japanese armed forces in the Netherland East Indies, east of Lombok, and those in Borneo.

Tojo, General Hideki. Born in Tokyo in 1884, into a low caste samurai family, he was commissioned into the infantry in 1902. An autocratic workaholic, he was nicknamed *Kamisori* (the Razor) and 'Fighting Tojo' by his classmates. He was tough and wiry, although quite small (5ft 4in) and completely dedicated to establishing Japanese supremacy through warfare. Deputy prime minister in three cabinets under Prince Konoye, he became minister of war in July 1941, then prime minister when Konoye resigned in October 1941. He supported Japan joining the Axis, and tried unsuccessfully to negotiate with the Allied powers but rapidly reached the conclusion that the only way forward for Japan was by force of arms. He took over as war minister as well as being PM, also home minister and briefly foreign minister into the bargain! In 1944 he took over as IJA CGS from Sugiyama, and tried to maintain power despite the succession of severe Japanese defeats. In July 1944 he faced a vote of no confidence and was forced to resign on 18 July 1945, although he continued to wield considerable influence. When Gen MacArthur ordered the arrest of the first batch of war criminals, Tojo was among them. However, he attempted suicide, shooting himself in the chest, but recovered, was put on trial and hanged at Sugamo Prison in December 1948.

Gen Hideki Tojo. He became minister for war and then Prime Minister and CGS, but was forced to resign in 1944. (Richard Fuller)

Umezu, General Yoshijiro. Born in 1904, he was commander of the China Garrison Army in 1934, became vice minister of war in 1936, C-in-C Kwantung Army in 1939 and CGS in 1944, replacing Tojo. He wanted to fight on even after the atomic bombs were dropped, but did not join the attempted army coup, remaining evasive (he said he 'did not disapprove' but then did not get personally involved). He signed the Instrument of Surrender on the USS *Missouri* and was arrested as a Class A war criminal. Sentenced to life imprisonment, he died of cancer in 1949.

Ushijima, General Mitsuru. Born in 1887, he commanded the 32nd Army in Okinawa, then the entire garrison when the American landings began.

He did not put his main defences on the beach areas where they were vulnerable to naval gunfire, but rather concentrated them inland, in three concentric circles around the Shuri Castle feature where he had his HQ at the southern end of the island. The fighting was bitter, with heavy casualties on both sides. It was to be the costliest operation of the Pacific war for the Americans, while the Japanese lost over 107,000 men, with many entombed in caves, etc., and only just over 10,000 captured. Ushijima committed ritual suicide and was then decapitated by his adjutant.

Ushiroku, General Jun. Born in 1884, he was commissioned in 1906 into the infantry. He held various appointments until 1944, when he was senior deputy CGS and as such advocated suicide tactics, namely that soldiers should carry satchel charges and be prepared to blow up enemy tanks – and themselves in the process! In March 1944 he was appointed commander of all forces on Saipan, but left before the Americans captured the island and was transferred in disgrace to Manchuria (apparently for ordering his troops to use the suicide tactics already mentioned). C-in-C 3rd Area Army when the Red Army invaded, he ignored the agreed plan to withdraw to defensive positions and ordered an immediate counter-attack. By mid-August 1945 his forces had been smashed with heavy losses. The

Gen Yoshijiro Umezu. He became CGS after Tojo in 1944 and signed the Instrument of Surrender on 2 September 1945. (Richard Fuller)

Manchurian troops then mutinied. He surrendered to the Russians and was held as a POW until repatriated in 1956.

Yamada, General Otozo. Born in 1881, he was commissioned into the cavalry in 1903. By 1938 he was commanding 3rd Army in Manchuria, then became C-in-C China Expeditionary Army. In 1940 he was promoted full general and became C-in-C General Defence Command and a member of the Supreme War Council. He was directly responsible for the control of secret bacteriological warfare 'Detachments 100 and 731'* and sanctioned the use of captured civilians for experimentation purposes (later he would authorize their destruction and the deaths of all the prisoners). His forces in Manchuria disintegrated when the Soviets attacked and he formally surrendered to them. Sentenced to twenty-five years in a labour correction camp, he was released in 1956 and repatriated.

* In fact this unit was set up in 1932 as an extension of the biological and chemical warfare centre, pioneered by Emperor Hirohito's father-in-law, *Chujo* Prince Kuniyoshi Kuni in the late 1920s.

Yamashita, General Tomoyuki (Hobun). Born in 1885, he was commissioned into the infantry in 1906. He was involved with the 'Imperial Way' faction. He was ambitious, ruthless and highly strung, and was considered by many to be Japan's greatest general. He was appointed commander of the 25th Army to invade Malaya and capture Singapore which he achieved by 15 February 1942, earning himself the nickname 'Tiger of Malaya', although he preferred to think of himself as 'The Great Cedar', being large and stern! He next became C-in-C 1st Area Army on the Siberian border, then, after the fall of Prime Minister Tojo, he became C-in-C 14th Area Army in the Philippines. He was always being obstructed by the incompetent Terauchi, who made him dissipate his forces, sending reinforcements to Leyte, where the IJA were fighting a losing campaign. Even when Terauchi moved his HQ to Saigon, he still retained operational control over the Philippines, until later in December 1944, when Yamashita was finally given authority to act on his own without interference from above. Leyte had now been lost. Yamashita had around 250,000 troops under his command, but many divisons were hardly trained and ill equipped, while the Americans had both air and sea superiority. Things went from bad to worse, although many consider his final delaying campaigns to have been carried out with considerable expertise. Eventually, however, all was lost and when the news of Japan's surrender came Yamashita is said to have 'aged 10 years overnight' and his staff thought he would commit suicide. Instead, he considered that it was his last duty to get what was left of his army safely back to Japan. He was tried as a war criminal in Manila, found guilty and hanged at New Bilibid Prison on 23 February 1946, writing after hearing his death sentence: 'The world I knew is now a shameful place. There will never be a better time for me to die.'

Gen Tomoyuki Yamashita. Known as the 'Tiger of Malaya', he was one of the most brilliant of the IJA commanders. He was hanged in Manila in 1946. (Richard Fuller)

CHAPTER 14

THE KEMPEITAI

This chapter is based on original research by Raymond Lamont-Brown for his book *Kempeitai: Japan's Dreaded Military Police* (Sutton Publishing, 1998).

Before looking in any detail at the Kempeitai, the infamous Japanese Military Police, a few words on the general way in which discipline was maintained in the IJA would not go amiss. At least one historian has written, with considerable justification, that the discipline in the IJA, 'could not be borne by any other army in the world, and the intention of that discipline was to reduce the individual to an automaton who would obey his orders absolutely and to the letter'.* He goes on to explain how physical violence played a major part in keeping discipline, even the most minor offence being dealt with immediately by physical punishment on the spot. This might be done by repeated slapping of the face, or using fists, boots, clubs, flats of officers' swords; in fact, any suitable way of administering violence was permitted and even encouraged. Such punishments could be effected by anyone, provided they were senior in rank. However, this 'faded into triviality in comparison with the expert treatment handed out by the military police to those who crossed their path'. This 'everyday violence' towards soldiers was known as *Bentatsu* and was carried out in the IJA code as *Shinetsu-na okonai* – an act of kindness!

However, the harsh treatment which was meted out by officers to their own troops pales into insignificance when one investigates the way in which the Japanese military police treated prisoners of war and the subject peoples in the countries which the IJA had invaded, so perhaps some word of explanation as to why this was done is necessary as a preface to this chapter. In his book *Kempeitai, Japan's Dreaded Military Police*, Raymond Lamont-Brown explains how foreigners (*Gaijin*) were considered to be sub-human by the entire Japanese nation, within which one's position in society was all-important, human worth depending upon status. As the *gaijin* were considered to be below even the lowest class in the pyramid – which had the Emperor and his family at the top and the *burakumin* (the untouchables) at the bottom – then everyone who was not Japanese was regarded as the lowest of the low. Soldiers who had surrendered† were held in complete

---

* *Tank Tracks to Rangoon* by Bryan Perrett.
† Article 2 of the IJA Military Training Regulations stated that it was the duty of the military to sacrifice their lives for the Emperor; hence the Japanese believed that by surrendering POWs had lost all honour and loyalty to their beliefs.

contempt as they had 'lost face' before the enemy. Thus, surrendering enemy soldiers, *gaijin* soldiers, were at the very bottom of the pile and would be treated as being less than dirt. He points out that there is a mistaken impression among some ex-POWs that the reason why they were treated so badly was because of the ancient military code of *Bushido* (the 'Way of the Warrior'), but that this was not the case: '*Bushido* in its original form never condoned cruelty, the Kempeitai made it a travesty.' Up to the end of the Second World War therefore, the Japanese attitude to human rights was one of complete indifference and the military police in particular would not think twice before using the most inhuman and brutal treatment to foreign soldiers and civilians alike, safe in the knowledge that their acts – even their worst excesses – would be ignored or condoned by everyone else. Notwithstanding this situation, the bestial behaviour which the Kempeitai used on civilian and POW alike went beyond the bounds of all reason.

ORIGINS

The Japanese civil police in prewar Japan had a wide range of duties which included functions well beyond normal everyday police matters such as crime prevention and the arrest of criminals. They 'regulated everything from public health to factory construction, from issuing permits for a wide range of activities to controlling businesses. When fighting broke out in China in 1937, the stringencies of war added responsibilities to the police mandate to include such functions as motivating labour and controlling transportation. They also had duties of social censorship on all branches of the media (within the press law of 1875), as well as the monitoring of political activities, particularly concerning public meetings'. These latter duties led in 1901 to the founding of the TOKKO – the Special Higher Police, known as the 'Thought Police'. They were the civilian counterpart of the Kempeitai, who had in fact been established before TOKKO came on the scene, having been formed in January 1881 as an elite corps of just 349 men, by order of the Meiji Council of State. By the 1920s they were responsible within the IJA for three main functions: the supply, organization and training of police units; security; and counter-intelligence. There was also a section called the TOKKO-Kempeitai which dealt with 'anti-ideological work'.

In peacetime, the Kempeitai were responsible to the Ministry of War for normal military duties, to the Home Ministry for civil police duties and to the Ministry of Justice for law administration. They built up an enormous network of influence throughout the empire and the occupied countries and it was in these latter areas, in the maintenance of 'law and order', that they gained their bad reputation. Overall they were a branch of the IJA under the Military Administration Bureau, with the Provost Marshal General directly answerable to the Minister of War. In war/fortress zones they came under the command of the commanders of these areas. They were never a gendarmerie (an armed police force). As Raymond Lamont-Brown says: 'In no other country was the ordinary man and woman so in awe of the *keikan* (policeman) or the Kempeitai functionary. They were the visible arm of the law, the guardians of the law, the public censors and overseers of private morals and thought as

Examples of Japanese Occupation banknotes. The calligraphy in the bottom centre of the note reads 'Japanese Government'. Some Kempeitai officers operated and condoned scams in counterfeit notes. (Author's collection)

Examples of Japanese propaganda leaflets. Those in English plugged the sex angle – brutal and licentious British/American troops seducing wives/sweethearts back home while others did the fighting. The Indian ones depicted Churchill raping the Indian economy. (Author's collection)

well as arbiters of decorum.' There was no such thing as a writ of 'habeas corpus', the individual having no rights and being presumed guilty on arrest. Couple this with the fact that the Kempeitai in several of the occupied countries made use of criminals and outlaws as law enforcers, and one can imagine the kind of justice that was meted out, especially as torture was almost always employed to extract 'confessions'.

Wartime duties. In the war theatres the Kempeitai continued to issue travel permits (thus giving them a virtual stranglehold on movement), recruited labour, discovered and arrested fifth-columnists, requisitioned foodstuffs and supplies, started propaganda programmes and put an end to any anti-Japanese propaganda or subversive rumours. Their power within the military was considerable, any member of the Kempeitai being empowered to arrest anyone three ranks higher in rank than themselves.

PERSONNEL

The Kempeitai consisted of: field officers (*sakan*), NCOs (*kashikan*) and superior privates (*jotohei*) When required, first and second class privates were also attached from other arms. In peacetime all officers were volunteers,

supposedly drawn from those of good character and high physical standard; in wartime, they were drawn from all branches of the service as and when needed. All were trained at special military police schools or special training units, as well as undergoing special Kempeitai training in unit barracks. The main Kempeitai schools were at Tokyo and Keijo (now called Seoul) in Korea, while others were set up at Singapore and Manila during the war. Peacetime officer training normally lasted for some six years, and even in wartime it was a year. NCO courses were six months long. Undoubtedly, the Kempeitai personnel were above the average both in educational background and physical appearance. Training courses included subjects such as espionage, use of explosives, fifth-column organization, code-breaking, effective burglary, horsemanship, and even the art of disguise (trainees were then sent incognito to companies to remain undetected while sending back reports); officers also received secret intelligence instruction. Foreign language study was kept low-key and in the field Kempeitai officers normally used interpreters.

UNIFORM AND EQUIPMENT

At the start of the war for normal duties Kempeitai personnel wore the uniform of the cavalry, with heavy black undressed leather boots, and

On 22 September 1945 some
twenty members of the Kempeitai,
who had been responsible for the
conduct of POW and internment
camps in Singapore, were marched
through the city to Pearl Hill Gaol.
Here civilians watch as the
erstwhile jailers go to get a taste of
their own medicine. (IWM:
SE 5010)

carried a cavalry sabre and pistol (officers), pistol and bayonet (other ranks). The normal pistol was the 8mm Nambu, carried in a leather holster. All wore a white armband on the left arm which bore two calligraphic characters for Kempeitai (*ken* = law, *hei* = soldier), while the upper arm insignia was black. Sometimes the calligraphy was in red on khaki. During the war the Kempeitai often wore the M1938 khaki field dress, while plain clothes could sometimes be worn on relevant occasions (but with badges of the correct insignia or the imperial chrysanthemum on the underside of their jacket lapels). Another item often carried by Kempeitai junior NCOs when looking after prisoners of war, was a pliable bamboo sword as normally used in the sport of *kendo*.*

STRENGTHS

In 1937 it was estimated that the Kempeitai comprised 315 officers and over 6,000 men. By 1942 these numbers had increased considerably, the TM-E 30–480 handbook quoting that there were at least 601 regular

---

* Kendo was a way of practising swordsmanship without serious injury, although the bamboo which made up the kendo sword was split to make it more pliable, so it could inflict a painful, stinging blow. The combatants in the sport wore special body armour; the Kempeitai NCOs used the swords to strike POWs.

Kempaitai surrender their swords at Saigon. On 16 November 1945 fifty Kempeitai from all over the northern provinces of French Indo-China were brought down to Saigon to ceremonially hand over their swords to the Allied Control Commission. Maj Gen Gracey delegated the honour of receiving them to Subedar Major Ahmed Sarda Bahadur OBE, IOM. (IWM: SE 5691)

officers, not to mention reserve officers, etc. They show the known distribution of these officers as being: Japan and Karafuto* – 142; Manchuria – 114; Korea – 23; Formosa – 24; North China – 100; Central China – 97; South China – 16; Southern Area (including field units) – 85.

In his book, Raymond Lamont-Brown gives the following figures for the Kempeitai strength at the height of the war:

Japan	10,679
Korea	1,927
Kwantung Army	4,946
North China	4,253
South China	1,094
Central China	6,115
French Indo-China	479
Malaya	758
Singapore	362
Thailand	937
Burma	540
Philippines	829
Java	538
Sumatra	387
Borneo	156
Formosa	745
South Seas	89
TOTAL	34,834

Other Duties

The Kempeitai also undertook other duties such as:

(a) **Ethnic 'help-groups'.** In occupied areas the Kempeitai organized groups to take on such duties as 'pacifying hostile natives' and 'settling disputes between

---

* Karafuto was the colonial administration centre of the Southern Sakhalin Islands.

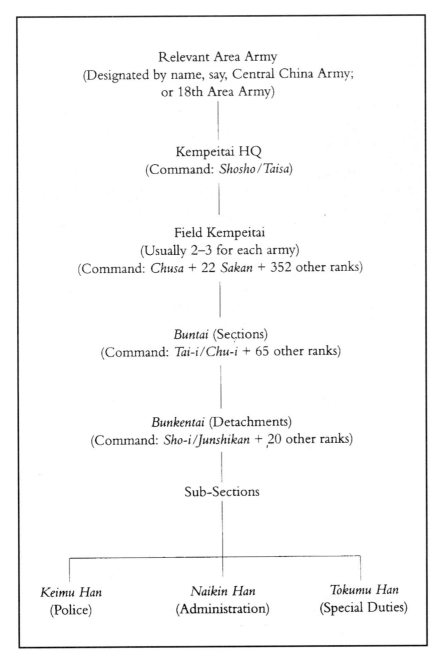

Relevant Area Army
(Designated by name, say, Central China Army;
or 18th Area Army)

Kempeitai HQ
(Command: *Shosho / Taisa*)

Field Kempeitai
(Usually 2–3 for each army)
(Command: *Chusa* + 22 *Sakan* + 352 other ranks)

Buntai (Sections)
(Command: *Tai-i / Chu-i* + 65 other ranks)

Bunkentai (Detachments)
(Command: *Sho-i / Junshikan* + 20 other ranks)

Sub-Sections

Keimu Han	*Naikin Han*	*Tokumu Han*
(Police)	(Administration)	(Special Duties)

Structure of the Kempeitai. (Source: Kempeitai, *by Raymond Lamont-Brown)*

natives and Japanese soldiers'. They also established native spy networks to work behind enemy lines, carry out reconnaissance work and generally harass the enemy. In one area at Lae (Papua New Guinea) the Kempeitai commander was directed to complete the training of the native 'army'.

(b) **Prisoner-of-War Camps**. All POW camps (*furyu shuyojo*) and POWs (*furyu*) were monitored and governed by the Kempeitai, who also searched and screened anyone bound for camps in Japan. Camp duties were normally undertaken by Kempeitai NCOs who were always trying to find diaries, radios and anything that the POWs could sell. One POW wrote about them: 'I noticed that the Kempeitai were feared as much by the Japanese as by the prisoners. Although of comparatively junior rank they walked into camps or workplaces without hindrance and shouted orders at officers and civilians alike. They were swaggering bullies and used physical attack as a matter of course.'* In addition, many POWs did not reach the camps, being murdered en route by the Kempeitai; one such repeated example being the beheading of Allied airmen shot down over Japan.

(c) **Reprisal operations**. These were carried out against both rebellious native populations and local guerrillas, with or without the support of Allied troops. For example, at Tenasserim near Moulmein in Burma in June 1945, where British paratroopers had been assisting local guerrillas to attack Japanese positions, the Kempeitai, together with soldiers from the 3rd Battalion, 215th Regiment, occupied the village, rounded up the inhabitants, raped and beat up all the women and children, but could get no information from them about the resistance fighters. Then, acting on Kempeitai orders, they massacred the entire village population, blindfolding and bayoneting 600 villagers.

(d) **Use of women**. The Kempeitai used women as both spies and informers, also as prostitutes. They were responsible too for running the general supply and administration of the organization which provided 'comfort women' (*jugun ianfu*) all over the battlefield areas, using IJA and IJN transport. They also regulated the accommodation of the brothels, checked the identity of customers, and controlled violence and even drunkenness.

(e) **Medical Experimentation**. I have already mentioned the 'human experimentation' Unit 731, to which the Kempeitai sent any 'difficult' prisoners: over 3,000 Americans, Chinese, Europeans, Koreans and Russians ended up in the 150-building compound in Harbin, Manchuria. The 'logs' – which is how the Kempeitai described the prisoners – were selected and moved by the 'Human Materials Procurement Arm' of the Kempeitai, where they would be experimented upon: 'horrific vivisection and artificially induced disease, frostbite and horrific simulated war wounds were all part of the experiments carried out on human beings'.† There were also numerous other such establishments which performed similar hideous experiments.

So much for the Kempeitai. Their appalling deeds, like those of the Nazi SS must never be forgotten.

---

* Jim Ford CB, MC of the Royal Scots, quoted in *Kempeitai* by Raymond Lamont-Brown.
† Quoted from *Kempeitai*, Raymond Lamont-Brown.

A N N E X A

JAPANESE MILITARY CONVENTIONAL SIGNS

GENERAL PRINCIPLES

Military Signs

Japanese military signs as used on their military maps and diagrams were supposed to be standard, although they did not always display a great degree of consistency in the formation of these signs, sometimes used signs that were supposed to be obsolete and, on occasions, condoned the use of extemporary signs. Nevertheless, what follows will provide a useful selection and has been taken from 'Supplement No. 1 of Japanese Field Service Regulation (Military Signs)' of August 1940 and repeated in TM-E 30–480.

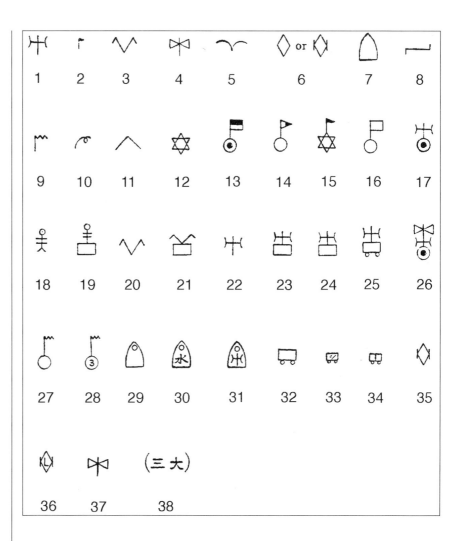

Basic signs

Basic signs. Examples of these are:

1. field artillery
2. cavalry
3. engineers
4. air (Army)
5. air (Navy)
6. tank

7. shipping
8. signal
9. radio
10. gas
11. established depot (when placed over the rest of the sign)

Headquarters. HQs down to and including battalion level were usually distinguished by flags and/or circles. However, brigade or group HQs were indicated by a six-pointed star (12). The appropriate basic sign may be added to indicate arm. For example:

13. area army HQ
14. divisional HQ
15. cavalry brigade HQ

16. infantry battalion HQ
17. field artillery RHQ

Units. The normal method of designating units was by adding a rectangle below the sign of the particular arm or weapon (in full or abbreviated). For example:

18. medium mortar   20. engineer (basic sign)
19. medium mortar unit   21. engineer unit

NB: An exception to this principle should be noted:

22. field artillery   23. field artillery ammunition train

Motorization. To show that a unit was motorized, two rings (representing wheels) were added either below or beside the particular sign, e.g.:

24. field artillery ammunition   25. field artillery ammunition train,
train   motorized

Compound signs. Basic signs such as those described already were combined into compound signs, e.g.:

26. anti-aircraft artillery RHQ

Classification. An appropriate symbol, number or abbreviation (either in English letters or Japanese characters) might be added to a sign when necessary, in order to further classify the unit or equipment indicated by the relevant sign, e.g.:

27. mobile ground radio station   31. armed ship
28. No. 3 type mobile ground radio   32. motor truck
station   33. repair truck
29. ship (general)   34. truck loaded with machine-guns
30. water supply ship (the character 35. tank
included meant 'water')   36. light tank

Boundaries, directions. Boundaries of districts or limits of fortified areas were shown by lines; directions of shooting, points of attack and changes of direction of troops were shown by arrows.

Numbers
The numbers of units or weapons were shown by placing the appropriate figure, either in Arabic or Japanese, with necessary additions in brackets, after the particular sign or abbreviation. For example:

37 (2) is two aeroplanes
38 is three battalions of field artillery. The two Japanese characters in brackets are respectively 'three' and the first character of the Japanese word for 'battalion'.

Identification

When it was necessary to distinguish between enemy and friendly forces, the Japanese showed signs in red for the enemy and blue for friendly forces.

If indicating the organizational numbers of units, Arabic numerals were used, except for battalions when Roman numerals were used. The number of the lower unit preceded that of the higher organization of which it was a part, the two being separated by a slanting line, e.g.:

18P = the 18th Engineers
III/2i = 3rd Battalion of 2nd Infantry Regiment
II St/1A = 2nd Battalion Ammunition Train of the 1st Artillery Regiment

Platoons and sections were usually shown as fractions of a company, e.g.:

¼ 2/1P = 1 Platoon of the 2nd Company of the 1st Engineer Regiment
¹⁄₁₆ 2/5i = 1 Section of the 2nd Company of the 5th Infantry Regiment

Missing units of an organization were indicated by numerals preceded by a minus sign in brackets. Units attached to an organization were shown in the same way, but with a plus sign instead of a minus, e.g.:

2i (-7/8) = 2nd Infantry Regiment less the 7th and 8th Companies
1 (+ iP)/2i = 1st Company plus a labour unit of the 2nd Infantry Regiment

ARMY SIGNS COMMON TO ALL ARMS

Symbol	Japanese	English
(symbol)	Daihon-ei	Imperial Headquarters.
(symbol)	Sogun shireibu	General Headquarters.
(symbol)	Homengun shireibu	Area army headquarters.
(symbol)	Gun shireibu	Army headquarters.
(symbol)	Gundan shireibu	Corps headquarters (not part of the Japanese Army organization.)
(symbol)	Shidan shireibu	Division headquarters.
(symbol)	Chutaicho	Company commander.
(symbol)	Shoko / Shotaicho	Commissioned officer—platoon commander.
(symbol)	Kashikan / Buntaicho	Noncommissioned officer. Section leader.
(symbol)	Hei	Private soldier.

Note. NCO's and privates may be classified by the addition of appropriate "kana," numbers, or signs, e. g.: (symbol), liaison NCO; (symbol), runner; (symbol), bugler; (symbol), No. 3 man in section; (symbol), private in charge of grenade discharger.

Symbol	Japanese	English
(symbol)	Kihei no hei	Cavalry private.

Symbol	Japanese	English
(symbol)	Butai no shudan	Group (mass) of troops.
(symbol)	Fuzokutai	Attached unit.
(symbol)	Butai no shudan chiki	Area containing groups (masses) of troops.
(symbol)	Tekidanto / Tekidanju	Grenade discharger. Grenade rifle.
(symbol)	Keikikanju	Light machine gun.
(symbol)	Kikanju	Machine gun (heavy).
(symbol)	Kikanjutai	Machine gun unit.
(symbol)	Kikanho	Machine cannon.
(symbol)	Jidoho	Automatic gun.
(symbol)	Jidohotai	Automatic gun unit.
(symbol)	Sokushaho	Antitank gun.
(symbol)	Sokushahotai	Antitank gun unit.
(symbol)	Keihakugekiho	Light trench mortar.
(symbol)	Keihakugekihotai	Light trench mortar unit.
(symbol)	Chuhakugekiho	Medium trench mortar.
(symbol)	Chuhakugekihotai	Medium trench mortar unit.

ARMY SIGNS COMMON TO ALL ARMS

Symbol	Japanese	English
(symbol)	Gasu kumo / Dokuen	Gas cloud. / Toxic or poison smoke.
(symbol)	Shukuei butai	Quartered or billeted troops: 2d Bn of the 4th Inf Regt.
(symbol)	Chugun butai	Troops stationed for a period; garrison troops: 2d Co of the 1st Inf Regt, 2d Bn of the 1st Field Arty Regt.
		NOTE. The boundary of a billeting area is shown by a thick continuous line. The symbols of the units are written inside or outside.
(symbol)	Keikyu shugojo	Alarm post.
(symbol)	Keikyu daishugojo	Grand alarm post.
(symbol)	Mizu kofujo	Water distributing center.
(symbol)	Imbajo	Place for watering animals.
(symbol)	Bakeijo	Horse lines.
(symbol)	Kikanjusho	Machine gun depot.
(symbol)	Hosho (yaho)	Gun depot (field artillery). NOTE: Depots for other types of artillery are shown by the appropriate symbol within a rectangle.
(symbol)	Shasho	Vehicle depot.
(symbol)	Jidoshasho	Motor transport depot.
(symbol)	Bunsho / Kashisho	Sentry group (infantry or cavalry) with noncommissioned officer in charge.
(symbol)	Sanninsho	Sentry group of 3 men.

Symbol	Japanese	English
(symbol)	Juhakugekiho	Heavy trench mortar.
(symbol)	Juhakugekihotai	Heavy trench mortar unit.
(symbol)	Shomeito	Searchlight (general); ground-flare (aero).
(symbol)	Yasen shomeitai	Field searchlight unit.
(symbol)	Kamo	Fire net; area covered by fire.
(symbol)	Karyoku jumbi no ichi-rei	Examples of fire preparation: 2 Fld Arty Cos, 1 Med Arty Co; 2 MG Cos, 1 Regt Gun Co, 1 Bn Gun Co.
(symbol)	Kogeki no juten. Shageki no hoko (mokuhyo)	Main point of attack. Direction of fire (target, objective).
(symbol)	Zenshin hoko nado	Direction of advance, etc.
(symbol)	Gasu butai hombu	Chemical warfare unit headquarters.
(symbol)	Gasu butai	Gas unit. NOTE. Sandoku (poison spreading), shodoku (disinfecting), and jodoku (decontaminating) units are shown respectively by (symbols).
(symbol)	Gasu-gakari shoko	Officer in charge of gas.
(symbol)	Gasu-gakari kashikan	NCO in charge of gas.
(symbol)	Gasu-gakari hei	Private in charge of gas.
(symbol)	Sandoku chiiki	Contaminated area.
(symbol)	Emmaku	Smoke screen.

ARMY SIGNS COMMON TO ALL ARMS

Symbol	Japanese	English
[symbol]	Nininsho	Sentry group of 2 men.
[symbol]	Tansho	Single sentry.
[symbol]	Kashikan wo cho to seru sekko	Patrol with noncommissioned officer in charge.
[symbol]	Tembosho	Observation group.
[symbol]	Kotsu seirihan	Traffic control section.

b. Infantry.

Symbol	Japanese	English
[symbol]	Hohei ryodan shireibu	Infantry brigade headquarters.
[symbol]	Hohei rentai hombu	Infantry regimental headquarters.
[symbol]	Hohei daitai hombu	Infantry battalion headquarters.
[symbol]	Hohei butai	Infantry unit.
[symbol]	Hohei butai (kogun taikei)	Infantry unit (in march formation.).
[symbol]	Hohei butai no sokai	Deployment of an infantry unit.
[symbol]	Dai-issen	Front line.
[symbol]	Rentaiho	Regimental infantry gun.
[symbol]	Rentaihotai	Regimental infantry gun unit.
[symbol]	Daitaiho	Battalion infantry gun.
[symbol]	Daitaihotai	Battalion infantry gun unit.
[symbol]	Heisha hoheiho	Infantry gun.
[symbol]	Kyokusha hoheiho	Infantry mortar.
[symbol]	Sagyotai	Working party; pioneer unit.
[symbol]	Hohei rentai (ryodan) tsushintai (han)	Infantry regiment (brigade) signal unit (section).
[symbol]	Senryo chiiki	Occupied area.

c. Cavalry.

Symbol	Japanese	English
[symbol]	Kihei shudan (shidan) shireibu	Cavalry group (division) headquarters.
[symbol]	Kihei ryodan shireibu	Cavalry brigade headquarters.
[symbol]	Kihei rentai hombu	Cavalry regimental headquarters.
[symbol]	Kihei butai	Cavalry unit.
[symbol]	Kihei butai no sokai	Deployment of a cavalry unit.
[symbol]	Dai-issen	Front line (cavalry).
[symbol]	Joba sankai butai	Deployment of mounted cavalry.
[symbol]	Toho sampei	Dismounted skirmishers.
[symbol]	Tohobutai	Dismounted unit.

ARMY SIGNS Cavalry (continued)

Symbol	Japanese	English
	Teuma	Led horses.
	Kihei rentai (ryodan) (shudan) tsushintai (han).	Cavalry regiment (brigade) (group) signal unit (section).

d. Artillery.

Symbol	Japanese	English
	Hohei shireibu	Artillery headquarters.
	Hoheidan (hoheiryodan) shireibu.	Artillery group (brigade) headquarters.
	Yahohei rentai hombu	Field artillery regimental headquarters.
	Yahohei daitai hombu	Field artillery battalion headquarters.
	Yahohei butai	Field artillery unit.
	Yahohei no danretsu	Field artillery ammunition train.
	Yahohei no horetsu	Line of guns (field artillery).
	Yahohei no renrakuhan	Field artillery liaison section.

NOTE. Horse, mountain, medium, and heavy artillery are represented by the signs [symbols] respectively, instead of [symbol].

Guns and howitzers are represented by the addition of ∧ and ● respectively to the top of the appropriate sign.

Symbol	Japanese	English
	Choshatei yaho	Long-range field gun.
	Juryu	10-cm (105-mm) howitzer.
	Juka	10-cm (105-mm) gun.
	Jugoryu	15-cm (150-mm) howitzer.
	Kikyutai	Balloon unit.

ARMY SIGNS Artillery (continued)

Symbol	Japanese	English
	Kikyu jinchi / Kikyu shoto ichi	Balloon position. / Balloon ascension point.
	Shikihan (shiki shotai)	Command section (platoon).
	Hoheidan (ryodan) kansokujo (hojo kansokujo).	Artillery group (brigade) observation post (auxiliary observation post).
	Rentai kansokujo (hojo kansokujo).	Regimental observation post (auxiliary observation post).
	Daitai kansokujo (hojo kansokujo).	Battalion observation post (auxiliary observation post).
	Chutai kansokujo (hojo kansokujo).	Company observation post (auxiliary observation post).

NOTE. Observation posts in general are represented by [symbol]. Auxiliary posts are distinguished by a blank triangle [symbol].

Symbol	Japanese	English
	Hyotei no tame no hojo kansokujo.	Auxiliary observation post for plotting.
	Hyotei shikijo	Plotting control post.
	Hohei johotai hombu	Artillery intelligence unit headquarters.
	Hohei johotai	Artillery intelligence unit.
	Hyoteitai	Plotting unit.
	Hyoteisho	Plotting station.
	Shotai hyoteisho	Platoon plotting station.
	Chutai hyoteisho	Company plotting station.
	Ongentai	Sound locator unit.

ARMY SIGNS Artillery (continued)

Symbol	Japanese	English
	Cho-onsho	Listening post.
	Cho-on shusho	Main listening post.
	Cho-on zenshinsho	Forward listening post.
	Sokuchitai	Land survey unit.
	Kisosokuchi no kijunten	Base point of a primary survey.
	Jinchi oyobi zenchi no sokuchi no kijunten.	Base point of a military survey (position and advanced position).
	Kisen	Base line.
	Hoko kisen	Directional base line.

e. Engineers.

Symbol	Japanese	English
	Kohei shireibu	Engineer headquarters.
	Kohei rentai hombu	Engineer regimental headquarters.
	Kohei butai	Engineer unit.

NOTE. The denomination of a unit is shown within the rectangle, e. g. , "A" unit. , "B" unit. , battalion. , company.

Symbol	Japanese	English
	Gakyo zairyo chutai	Bridging matériel company.
	Toka zairyo chutai	River crossing matériel company.
	Yasen sokuryotai	Field survey unit.
	(?) Shuteicho	Boat (landing craft) commander.
	(?) Shutei kohei	Boat (landing craft) engineer.
	(?) Rikujo kohei	Land engineer.

ARMY SIGNS Anti-Aircraft

Symbol	Japanese	English
	Bokubutai shireibu	Antiaircraft defense unit headquarters.
	Koshaho rentai hombu	Antiaircraft artillery regimental headquarters.
	Koshaho daitai hombu	Antiaircraft artillery battalion headquarters.
	Koshahotai	Antiaircraft artillery unit.

ARMY SIGNS
f. Air antiaircraft and meteorological

Symbol	Japanese	English
	Koshahotai jinchi	Antiaircraft artillery position.
	Shoku butai hombu	Searchlight unit headquarters.
	Shokutai	Searchlight unit.
	Shokuto	Searchlight.
	Kuchu cho-onki	Sound locator.
	Dempa tanshingi	Radar.
	Boku kikyu	Barrage balloon.
	Kosha kikanju	Antiaircraft machine gun.
	Kosha kikanho	Antiaircraft machine cannon.

NOTE. In connection with antiaircraft defense if it be necessary to distinguish between field troops and troops protecting important strategic points, the latter are represented by a stroke under the appropriate sign, e. g.

ARMY SIGNS
g. Armoured Forces

Kikogun shireibu		Mechanized army headquarters.
Sensha shidan shireibu		Armored division headquarters.
Kido shidan shireibu		Motorized division headquarters.
Sensha ryodan shireibu		Tank brigade headquarters.
Sensha rentai hombu		Tank regimental headquarters.
Sensha (tai)		Tank (unit).
Sensha kogun taikei		Tank march formation.
Sensha sokai taikei		Tank deployment formation (arrow indicates direction of advance).
Sensha sento taikei		Tank battle formation.
Sensha chutaicho		Tank company commander.

ARMY SIGNS
Armoured Forces (continued)

Symbol	Japanese	English
	Sensha shotaicho	Tank platoon commander.
	Keisensha (tai)	Light tank (unit).
	Chusensha (tai)	Medium tank (unit).
	Jusensha (tai)	Heavy tank (unit).

NOTE. The equipment of individual vehicles is shown by the addition of appropriate signs, e. g., ⬦ represents a tank equipped with radio.

To indicate a cavalry unit ⌐ is added to the top portion of the sign, e. g. ⬦.

Symbol	Japanese	English
	Jisoho (tai)	Self-propelled artillery (unit).
	Hosensha (tai)	Tank destroyer (unit).
	Keninho (tai)	Truck or tractor-drawn artillery (unit).
	Sokosha (tai)	Armored car (unit).
	Suiriku ryoyo sensha (tai)	Amphibian tank (unit).
	Soko sagyo sensha (tai)	Armored construction tank (unit).
	Rikisakusha (tai)	Generator car (unit).
	Soko heisha (tai)	Armored troop carrier (unit).
	Sokiteisha (tai)	Half-track reconnaissance car (unit).
	Senshatai no danretsu	Tank unit ammunition train.
	Senshatai no seibi	Tank unit maintenance.

Symbol	Japanese	English
	Jidoteisha	Scout car.
	Shuri jidosha	Maintenance car.

NOTE. When it is necessary to differentiate between light and heavy, ⬛ is used for the heavy.

Symbol	Japanese	English
	Joyosha	Passenger car.
	Kogata joyosha	Small model passenger car.
	Shikisha	Command car.
	Sokusha	Side-car.
	Jidokasha	Motortruck.

NOTE. The type of truck or the load carried may be shown by appropriate characters or signs, e. g., ⬛ repair truck; ⬛ truck loaded with machine guns.

Symbol	Japanese	English
	Jidokasha kusha	Empty motortruck.
	Sokikasha	Caterpillar truck or tractor.
	Sosakutai	Reconnaissance unit.
	Sosakutai hombu	Reconnaissance unit headquarters.
	Soko tsushintai	Armored signal unit.
	Soko tsushintai hombu	Armored signal unit headquarters.

h. Field works.

Symbol	Japanese	English
	Sampeigo, kotsugo	Firing trench, communication trench.

NOTE. Portions of the communication trench defended by fire are shown by a thick line.

ARMY SIGNS
Field Works (continued)

Symbol	Japanese	English
[symbol]	Keikikanjuza	Light machine gun emplacement.
[symbol]	Kikaijuza	Machine gun (heavy) emplacement.
	NOTE. The presence of weapons in the emplacement is shown by the appropriate symbol, e. g. [symbol]	
[symbol]	Yasenhohei no entai	Field artillery shelter.
[symbol]	Juhohei no entai	Heavy artillery shelter.
[symbol]	Tetsujomo	Wire entanglements.
[symbol]	Ido tetsujomo	Movable wire entanglements.
[symbol]	Rokusai	Abatis.
[symbol]	Jirai	Land mines.
[symbol]	Taisenshago	Antitank ditch.
[symbol]	Jukkobutsu no hakaibu	Artificial obstacles which have been demolished.
[symbol]	Shinrin no bassaibu	Cleared area in woods, forest, etc.
[symbol]	Doro, kyoryo, nado no sozetsubu.	Barricade across road, bridge, etc.
[symbol]	Shogaibutsu no hakaiko oyobi sandoku chiiki ni mokuru tsuro.	Breach made in obstacles or passage opened through an area contaminated with gas.
[symbol]	Empeibu	Dug-out; shelter.
[symbol]	Engai	Cover; shelter.
[symbol]	Konkuritosei engai	Concrete shelter.
	NOTE. The type of fire-arm within a shelter is shown by the appropriate sign, e. g. [symbol].	
[symbol]	Jinchi no zensen wo senryo seru butai.	Unit in occupation of front line of position.
[symbol]	Jinchi wo senryo seru butai	Unit in occupation of position.
	NOTE. Dummy works and dummy positions are indicated by dotted lines.	

ARMY SIGNS
i. Railway

Symbol	Japanese	English
[symbol]	Tetsudo yuso shireibu	Railway transport headquarters.
[symbol]	Tetsudo yuso shireibu shibu	Railway transport headquarters, branch office.
[symbol]	Teishajo shireibu	Railway station headquarters.
[symbol]	Teishajo shireibu shibu	Railway station headquarters, branch office.
[symbol]	Yasen tetsudo shireibu	Field railway headquarters.
[symbol]	Yasen tetsudo shireibu shibu	Field railway headquarters, branch office.
[symbol]	Tetsudo kambu	Railway inspectorate.
[symbol]	Tetsudo rentai hombu	Railway regimental headquarters.
[symbol]	Tetsudo daitai hombu	Railway battalion headquarters.
[symbol]	Tetsudotai	Railway unit.
[symbol]	Soko resshatai	Armored train unit.
[symbol]	Tetsudo zairyosho	Railway supply depot.
[symbol]	Tetsudo rentai zairyosho	Railway regiment supply depot.
[symbol]	Teoshi keiben tetsudotai	Hand-car unit.

ARMY SIGNS
Railway (continued)

Symbol	Japanese	English
	Yasen tetsudosho	Field railway depot.
	Fukusen	Double track.
	Teishaba	Station.
	Tansen	Single track.

ARMY SIGNS
k. Signal

Symbol	Japanese	English
	Tsushintai hombu	Signal unit headquarters.
	Tsushintai	Signal unit.
	Tsushin chutai mata wa yusentai	Signal company or wire unit.
	Heitan tsushintai hombu	Line of communications signal unit headquarters.
	Heitan tsushin chutai	Line of communications signal company.

ARMY SIGNS
Signal (Continued)

Symbol	Japanese	English
	Soko tsushintai hombu	Armored signal unit headquarters.
	Soko tsushintai	Armored signal unit.
	Musentai	Radio unit.
	Idoshiki musentai	Mobile (ground) radio unit.
	Kotei musentai	Fixed radio unit.
	Musen johotai (tokushu musentai) hombu.	Radio intelligence (special radio) unit headquarters.
	Musen johotai (tokushu musentai).	Radio intelligence (special radio) unit.
	Shidan tsushintai	Division signal unit.
	Hohei rentai (ryodan) tsushintai (han).	Infantry regiment (brigade) signal unit (section).
	Kihei rentai (ryodan) (shudan) tsushintai (han).	Cavalry regiment (brigade) (group) signal unit (section).
	Denshin tsushinjo	Telegraph signal station.
	Denwaki. NOTE. ⋈, telephone with bell, when it is necessary to distinguish.	Telephone instrument.
	Denwa kokanki	Telephone switchboard.
	Tenkanki	Change-over switch; switch.
	Denshinki	Telegraph instrument (one-way buzzer).
	Taju denshinki	Multiplex telegraph instrument (duplex buzzer).

Symbol	Japanese	English
	Taju denshinki	Multiplex telegraph instrument (quadruplex buzzer).
	Gempaki	Modulator.
	Jidoki	Automatic instrument.
	Jido teisoki	Automatic relay instrument.
	Insatsu denshinki	Teleprinter; teletype.
	Insatsu denshinki (musen)	Radio teleprinter or teletype.
	Shashin densoki (yusen)	Telephoto instrument (by line).
	Shashin densoki (musen)	Telephoto instrument (radio).
	Rensetsu tsushinjo	Relay signal station.
	Tsushinsen (denwa). NOTE. When necessary, insulated and submarine cables are represented by a wavy line, thus:	Signal line (telephone).
	Kisetsu tsushinsen	Existing signal line.
	Ofukusen	Duplex circuit.
	Fukusen	Twisted (or parallel) pair.
	Tenkasen	Supplementary line.
	Hansosen	Carrier circuit.
	NOTE. For a telegraph line ○ is used instead of ⋈.	
	Denshin denwa soshinpo	Line using both telegraph and telephone (simplexed).
	Idoshiki chijo musen tsushinjo.	Mobile ground radio station.

NOTE. 1. A control station is represented by [symbol].

NOTE. 2. The type of radio set may be indicated by inclosing within the circle the appropriate figure or symbol. Examples follow:

ARMY SIGNS
Signal (continued)

Symbol	Japanese	English
	Jitensha teidensho	Bicycle relay post.
	Inu no renrakuro	Dog messenger route.
	Fuban shingosho	Panel signal station.
	Yubin ukewatashijo	Postal clearing house.
	Yasen yubinkyoku (tai)	Field post office (unit).
	Yasen yubinkyoku (teisokyoku)	Field post office (relay station).

1. Transport, Supply, and Medical Services.

Symbol	Japanese	English
	Danyakuhan (shotai)	Ammunition section (platoon).
	Kori	Baggage train.
	Shichohei rentai hombu	Transport regimental headquarters.
	Shichohei daitai hombu	Transport battalion headquarters.
	Shichohei dokuritsu daitai hombu	Independent transport battalion headquarters.
	Bamba hensei shichohei butai	Horse-drawn transport unit.
	Daba hensei shichohei butai	Pack horse transport unit.
	Jidosha hensei shichohei butai	Motor transport unit.

Symbol	Japanese	English
	Heiki kinmutai	Ordnance service unit.
	Keiri kinmuhan	Intendance service section.
	Boeki kyusuibu	Water supply and purification unit.
	Eiseitai hombu	Medical unit headquarters.
	Yasen byoin	Field hospital.
	Shidan hyobasho	Division veterinary depot.

NOTE. Established field hospitals and veterinary depots are distinguished by the addition of ∧ to the top of the sign.

Symbol	Japanese	English
	Kanja shuyotai	March casualties collecting unit.
	Eiseitai tanga chutai	Medical unit stretcher company.
	Hotaijo	Dressing station.
	Byoba shugojo	Veterinary collecting station.
	Byoba kyugosho	Veterinary first-aid station.
	Yasen soko	Field warehouse.
	Ryomatsu kofujo	Rations and forage distributing point.
	Danyaku kofujo	Ammunition distributing point.
	Nenryo kofujo	Fuel distributing point.

ARMY SIGNS

1. Transport, Supply and Medical Services

Symbol	Japanese	English
	Kagakusen shizai kofujo	Distributing point for chemical warfare material.
	Heiki, hifuku nado no shurijo	Repair depot for ordnance, clothing, etc.
	Gunjuhin no sekisae	Loading war material.
	Gunjuhin no shaka	Unloading war material.
	Gunjuhin no tsumikae	Trans-shipping war material.

m. Line of Communications.

Symbol	Japanese	English
	Heitan shuchi	Line of communications main base.
	Heitan chiku shireibu	Line of communications sector headquarters.
	Heitanchi	Line of communications intermediate base.
	Yotei heitanchi	Projected line of communications intermediate base.
	Heitanchi igai no hokyuten	Supply point other than a line of communications intermediate base.
	Yasen heiki honsho	Main field ordnance depot.
	Yasen heikisho	Field ordnance depot.
	Yasen heiki shisho	Branch field ordnance depot.
	NOTE. Subbranch (forward) depots and mobile repair sections are shown respectively by and	
	Yasen koku honsho	Main field air depot.
	Yasen kokusho	Field air depot.

Symbol	Japanese	English
	Yasen koku shisho	Branch field air depot.
	Yasen jidosha honsho	Main field motor transport depot.
	Yasen jidosha sho	Field motor transport depot.
	Yasen jidosha shisho	Branch field motor transport depot.
	NOTE. Subbranch (forward) depots and mobile repair sections are shown respectively by and	
	Yasen kamotsu honsho	Main field freight depot.
	Yasen kamotsu sho	Field freight depot.
	Yasen kamotsu shisho	Branch field freight depot.
	NOTE. Subbranch (forward) depots and mobile repair sections are shown respectively by and	
		The nature of the material in a depot or dump is shown by the proper abbreviation, e.g. represents an artillery ammunition depot.
	Yasen yusotai shireibu	Field transport unit headquarters.
	Jidosha daitai hombu	Motor transport battalion headquarters.
	Heitan shichohei butai	Line of communications transport unit.
		NOTE. Details of the organization are shown by appropriate lettering.
	Ken-in jidoshatai	Tractor unit.
	Yuso kanshitai	Transport escort unit.
	Yasen hoju basho	Field remount depot.

ARMY SIGNS

m. Line of Communications (continued)

Symbol	Japanese	English
	Heitan byobasho	Line of communications veterinary hospital.
	NOTE. Established depots are distinguished by the addition of ∧ to the top of the sign.	
	Gumba bœkisho	Veterinary quarantine hospital.
	Heitan eiseitai hombu	Line of communications medical unit headquarters.
	Heitan byoin	Line of communications hospital.
	NOTE. Established depots are distinguished by the addition of ∧ to the top of the sign.	
	Heitan eiseitai ido chiryohan	Mobile treatment section of line of communications medical unit.
	Yasen boeki kyusuibu	Field water supply and purification section.
	Kanja yusotai	Sick transport unit.
	NOTE. The position of headquarters is represented by the addition of ⊓ to the top of the sign.	
	Kanja ryoyojo	Convalescent station.
	Kanja shugojo	Collecting station for sick and wounded.
	Yasen sakuseitai hombu	Field well-construction unit headquarters.
	Yasen sakuseitai	Field well-construction unit.
	Yasen kimmutai hombu	Field service unit headquarters.
	Yasen kenchikutai hombu	Field construction unit headquarters.
	NOTE. Headquarters of similar units are represented by inserting the appropriate kana symbol within the rectangle.	

Symbol	Japanese	English
	Rikujo kimmu chutai	Land service company.
	NOTE. Similar companies may be represented by inserting the appropriate kana symbol within the rectangle. For example:	
		Water service company.
		Road service company.
		Barge service company.
	Heitan tsushintai hombu	Line of communications signal unit headquarters.
	Heitan tsushin chutai	Line of communications signal company.
	Yubin ukewatashijo	Postal clearing office.
	Yasen yubinkyoku (tai)	Field post office (unit).
	Yasen yubinkyoku (teisokyoku)	Field post office (relay station).
	NOTE. A branch office is represented by $\frac{\overline{\top}}{(\text{®})}$	

n. Siege and fortress defense.

Symbol	Japanese	English
	Yosai shireibu	Fortress headquarters.
	Yosai juhohei rentai hombu	Fortress heavy artillery regimental headquarters.
	Yosai hohei shikikan	Fortress artillery commander.
	Yosai juhohei daitai hombu mata wa chikutai hombu	Fortress heavy artillery battalion headquarters or sector unit headquarters.
	Yosai byoin	Fortress hospital.
	Yosai bun-in	Branch fortress hospital.
	Yosai tanshoto	Fortress searchlight.

ARMY SIGNS
n. Siege and Fortress Defence (continued)

Symbol	Japanese	English
	Suichu chosokuki	Under-water sound locator.
	Kyuryu yaho	Field gun under shelter.
	Eikyu horui	Permanent fort.
	Haneikyu horui	Semipermanent fort.
	Rinji horui	Temporary (improvised) fort.
	NOTE. Forts are drawn according to actual shape.	
	Heisha eikyu hodai	Permanent gun emplacement.
	Heisha haneikyu hodai	Semipermanent gun emplacement.
	Heisha rinji hodai	Temporary (improvised) gun emplacement.
	Kyokusha eikyu hodai	Permanent mortar emplacement.
	Kyokusha haneikyu hodai	Semipermanent mortar emplacement.
	Kyokusha rinji hodai	Temporary (improvised) mortar emplacement.
	Hoto	Turret.
	Eikyu kyosha	Permanent block-house.
	Rinji kyosha	Temporary (improvised) block-house.
	Heisha	Barracks.
	Shosha, makuei	Barracks, tents.
	Kodo	Gallery, underground passage.
	Koro	Approach trenches, saps.
	Dangansho, dangan honko	Main shell magazine.

Symbol	Japanese	English
	Dansho	Shell magazine.
	Kayakusho, kayaku honko	Main powder magazine.
	Kayaku shisho	Branch powder magazine.
	Danyakusho, danyaku honko	Main ammunition depot.
	Danyaku chukansho; danyaku shiko	Intermediate ammunition depot, branch ammunition depot.
	Kohei kizai kofujo	Distributing center for engineer equipment and matériel.
	Yuso zairyosho	Transport supply depot.
	Heiki shuri kojo	Ordnance main repair shop.
	Heiki shurijo	Ordnance repair shop.
	Kanon	Gun.
	Ryudampo	Howitzer.
	Kyuho	Mortar.

NOTE. The caliber in centimeters of guns, etc., is shown by figures, the number of guns by short cross strokes, e. g. ⊣⊢ represents four 15-cm guns.

Example: Fortress with 4 12-cm guns, 2 7.5-cm guns, 2 15-cm guns, and 4 15-cm howitzers.

	Sanjuka shi-mon no dai ichi eikyu hodai.	Four 30-cm guns in No. 1 permanent battery.

ARMY ABBREVIATIONS

GENERAL

English letters, both capital and small, were used in such abbreviations. In most cases they derived from German words, but later additions used the romanized forms of Japanese words, e.g.:

BA = mountain artillery (i.e. *Bergartillerie*)
SeE = shipping medical unit HQ (i.e. *Sempaku eiseitai hombu*)

Abbreviation	Japanese	English
A	Gun	Army.
A	Yahohei	Field artillery.
AA	Koshahotai; koshaho jinchi.	Antiaircraft artillery unit; antiaircraft artillery position.
AAS	Dokuritsu koshahotai	Independent AA unit.
ab	Hikojo daitai	Airfield battalion.
ac	Hikojo chutai	Airfield company.
AE	Yasen kisho butai	Field meteorological unit.
AL	Hyoteitai	Plotting unit (artillery).
AM	Hohei danyaku	Artillery ammunition.

NOTE. The kind of ammunition is represented as follows:
BAM, Mountain artillery ammunition.
SAM, Medium artillery ammunition.

Abbreviation	Japanese	English
AMT	Hohei danyaku chutai	Artillery ammunition company.
AN	Hohei johotai	Artillery intelligence unit.
AP	Keikyu shugojo	Alarm post.
AQ	Shokutai	Searchlight unit.
AQS	Dokuritsu shokutai	Independent searchlight unit.
AS	Ongentai	Sound locator unit (artillery).
AT	Sokuchitai	Land survey unit (artillery).
ATK	Hosensha (tai)	Tank destroyer (unit).
ATL	Tsushintai hombu	Army signal unit headquarters.
B	Ryodan, mata wa kore ni junzuru mono.	Brigade, or its equivalent.
b	Daitai	Battalion.
BA	Sampohei	Mountain artillery.
BAS	Dokuritsu sampohei	Independent mountain artillery.
BAM	Sampohei danyaku	(See AM above.)
BG	Yasen sakuseitai	Field well-construction unit
biA	Daitaihotai	Infantry battalion gun unit.
BiZ	Hohei ryodan gasu butai	Infantry brigade gas unit.
BK	Gakyo zairyo chutai	Bridging matériel company.
BM	Ryodan danyakuhan	Brigade ammunition section.
Bo (BO)	Boeki kyusuibu	Water supply and purification unit.
BS	Dokuritsu konsei ryodan	Independent mixed brigade.
BSAA	Dokuritsu konsei ryodan koshahotai.	Independent mixed brigade AA unit.
BSP	Dokuritsu konsei ryodan kohei.	Independent mixed brigade engineer unit.
BTL	Hohei ryodan tsushintai (han).	Infantry brigade signal unit (section).
C	Gundan	Corps (not part of the Japanese Army organization).
c	Chutai	Company.
D	Shidan	Division.
DK	Shidan kihei	Division cavalry.
DO	Yasen dorotai	Field road unit.
DP	Shidan kohei	Division engineers.
DT	Shidan shicho	Division transport.
DTL	Shidan tsushintai	Division signal unit.
E	Tetsudotai	Railway unit.
EB	Tetsudo ryodan	Railway brigade.
F	Teki	Enemy.
FA	Kokugun (formerly kokuheidan).	Air army.
FA	Yosai hohei	Fortress artillery.
FB	Hiko (ryo) dan	Air brigade.
Fc	Hikochutai	Air company.
FD	Hikoshidan	Air division.
FeA	Juhohei	Heavy artillery.
FeAS	Dokuritsu juhohei	Independent heavy artillery.
FIS	Dokuritsu koku chikutai	Independent air sector unit.
FL	Yasen byoin	Field hospital.
FM	Hikobutai	Air unit.
FN	Koku johotai	Air intelligence unit.
FP	Yosai kohei	Fortress engineers.
FR	Hikosentai (rentai)	Air regiment.

NOTE. Reconnaissance, fighter, or bomber aircraft are shown by putting O, C, or B respectively on the lower right side of the abbreviation. Similarly light, heavy, or long-range aircraft are shown by L, S, or T, respectively.
Examples:
FR_O, Air regiment (reconnaissance aircraft).
FR_{SC}, Air regiment (heavy fighter aircraft).
FR_{LB}, Air regiment (light bomber aircraft).

Abbreviation	Japanese	English
FS	Yasen kanja shuyotai	Field casualty collecting unit.
FTL	Koku tsushintai	Air signal unit.
FW	Hikojo setteitai	Airdrome construction unit.
G	Konoe	Imperial Guards.
GAP	Keikyu daishugojo	Grand alarm post.
Gr	Jidosha (hikoki) nenryo	Automobile (aviation) fuel.
H	Ryudampo	Howitzer.

Army abbreviations

Abbreviation	Japanese	English
HA	Koshaho	AA gun.
HeF	Hansui sagyotai	Boat launching unit.
HFL	Heitan byoin	Line of communications hospital.
HMA	Kosha kikanho	Antiaircraft machine cannon.
HMG	Kosha kikanju	Antiaircraft machine gun.
Hr	Eisei zairyo	Medical supply.
i	Hohei	Infantry.
iA	Hohei hotai	Infantry gun unit.
iB	Hohei ryodan	Infantry brigade.
iH	Kyokusha hoheiho	Infantry mortar.
iK	Heisha hoheiho	Infantry cannon (gun).
iM	Hohei danyaku	Infantry ammunition.

NOTE. The kind of ammunition is represented as follows:
iM (MG). Machine gun ammunition.
iM (TA). Antitank gun ammunition.

iMT	Hohei danyaku chutai	Infantry ammunition train.
iP	Sagyotai	Labor unit (infantry pioneers).
iR	Hohei rentai	Infantry regiment.
iRS	Dokuritsu hohei rentai	Independent infantry regiment.
iS	Dokuritsu hohei	Independent infantry.
iTL	Hohei rentai tsushintai (han).	Infantry regimental signal unit (section).
K	Kanon	Cannon (gun).
K	Kihei	Cavalry.
KA	Kihohei	Cavalry (Horse) artillery.
KaY	Kaijo yuso daitai hombu	Sea transport battalion headquarters.
KB	Kihei ryodan	Cavalry brigade.
KBA	Kihei ryodan hotai	Cavalry brigade artillery unit.
KBAA	Kihei ryodan koshahotai	Cavalry brigade AA unit.
KBT	Kihei ryodan shicho	Cavalry brigade transport.
KBTAS	Kihei ryodan dokuritsu sokushahotai.	Cavalry brigade independent antitank unit.
KBTK	Kihei ryodan senshatai	Cavalry brigade tank unit.
KBTL	Kihei ryodan tsushinhan (tai).	Cavalry brigade signal section (unit).
KD	Kihei shidan	Cavalry division.
Kg	Shubitai	Guard detachment, garrison.
KgS	Dokuritsu shubitai	Independent garrison.
Ki	Kikyutai	Balloon unit.
KK	Kihei shudan	Cavalry group.
KKTL	Kihei shudan tsushinhan	Cavalry group signal section.
KS	Dokuritsu kihei	Independent cavalry.
KTK		(See TK below.)
KTL	Kihei rentai tsushinhan (tai).	Cavalry regimental signal section (unit).
LBK	Toka zairyo chutai	River crossing matériel company.
LG	Keikikanju	Light machine gun.
LM	Keihakugekihotai	Light trench mortar unit.

Abbreviation	Japanese	English
LTK		(See TK below.)
M	Kyuho	Mortar.
M	Danyakuhan (shotai)	Ammunition section (platoon).
MA	Kikanhotai	Machine cannon unit.
MD	Kido shidan	Motorized division.
MG	Kikanjutai	Machine gun unit.
MM	Chuhakugekihotai	Medium trench mortar unit.
MS	Dokuritsu hakugekihotai	Independent mortar unit.
MTK		(See TK below.)
MW	Tekidanto, tekidanju	Grenade discharger, grenaderifle.
N	Kori	Baggage or train.
N	Johotai	Army intelligence unit.
NA	Kaigunho	Naval gun.
NSF	Kotei musentai	Fixed radio (wireless) unit.
P	Kohei	Engineers.
PA	Kikogun	Mechanized army.
PD	Shidan byobasho	Division veterinary hospital.
Pr	Ryomatsu	Provisions and forage.
PrT	Ryoshoku chutai	Provision train.
PS	Dokuritsu kohei	Independent engineers.
PT	Hatotai; shikyutai	Carrier pigeon unit.
PW	Sokoshatai	Tankette unit.
PWS	Dokuritsu sokoshatai	Independent tankette unit.
R	Rentai	Regiment.
RD	Tokushu musentai	Special radio unit.
RiA	Rentai hotai	Infantry regimental gun unit.
RSt	Rentai danretsu	Regimental ammunition train.
S	Dokuritsu	Independent.

NOTE. Added at the end of the unit abbreviation.

S	Kanja shuyotai	March casualties collecting unit.
SA	Yasen juhohei	Medium artillery.
SAM	Yasen juho danyaku	(See AM above.)
SAS	Dokuritsu yasen juhohei	Independent medium artillery.
SeA	Sempaku hohei rentai	Shipping artillery regiment.
SeAA	Sempaku koshahotai	Shipping antiaircraft unit.
SeC	Sempaku shireibu	Shipping headquarters.
SeD	Sempaku dan shireibu	Shipping group headquarters.
SeE	Sempaku eiseitai hombu	Shipping medical unit headquarters.
SeH	Sempaku heidan shireibu	Large shipping group headquarters.
SeK	Sempaku kosakusho	Shipping repair depot.
SeP	Sempaku kohei rentai	Shipping engineers regiment.
SeS	Byoinsen eiseihan	Hospital ship medical section.
SeT	Teihakujo shireibu	Anchorage headquarters.
SeTi	Sempaku yuso chikutai shireibu	Shipping transportation area unit headquarters.
SeTL	Sempaku tsushin rentai	Shipping signal regiment.
SeU	Sempaku yuso shireibu	Shipping transportation headquarters.
SeUb	Kaijo yuso daitai	Sea transport battalion.

1. ARMY ABBREVIATIONS—Continued.

Abbreviation	Japanese	English
SeY	Yorikutai	Disembarkation unit.
SF	Musentai	Radio unit.
SM	Juhakugekihotai	Heavy trench mortar unit.
SO	Sosakutai	Reconnaissance unit.
STK		(See TK below.)
St	Danretsu	Ammunition train.
SuB	Suijo shireibu	Headquarters at sea.
SW	Yasen shomeitai	Field searchlight unit.
T	Shicho	Transport.
TA	Sokushahotai	Antitank gun unit.
TAS	Dokuritsu sokushahotai	Independent antitank gun unit.
TD	Sensha shidan	Armored division.
TG	Yusosentai	Group of transport; convoy.
TG		Tommy gun.
TK	Sensha (tai)	Tank (unit.)

NOTE. Light medium, or heavy tanks are represented by putting L, M, or S, respectively, in front of the abbreviation. For example, STK represents a heavy tank unit. A tank unit employed as cavalry is represented by KTK.

TKP	Senshatai kohei	Tank unit engineers.
TKS	Dokuritsu senshatai	Independent tank unit.
TKTL	Senshatai tsushintai	Tank unit signal unit.
TL	Tsushin chutai, mata wa yusentai.	Signal company; wire unit.
TLS	Dokuritsu tsushin chutai	Independent signal company.
TP	Kikaika butai	Mechanized unit.
TZ	Senshatai no seibi butai	Tank unit maintenance unit.
V	Yasen sokuryotai	Field surveying unit (engineers).
Vr	Jui zairyo	Veterinary supply.
Z	Gasu butai	Gas unit.
Zid	Jidohotai	Automatic gun unit.
Zr	Kagakusen shizai	Chemical warfare.
ZS	Dokuritsu gasu butai	Independent gas unit.

JAPANESE GROUND RADIO EQUIPMENT

Classification	Transmitter output (watts)	Form	Model	Type No.	Date of original model	Function	Type transmission	Range (miles)
Transmitters	100	Portable	TE-MU	3		Used on some islands in local radio net.	Unknown CW, phone, or both.	15-20
	50 or 250	Fixed station	TE-MU	2	1942	Ground to air	CW, phone	50
	275	Semiportable. Fixed station.	94	1	1934	Hq-Army Div	CW, MCW, phone.	
	300	Semi-fixed station	Not known	Not known		Marine ground unit.	CW only	
	500	Fixed station	95	4	1935, modified 1941.	High power, island to island.	Phone	Long distance
	1,000	do	92	3	1932, modified 1941.	do	CW	do
	1,000	do	95	Not known	1935	do	Unknown if CW, phone, or both.	do
	1,000	do	94	1	1934	Army Div Hq	CW phone	150
	2,000	do	87	1	1927	Comm. GHQ		300
	1-2	Man pack	94	5	1934	Limited range. Comm. between Inf. units.	CW phone	5-CW, 1-2-phone
Transmitter-receiver.	4.5 - C W. 3 phone.	Portable	Not known	Not known		Portable field set	do	
	10	Pack	94	do	1934	Field equipment in div.	CW only	
	15	3-Man pack	94	SP-3A-36	1934	Comm. in Inf. Cav. and F. A. from brigade down to Inf.	do	Approximate 25
	20	do	87	2	1927	Field, ground, and air.		Field-25 G/A190
	80 - C W. 200 phone.	2-Man pack	94	2-B	1934	Commd. set in Inf. div.	do	
		2-3 man pack	94	3-A-36D	1934		Receives C W, MCW, phone.	
			99	3	1939		CW, MCW, phone	
	0.5	Man pack	94	6	1934	Walkie-talkie type. In Inf.	CW, MCW, phone	1-2
	1	2-3 man pack	TM	2	Revis. 1942		CW only	1-2
Transceivers	1-2	Walkie-talkie	97	3	1937	Walkie-talkie, also air Gnd.	CW, phone	2-3
		do	Not known	66		Infantry squads, platoons.	do	1
	2		do	Not known			CW only	
	2.5	Portable	do	do		Infantry ground; portable.		Several
		Fixed sta	92	do	1932	Comm. bet. Corps and Div.		
Receivers		Direction finder and intercept receiver.	94	1	1934	Direction finder and intercept receiver.		

RF coverage in MC	Frequency shifting capabilities	Present frequency	Antenna system	Tuning—MO or crystal (number of crystals)	Selectivity receiver	Sensitivity receiver	Receiving circuit
1.5–15.0 (plug-in-coils)		Unknown (At least 1).	Wire	MO or crystal. (Number of crystals unknown.)			
3.38–10.4; 12.2–14.0 (4 bands, tapped coils and switches.)	Good. Continuous coverage.		Wire-link coupling from PA to ant. coupler. Coupling adjusted from transmitter panel.	MO			
0.14–15.0 shift bands by plug-in coils. No. of bands and coils unknown.	Good	Unknown	Wire–2 ant. ckts. in transmitter—Series resonant for high freq., Parallel resonant for low freq.	Crystal. (Number of crystals unknown.)			
3.0 –10.0.							
3.7–18.2			Wire				
0.05–0.6.			Wire—Uses loading coils in antenna system.				
3.7–8.0 (plug-in coils)		Unknown (at least 1).	Wire	MO or crystal (number of crystals unknown).			
0.02–0.5. 0.1–(?). *Transmitter:* 0.779–3.061 (3 bands) tapped coil and switch. *Receiver:* 0.779–7.0 (4 bands) tapped coil and switch.	Continuous coverage on MO.	10	Wire—Same ant. for both Xmtr. and Rec. connected by Send-receive switch. Counterpoise wires incl.	MO or XTAL (number of XTALS–10).	Fair	Poor	1 Stage RF. Regen. Det. 1 Stage AF.
0.9–5.3 (3 bands)		1	Crystal				4 Tube TRF Regn. Det.
0.4–6.0 (5 bands) plug-in coils. Both Xmtr. and receiver.	Continuous coverage on band used.	Unknown (at least 1).	Wire	MO or Crystal (number of crystals unknown.			
XMTR. 0.4–5.7 Rec.—0.35–6.0 (5 plug-in coils).	Continuous coverage for band used on MO.	1	do	Crystal or MO (number of XTALS, 1).	Fair	Very sensitive.	5 Tube Superhet. Regen. 2d Det.
0.33–0.60.							
Rec.: 0.14–15.0 (7 plug-in coils) XMTR: 0.95–6.675.	Continuous coverage on band used.	Adjustable presets on dials.	Wire "L" type. Total length 29.7 yds. Counterpoise wires 22′ long.	Crystal or MO (Number of XTALS 1).			5 Tube Superhet.
0.4–5.75 (5 plug-in coils)	Continuous coverage for band used.		Wire-rubber covered lead in 6 feet long. Gnd. wire same length.		do	Good	4 tubes, 1 stage RF., Regen Det. 2 stages AF.
Rec. 1.5–6.7 (3 plug-in trays of coils).	do	3		MO–Crystal (Number of Crystals 3).			do
24. 2–49, 3 (3 bands)			Rod, 5 feet	MO			Super-regen. Det and one stage AF.
4.0–12.0	Continuously variable.		Wire with reel—to vary length, and tune ant. ckt.	do	Poor-except when on verge of Osc.	Extremely poor	Regen. Det. one stage AF.
25. 5–31 (tapped coil and switch).	Continuous coverage.		Dipole— each half 23 inches long. Elements fasten to case.	do	Poor	Poor	Super-regen. Det. and One stage AF.
2.5–4.5	Continuous cover on MO	1	Either long or short antenna. Ant. tune system.	Crystal or MO. (No. of XTALS–1).			3 Tube. Regen. Det
0.1–2.0; 4.0–5.0.	5 crystals	1	Rod 6 feet long	Crystal			
4.5–11.0.			Wire				
0.2–20.0 (Use total of 7 plug-in coils at one time.)	Continuously var. for coils used.	None	do		Fair	Fair	7 Tube comb. TRF and Superhet. No AVC.
0.1–2.0 (In 5 bands) switches and taps on coils.	Continuously variable for range of coils used.	None	Square loop—ea. side, 4-foot long. 6 turns, unshielded rotation—400° to stops.		Very selective	Poor	6 tube TRF., 3 stages RF., Regen. Det., 2 stages AF.

GROUND RADIO EQUIPMENT

Classification	Transmitter output (watts)	Transmitter circuit	Frequency stability	Meters used	Power source	Remarks
Transmitters	100	MOPA. Tubes used—UV202A, UX814, and UV812. 3 stages—Osc., Buffer, PA. No freq. multiplication. Keyed in buffer and PA.	Good		220 volts, 3 phase, 50–60 cycle AC. Half wave rect. Uses 3 X968 tubes.	Medium power. Short wave portable station. Used primarily in local radio nets on island.
	50 or 250		Fair	Osc. indicator. Osc. plate current. Buffer plate current. PA plate current. Ant. ammeter.	Rectified AC; low power 1,000 v; high power–2,000 v.	Used with rectifier unit. Carried in 2 cases, slung on poles. Fixed station operation. Buffer and PA tubes, screen grid type. No neutralization used. Capable of low or high power operation by switching arrangement.
	275	MOPA–Hartley Osc. MO–UY511B. PA—two UV812 in parallel screen grid voltage keyed for CW. Grid modulation for MCW and phone.	do	Ant. ammeter. PA plate current. PA grid current. Osc. plate current. Fil. voltmeter.	Motor generator: 2,000 volts DC; 1,000 volts DC; 400 volts DC; 100 volts DC; 12 volts DC.	Semiportable. Fixed station operation. Weight with Mot. gen. approx. 500 pounds. 2 cases and Mot. Gen. Each case carried by 2 men. Has neon osc. indicator. Various voltages go through power distribution panel.
	300					
	500	Grid modulated tubes—UV202, UV865, UV814, UV860, UV861.	Good		220 volts, 3 phase 50–60 cycle AC. output voltages 3,000 volts—2,000 volts—500 volts—300 volts. Fil. 16V rect. tubes used 9-H 830, 6-X968.	Transmitter modification No.1: High-power, short wave fixed station. Used island to island over long distances. Has emergency power supply gas-driven generator. All filaments on DC. Tubes replicas of American types. Uses speech amplifier and modulator—4 tubes in all; 1-58, 1-56, 2-2A3. Legend on name plate for mod. unit "Modulator for type 95 Short Wave No. 4 transmitter modification No. 1".
	1,000	MOPA. Final tube SN 146.	do		220 volts, 2 phase, 50–60 cycle AC output voltages 2100 volts–1000 volts and 16 volts. 6 Rect tubes. Type H-836.	Transmitter modification No. 1: high power, long wave, long distance. Fixed stations. Used island to island. All filaments on DC. Final tube Japanese type; all others replicas of American tubes.
	1,000	MOPA. Tubes used—202, 865, 814, 812. Final—SN146.	do		220 volts, 3 phase, 50–60 cycle AC. Output voltages 3,000 volts–2,000 volts–500 volts–300 volts and 16 volts. Uses 9–H830 and 6-X968 rect. tubes.	High power, short wave, fixed station. Used over long distances. Not known if used on phone or CW or both.
	1,000					Transmitter.
Transmitter-receiver.	2,000					
	1–2	XTAL or MO control (Hartley ckt.) Osc. connected to antenna.	XTAL – Fair MO–Poor.	Ant. current 0–200 Ma.	Transmitter: Hand generator in separate case. Fil.-6 volts. Plate—150 volts. (Model F) receiver: batteries. In case with receiver. Fil.—1.65 volts. Plate-90 volts.	Stationary use. One twin triode tube. Triodes in parallel for CW operation. For phone, one triode becomes mod. Two man pack and operation. Throat mike used. Model 32 transmitter; Model 32 receiver.
	4.5–C W. 3 phone.					Transmitter-receiver.
	10	Hartley Oscillator		Ant. Ammeter, Plate current.	Hand generator: 7 volts filament, 500 volts plate.	Pack transmitter-receiver.
	15	1 Tube Hartley oscillator.	Poor	Plate voltmeter. Ant. ammeter.	Transmitter, hand generator receiver; batteries.	Pack animal or 3 man pack. Carried in 2 wooden cases. Transmitter keyed in high volt. Neg. ckt. Transmitter-receiver type.
	20					
	80 – C W. 200 phone.	1 Tube Hartley oscillator.	Fair		Rec.—Batteries; Xmtr.—Gasoline; driven motor generator; 12V–Fil. 1,300V-plate.	Receiver can be used for intercept. Transport by 2 man pack or car; No. 55 D transmitter; No. 27 receiver.
			do		Batteries: 1.5V-Filament; 22.5V-Plate; 1.5V-Bias.	Receiver only. Dials marked with luminous paint and have clamps for locking. Straps provided for carrying on back. Not a "Walkie-Talkie."
		2 Beam Type Tubes. Osc.-Plate Mod.	do			
	0.5	Oscillator and Mod.		Antenna Ammeter	Batteries-separate case. Fil. 6V ;plate 135V.	Transceiver. One coil with 3 taps and switch, 2 to 3 men to pack and operate. No. 23 Model H.
	1	2 tubes in parallel. Hartley osc.	Poor-Freq. shift when keyed.	Fil. voltmeter Ant. ammeter.	Rectified AC. DC voltages—150 and 180 V.	Transceiver. Portable 2 or 3 man pack, cycle, or car. Revision 2. Transmitter output also reported as 2½ Watts, and R. F. coverage as 4.5-11 M. C.
Transceivers	1–2	Master Osc. (Hartley) and modulator.	Poor	Antenna ammeter	Hand generator: Fil.—3 volts, Plate—135 volts.	Transceiver—Uses one twin triode, UX 19, for all functions. Dipole elements of ant. fasten to each end of case. Case intended to be strapped to back; Generator to chest.
		.3 tube Hartley oscillator.	do	Plate current Ant. ammeter.	Batteries: 1.5V filament; 135V plate	One man pack. Transmitter carried on chest, and batteries on back, by means of straps. Model A.
	2					Transceiver.
	2.5					Do.
Receivers					Rectified AC	Used in conjunction with transmitter Model 94 Type 2B. Fixed station Receiver. Total of 25 plug-in coils used.
			Freq. calibration not good.	No visual bearing indicator used.	Batteries—1.5V filament; 4.5V bias; 135V Plate.	Receiver only. 4 wooden chests. Weighs 350 pounds complete. Numerous controls. Slow and difficult to get a "fix." Set installed under shelter over which loop is mounted.

BIBLIOGRAPHY

PUBLISHED BOOKS

Anon., *Japanese tanks and tank tactics*, ISO Publications (Facsimile reproduction of the original study published in 1944), 1987

Appleman, Roy E. and others, *The War in the Pacific, OKINAWA: THE LAST BATTLE*, Historical Division, Dept of the Army, Washington, 1948

Barker A.J., *Japanese Army Handbook 1939–45*, Ian Allan Ltd, 1979

Bateson, Charles, *The War with Japan, a concise history*, Barrie & Rockliff, 1968

Boatner, Mark M., III, *Biographical Dictionary of World War II*, Presidio, 1996

Cross, J.P., *Jungle Warfare*, Guild Publishing, 1989

Forty, George, *World War Two Tanks*, Osprey Automotive, 1995

——, *World War Two AFVs*, Osprey Automotive, 1996

Fuller, Richard, *Shokan, Hirohito's Samurai*, Arms & Armour Press, 1992

Georgano, G.N., *World War Two Military Vehicles, Transport and Halftracks*, Osprey Automotive, 1994

Keegan, John, *World Armies*, Macmillan Publishers, 1979

Lamont-Brown, Raymond, *Kempeitai, Japan's Dreaded Military Police*, Sutton Publishing, 1998

McLean, Donald B., *Japanese Infantry Weapons*, Normont Armament Company, 1966

Nakata, Tadao and Nelson, Thomas B., *Imperial Japanese Army & Navy – Uniforms and Equipment*, Arms & Armour, 1987

Perrett, Bryan, *Tank Tracks to Rangoon*, Robert Hale Ltd, 1978

Slim, FM Viscount, *Defeat into Victory*, Cassell, 1956

Tamayama, Dr Kazuo, *Japanese Soldiers of the Burma Campaign*, published privately, 1997

Vanderveen, Bart, *Historic Military Vehicles Directory*, After the Battle, 1989

Weeks, John, *The Airborne Soldier*, Blandford Press, 1982

MILITARY PAMPHLETS

US War Department Technical Manual: *Handbook on Japanese Military Forces* TM-E 30–480, Washington, 15 September 1944

Military Intelligence Service, US Army: *Soldier's Guide to the Japanese Army*, Special Series No. 27, 15 November 1944

Notes from Theatres of War, No. 19: Burma 1943–44, May 1945

INDEX

Numbers in italics indicate illustrations.

Abbreviations, army 259 *et seq.*
Airborne forces 76 *et seq.*, 77
Air Service vi *et seq.*
Amphibious tanks, see under Tanks
Anami, Gen Korechika 11, 223
Anti-Comintern Pact 5, 6
Apprentices, army 25
Araki, Gen Baron Sadao 223 *et seq.*
Armies,
    Burmese Independent 20, *22*
    Formosan 7, 15
    Free Burma 10
    Indian Liberation (INLA) 10, 20, *21*
    Korean 7, 15
    Kwantung (Manchuria) 3(n), 7, *29*, *31*
Armour 68 *et seq.*
Armoured fighting vehicles, see under type (e.g. Tanks)
Armoured cars,
    Crossley Type 87, *170*, 171, 173
    Osaka Type 92, 173
    Sumida Type 2593, 5, *81*, *172*, 173, *214*
    Sumida Type ARM, 173
    Type M2592, 173
Armoured trains 188
Artillery 62 *et seq.*, 73
    Anti-aircraft 73, *147*, *149*, *151*
    Anti-tank 73, 132, *146*, 147 *et seq.*, 150
    Field 71 *et seq.*, *71*, 153, *154*
    Heavy 155, *155*, 156
    Medium 72 *et seq.*, 154, *154*, 155
    Mountain 72, *151*, 152, *152*
    Self-propelled *156*, 157, *157*, 158
    (See also Weapons)
Assault boats 192 *et seq.*, *193*
Assault landing barges 77, 194
Assault rafts *193*

Badges of rank 19, 109 *et seq.*
Bands 89
Banners and flags *2*, *14*
Banzai! *v*, *9*, *29*
Barrage mortars, see under Mortars
Bayonets 25, 124
Bicycles 161
Booby traps and mines 121 *et seq.*, *123*, *124*, 221
Bose, Subhas Chandra 20, *22*
Brothels, see Comfort girls
Bridging 189 *et seq.*

Assault 74, *190*
    Bridgelayer, armoured *183*
    Infantry pontoon *190*, *191*
    Trestle 192, *192*
Burma 10, 11, 49, *50*
Burma Road 5
Bushido ('Way of the Warrior') 233

Canteens *85*
Cars, see under Vehicles
Casualty evacuation 85
Cavalry 63, *70*, *107*
Chemical warfare 78, 201, *201*, *202*
China 3, *4*, 11, 15, *41*, 52, 170, 173
Christmas Island 9
Clothing and equipment 85, 95 *et seq.*
    (See also Uniforms and personal equipment)
Comfort girls 85, 86, 240
Conscription 13 *et seq.*
Conscripts,
    Active service 15 *et seq.*
    Training 25 *et seq.*
Control Faction 5 *et seq.*
Conventional signs, military 241 *et seq.*
Crane, armoured *182*

Decorations and medals *111*, 112 *et seq.*
Defence Units, Special 50
Defence works 205, 208, 209, 211
Depots, divisional 40 *et seq.*
Districts, army, divisional and regimental 38, 39
Dutch East Indies 11, 48, 77

Empire, Japanese 1 *et seq.*, 6, 10
Engineer equipment 194 *et seq.*
    Construction equipment 195
    Demolition equipment 195
    Electric power units 195
    Komatsu tractor *194*
    Water purification equipment 195 *et seq.*
Engineers 64, 74 *et seq.*

Field organisations 43 *et seq.*
Flags, see under Banners and flags
Flame-throwers *196*, *197*, *198*
Fortress units 53
Fulltrack vehicles, see under Vehicles, Tanks

Geisha *86*
Gliders 203
Graves *vii*
Grenades and grenade launchers, see Small arms
Guns, infantry,
    Regimental (75mm) *37*
    Type 11, 135
    Type 41, 136, *136*
    Type 92, *135*, 136
    Type 94, 136
    Type 99, *134*

Halftrack vehicles, see under Vehicles
Helmets, tropical *vii*, 99
High Command 34 *et seq.*
Higher Organisations, see Chapter 4
Hirohito, Emperor *1*, 11, *33*
Hiroo, 2Lt Onoda 224
Hitler, Adolf 5, *20*
Honda, Gen Masaka 224, *224*
Hong Kong *8*, 10
Honma (also Homma), Gen Masharu 224 *et seq.*, *225*
Hyakutaku, Gen Seikichi 225

Imamura, Gen Hitoshi, 225 *et seq.*
Imperial Guard *45*, *105*, 109
'Imperial Way' faction 6
India 10
Infantry *41*, *48*, *49*, *50*, *51*, 51, 52, 53, 57, 60, 61
Insignia, Arm 110
Intendance *52*, 82 *et seq.*

Judiciary 89

Kai Shek, Gen Chiang 5
Katana *11*, *37*, *41*, 126, *127*
Kawabi, Gen Masakazu 226
Kempeitai 22, 232 *et seq.*, *237*, *238*
Kendo *26*, *32*
Kimura, Gen Heitaro 226
Konoye, Prince 6 *et seq.*
Korea 2, 3, 12
Kuala Lumpur 7
Kuribayshi, Gen Tadamichi 226
Kuroki, Gen Baron Yamemoto 2
Kwantung Army 3(n), 7, *29*, *31*

Ladders, scaling *52*

MacArthur, Gen Douglas 12
Machine-guns,
    Heavy: Type 3, 129, *129*; Type 92, *37*, 129, *130*; Type 93, 131; Type 99, 129
    Light, see under Small arms
Malaya 10, 48
Manchuria (Manchukuo) 3, *5*, 11, *15*, *16*, 48, 52, 69
Maps,
    Defeat of Japan 10
    Expansion of Japan 6
    Military Districts of Japan 38
Mazaki, Gen Jinsaburo 6

Medals, see under Decorations and medals
Medical 64 *et seq.*, 87 *et seq.*
Medical Classification 13
Military Academy 27
Mines 124, *124*, *125*, *126*
Mobilisation 13 *et seq.*
Morale 26 *et seq.*
Mortars,
    Barrage mortar (70mm) 143, *144*, 146
    Rocket projectors (200mm) 145, 146 *et seq.*
    Spigot mortars (320mm) *142*, 142, 146
    Type 11 (70mm) *137*, 141
    Type 94 (90mm) *140*, 141 *et seq.*
    Type 97 (81mm) *139*, 141
    Type 97 (90mm) 144
    Type 97 (150mm) *141*, 144
    Type 98 (50mm) *137*, 138, 140
    Type 99 (81mm) *139*, 141
Motorcycles, see under Vehicles
Mountbatten, Lord Louis 12
Mukden 3
Mutaguchi, Gen Renya 226, 227

Nagata, Gen Tetsuzan 6
Naval land forces viii, 76(n), *170*
New Guinea 48
Nishmura, Gen Takuma 227
Numbering, Japanese system of viii

Occupation banknotes *234*
Officers,
    Ranks 18, 109
    Regular 16
    Reserve 18, 30
    Training 28 *et seq.*
Ordnance 65, 87
Organisation,
    Artillery regiment 62 *et seq.*
    Cavalry regiment 63
    Engineer regiment 64
    Independent infantry brigade 52 *et seq.*, 57
    Independent infantry regiment 53, 61
    Infantry battalion 60 *et seq.*
    Infantry division 51 *et seq.*, 53 *et seq.*
    Medical units 64
    Reconnaissance regiments 69
    Tank regiments 68 *et seq.*

Pack animals *89*, *91*, *92*
Pay, rates of 85 *et seq.*
Pearl Harbor 5, 7, 15
Percival, Lt Gen A. 8
Personal equipment, see under Uniforms and personal equipment
Pistols, see under Small arms
Port Arthur 2
Prisoner of war camps 240
Propaganda leaflets *235*, *236*

Radios, see under Signal equipment
Raiding forces 50

Railways, use of *5*, 69, 81, *81*, *172*, *214*
Rangoon 9, *93*
Rations 82 *et seq.*, *82*, *83*
Regimental colours *14*
Rifles, see under Small arms
Rocket projectors, see under Mortars
Roosevelt, President 7

Safe conduct pass 10
Sakai, Lt Gen Taikaishi *8*, 227
Sakhalin Island 3
Samurai 1, 2
San Aung 22
Schools, military 30 *et seq.*
Self-propelled guns
    HO-NI (75mm) *157*, 158
    HO-RO (150mm) *158*, 158
    SO-KI (20mm) *156*, 188
Senninbari (good luck belt) 98
Sensha, see Tanks
Seppuku (ritual disembowelling) 1, 11, 94
Services, the 79 *et seq.*
Signal equipment
    Line 198 *et seq.*, *199*
    Miscellaneous 200 *et seq.*
    Radios *199*, 200, 264 *et seq.*
    Signal units 75 *et seq.*
Signallers *28*, *42*, *75*, *76*, 198
Singapore *8*, 10
Slim, Gen (later Field Marshal) Sir William viii
Solomon Islands 48
Small arms,
    Grenades 119, *120*, 122
    Grenade launchers 118, *118*, *119*, 121
    Light machine-guns *37*, 126, 127, *128*
    Machine-carbines 117, *117*, 118
    Pistols 113 *et seq.*, 115, 128, *128*
    Rifles *24*, *37*, *45*, *48*, 115 *et seq.*, *116*
Snipers 216
Soldiers' code 7
Spigot mortars, see under Mortars
Staff training 30
Sugiyama, Field Marshal Hajime 227, *227*
Supply system 89 *et seq.*
Surrender *11*, *12*

Tabi (footwear) *95*, *96*
Tactics 204 *et seq.*
    Attack 204 *et seq.*
    Counter-attack 210
    Defence 207 *et seq.*, 211
    Night attack 206 *et seq.*
    Ruses 206, 218 *et seq.*
    Withdrawals 210
Tanaka, Baron Shinichi 228
Tankettes *4*, *17*, *46*, *47*, *67*, *106*, *174*, *175*, 175 *et seq.*
Tanks (Sensha),
    Amphibious: Type 2 (KAMI-SHA), *176*, 187; Type 3 (KA-CHI), *186*, 187; Type 5 (TO-KU), 187
    Bridgelayer, armoured *183*
    Crane, armoured *182*

    Heavy: 185 *et seq.*; Type 91, *184*, 185; Type 95, 185
    Light: 176, 177 *et seq.*, *177*, 179; HA-GO (Type 95), 176, *177*, 179
    Medium: *4*, *17*, *31*, *193*; CHI-HA (Type 97), 66, *180*, 181, *212*, *213*; CHI-HA (Shinto), *180*, 185; HA-TO (300mm mortar), *184*, 188; OT-SU (Type 89), *41*, *67*, *178*, *179*, 181, 185; SHI-KI (Command), 66, *181*
    Recovery: SE-RI *182*, 183
Task forces 44 *et seq.*, 48
Tenno, Emperor Maiji 1, 26 *et seq.*
Terauchi, Field Marshal Count Hisichi 228, *228*
Teshima, Gen Fusataro 229
Tojo, Gen Hideki 7, 33, 229, *229*
Tokko 233
Trailers 167
Training 23 *et seq.*
Training, Inspectorate General of 36
Transport 64, 79 *et seq.*
(See also Vehicles)

Umezu, Gen Yoshigiro 229, *230*
Uniforms and personal equipment *51*, *93*, *95*, *95 et seq.*, *96*, *97*, *98*, *99*, *100*, *101*, *102*, *103*, *104*, *105*, *106*, *107*, 236 *et seq.*
Ushijima, Gen Mitsuru 229
Ushiroka, Gen Jun 230

Vehicles
    Bicycles 161
    Cars: Nissan passenger sedan *163*; Staff cars 165 *et seq.*; Type 95 Kurogane (scout car) *162*, 165
    Fulltracks *168*, *169*, 170
    Halftracks 167, *167*, *168*
    Handcarts *161*, 162
    Motorcycles: 159 *et seq.*; Type 97 (solo) 159, *159*; Type 97 (sidecar) *160*; Trike (Kurogane) *160*, 161
    Trucks: 166 *et seq.*, Amphibian (2 ton) 166, *166*; Cargo Type 1 (3 ton) 167; Cargo Type 2 (7 ton) 167; Dump (20 ton) 167; Isuzu TU10 (1.5 ton) *164*, *165*, 166; Isuzu TX40 (2 ton) 166; Nissan 180 (1.5 ton) *79*, *163*, *164*, 166
Veterinary 65, 89
Volunteers 16

War Ministry 35
Warrant officers and NCOs 18 *et seq.*, 30
Wars,
    Great East Asia 7
    Russo-Japanese 1
    Sino-Japanese 1, 2
Water transport 81 *et seq.*
Weapons 133 *et seq.*
    Anti-aircraft guns: 20mm Type 80, *147*, 151; 20mm Type 98, 151; 25mm cannon, *149*, 151; 75mm Type 98, *149*, *150*, 151; 105mm Type 14, 151
    Anti-tank guns: 37mm, 147 *et seq.*, 150; 47mm, *146*, 150
    Field guns: 75mm Type 38(I), 153, *153*; 75mm Type 90, 153; 75mm Type 95, 153

Heavy guns: 150mm (Howitzer) Type 4, *155*, 156; 150mm (Howitzer) Type 38, 155; 150mm Type 89, 155, 156; 150mm (Howitzer) Type 96, 155, *155*, 156

Medium guns: 105mm Type 14, 154; 105mm Type 38, 154; 105mm (Howitzer) Type 91, *154*, 155; 105mm Type 92, 71 *et seq.*, *71*, *72*, 155

Mountain guns: 72; Type 94 (75mm), *151*, *152*, 152

Naval guns 151, 152

Self-propelled guns: 20mm (AA) SO-KI *156*; 75mm HO-NI I 157, 158; 75mm HO-NI III *157*, 158; 150mm HO-RO 158, *158*

Wounded *vi*, 87
(See also Casualty evacuation)

Yamada, Gen Otozo 230
Yamashita, Gen Tomoyuki 231, *231*